Necessary Knowledge

Necessary Knowledge

Henry Plotkin

Emeritus Professor of Psychology, University
College London, UK

OXFORD

UNIVERSITY PRESS

Great Clarendon Street, Oxford OX2 6DP

Oxford University Press is a department of the University of Oxford.
It furthers the University's objective of excellence in research, scholarship,
and education by publishing worldwide in

Oxford New York

Auckland Cape Town Dar es Salaam Hong Kong Karachi
Kuala Lumpur Madrid Melbourne Mexico City Nairobi
New Delhi Shanghai Taipei Toronto

With offices in

Argentina Austria Brazil Chile Czech Republic France Greece
Guatemala Hungary Italy Japan Poland Portugal
Singapore South Korea Switzerland Thailand Turkey Ukraine Vietnam

Oxford is a registered trade mark of Oxford University Press
in the UK and in certain other countries

Published in the United States
by Oxford University Press Inc., New York

© Oxford University Press, 2007

The moral rights of the author have been asserted
Database right Oxford University Press (maker)

First published 2007

A catalogue record for this title is available from the British Library
Library of Congress Cataloging in Publication Data
Plotkin, H. C. (Henry C.)
  Necessary knowledge / Henry Plotkin. -- 1st ed.
    p. cm.
  Includes bibliographical references and index.
  1. Evolutionary psychology.
    2. Knowledge, Theory of. 3. Nature and nurture. I. Title.
  BF698.95.P58 2007
  155.7--dc22

                                                         2006037289

Typeset by Cepha Imaging Private Ltd., Bangalore, India
Printed in Great Britain
on acid-free paper by
Biddles Ltd., King's Lynn

ISBN 978-0-19-856828-5 (Hbk: alk paper)

10 9 8 7 6 5 4 3 2 1

For Isobel Mae

Preface

This book presents the case for innate representational knowledge within the more general context of the relationship between the processes of the evolution of species and the learning of individuals. The general argument and the evidence are presented in Chapters 4, 5 and 6. The first chapter is an introduction to the issues, and a brief comment on the continuing scepticism, and often unnecessary disdain, for the introduction of evolutionary biology into matters of the mind, including cognition. Chapters 2 and 3 are historical, and Chapter 7 deals with matters philosophical. The science needs no justification. But why the history? And what place does philosophy have in a scientific monograph, the author of which is not a philosopher?

The short answer to both questions is that history and philosophy are important to all forms of scholarship. One of the dismaying features of the rise in the mid- and late 1980s of evolutionary thinking amongst a comparatively small number of psychologists was the seemingly dismal lack of knowledge of previous attempts to instil into the subject, in a viable form, evolutionary considerations. Evolutionary psychology was not born just two decades ago. Behaviourism inflicted enormous damage on psychological science, not least of which was the destruction of evolutionary thought in psychology which, under the likes of William James, Conway Lloyd Morgan and James Mark Baldwin, had thrived in the last decades of the nineteenth and for a decade into the twentieth century. It is to the shame of our discipline that so few students have any idea who these people were.

As to the philosophy, it is simply the case that for much of the last two and a half millennia, philosophy has comprised the single consistent and systematic analysis of all problems of human existence. Amongst these has been the issue of whether humans can know anything at all and, if we can, what that knowledge is, and the extent to which we can place trust in it. From the rationalism of ancient Greece to the empiricist epistemology of more recent centuries, two schools of thought have been at odds with one another. Modern cognitive science wedded to a modest evolutionary stance on cognition has something to tell philosophy about this schism.

I thank Carol Maxwell and Martin Baum of Oxford University Press for the help given in the production of this work. As is always the case, my greatest debt is to all those whose names appear in the following pages.

London, 2006.

Contents

CHAPTER 1

Pervasive problems

The philosopher Karl Popper wrote that '...*tabula rasa* theory is absurd: at every stage of the evolution of life and of the development of an organism, we have to assume the existence of some knowledge in the form of dispositions and expectations' (Popper 1972 p. 71). This assertion arose from Popper pursuing an evolutionary epistemology, i.e. a philosophy of knowledge based on evolutionary principles, which in the hands of others (notably Campbell 1974) is also a science of knowledge. It is a claim that, in transmuted and more specific form, will be pursued throughout this book. The transmuted claim is that some minimal representational knowledge is innate in all animals that can learn. This is the necessary knowledge in the title of this book, necessary knowledge which is already written onto our cognitive slates at birth.

This is, in fact, the strong form of the claim or hypothesis, and in that form it applies to most forms of human learning. In the final chapter, a modified, somewhat weaker, version is presented which embraces almost all forms of learning in most species of learners. However, for the sake of simplicity, it is the strong form that is pursued in most of what follows.

Behind this claim of innate representational knowledge is the answer to a fundamental question. The question is what is the relationship between the knowledge that each one of us has, and the evolution of our species? More generally, what is the relationship between evolution and the ability of any species of animal to learn?

Popper, though immensely erudite, was not playing the role of scientist in general or of psychologist specifically, and so cited no empirical findings against the notion of the *tabula rasa*. If he had been a scientist, and if he had sought to buttress his case at that time with evidence from within those areas of psychology, such as learning and reasoning, that deal with the acquisition and manipulation of knowledge, then he would have found very little to help his position. The notable exception would have been language and the Chomskian premise that innate knowledge of some kind is the only possible explanation of a number of features of language acquisition—though it might be noted that at least since Descartes drew his distinctions between humans and animals, language has been treated as an exception in one context or another for over 400 years. Nor would Popper have gained much *theoretical* support from scientists working within these disciplines, though again linguistic analysis would have been the exception.

Yet not much more than a quarter of a century later, another philosopher was able to extol the rise of what he called the 'new rationalism' (Fodor 1998), an essential element of which is the existence of innate knowledge. Fodor's position, though, which he first expressed in the 1980s (Fodor 1983), apart from the central notion of innate knowledge, was very different from that of Popper. In addition to his often expressed scepticism about the application of neoDarwinian evolutionary theory to human cognition, in arguing against the *tabula rasa* Fodor had at least the beginnings of empirical support by 1998 from studies in a number of different areas of cognition, and substantial numbers of psychologists and cognitive scientists by then believed that human and non-human learners alike come into the world with their cognitive slates already written on, quite apart from language. Not everyone, of course, was a convert from psychology's traditional empiricism, but there were enough, sometimes eminent, voices for the new rationalism to stand as an equal to other approaches in cognitive science.

What marks this period in psychology from the early 1970s to the mid 1990s is the entry of the nature–nurture dimension into the science of learning and reasoning itself. Whilst this has at times been done with reluctance, it has been important not only to cognitive science but also to how the nature–nurture issue itself has been considered. It raises two immediate points, which are the pervasive problems referred to by this chapter's title. The one concerns that reluctance; why is it that the nature–nurture question continues to be an emotive aspect of psychology, and indeed of all the social sciences? The second is why it simply cannot be ignored or even played down in importance; why the nature–nurture issue is actually one of the most enduring problems in all of psychology.

The demonization of nature

Pinker (2002) notes the derision in which the nature–nurture distinction is held by many, who consider it either outmoded or, if it ever was a problem, one which is now solved. Such disdain, however, is inappropriate. One of the aims of science is to seek generative (as opposed to successional) causal explanations of the phenomena of the world: 'to explain some pattern of happenings, we must be able to describe the causal mechanism which is responsible for it' (Harré 1972, p. 178). Psychology, then, is concerned with causal explanations of the human mind and behaviour (as well as the behaviour of other animals). The sources of those causes, which is what the nature–nurture distinction is about, is then also of central concern. This is not, and should not, be controversial. Nor should the human mind and behaviour most probably being always multiply caused and hence potentially multiply sourced be a contentious issue. Yet it is, which is why the nature–nurture issue still raises the hackles of some psychologists and other social scientists, and which gives rise to the disdain often still associated with the phrase. The hostility arises because these issues are inexorably related to the application of evolution, and hence also genetics, to the human mind, which whilst it has lessened in recent years, still gives rise to publications vituperative in tone such as 'Alas Poor Darwin' (Rose and Rose 2000), and, if anecdotal evidence be allowed, reference to psychologists of an evolutionary bent as 'the enemy' at a well-attended seminar on cognition in London in the autumn of 2003. There is no reason to doubt that such sentiments are still to be found in the academic community of 2006.

The problem arises from psychology, and in the context of the nature–nurture issue its scientific bed-fellow evolution, lying as close as any sciences can be to ideologies dealing with what it means to be human. Since the emergence of both evolution and psychology as sciences in the nineteenth century this has been a persistent difficulty, and one with which most other sciences have never had to deal (Plotkin 2004). One of the ways it has manifested itself, even amongst the most eminent of scientists, has been the difficulty so many of us have, perhaps all of us, in preventing our views of what is good and important about human life from penetrating our judgements about the social sciences and how they relate to the natural sciences. Given the certainty that human minds and behaviour are multiply caused with multiple sources of those causes, including genes, this has long given rise to sometimes irrational positions at best, and often intemperate and extreme stances at worst. The history of the nature–nurture distinction has not, though, always been emotionally and ideologically charged. It became so with the dawn of evolutionary science in the nineteenth century.

The distinction and argument about nature and nurture in determining human dispositions and behaviour goes back at least to Plato, though he did not, of course, use those words. The *Oxford English Dictionary* traces first usage of both terms to the early fourteenth century. Instincts as the acts of automata came to be identified with nature, and distinguished from learning through, and reasoning about, experience. No one did this with greater clarity than Descartes in his *Discourse on Method*. Considering 'automata, or moving machines' he argued that 'if there were such machines which had the organs and appearance of a monkey, or some other animal, we should have no way of recognizing that they were not entirely of the same nature as these animals, but that, if there were any machines that resembled our own bodies, and imitated our actions as much as possible, we should still have two certain ways of knowing that they were not real men'. The first of these ways is language and the second reasoning. Descartes continued thus: 'It is very remarkable that there are no men, however dull-witted and stupid, without excepting even imbeciles, who are incapable of putting words together and composing some sort of expression of their thoughts, while, on the contrary, there is no animal, however perfect and happily nurtured, capable of doing the same'. He went on to mention the existence of sign language in the deaf and parrots who imitate human speech, and on that basis concluded that 'this does not only show that animals have less reason than man; it shows that they have none at all' (Descartes 1637/1960, quotations from pp. 79–81). This was a stark distinction. On the one hand there are reasoning human beings possessed of language, the products of nurture, and on the other unreasoning animals devoid of language, wholly within the sphere of nature.

In the eighteenth century, the Cartesian distinction, though supported by Aristoteleans, who agreed with the notion that the human soul is rational but not that of animals, became muddied by the sensationalists (Richards 1987). The latter, represented by notables such as La Mettrie, Cabanis and Charles Darwin's grandfather, Erasmus, were of an empiricist stamp. They believed that humans and animals share the same source of knowledge, which is the senses. They also generally subscribed to the view that rational intelligence, whether in beast or man, arises out of some kind of associative process. Instincts were somewhat airily explained in terms of well-learned behavioural routines rather than being inborn patterns of behaviour. It is worth noting though that a field biologist of great stature, Réaumur, was inclined to dismiss the Cartesian beast–machine depiction even of invertebrates, though other biologists such as Buffon and Fabré were acutely aware of the existence of behaviours in many different kinds of animals that seemed to characterize particular species, and whose appearance seemed to have nothing to do with experience.

The theories of evolution of the nineteenth century changed everything. The Lamarckian and Darwinian approaches to learning (a force for nurture) and instinct (the product of nature) dominated writings on the distinction, or lack of it, between nature and nurture, and will be considered in the next chapter. All that need be said here is that it was with the appearance of Darwin's theory specifically, though certainly not through his personal agency, that the nature–nurture issue took an unpleasant turn. Herbert Spencer was one of the principal forces for bringing evolution into social philosophy. However, it was Darwin's cousin, Francis Galton, who was the villain of the piece. Galton was a fanatical hereditarian. His advocacy of the hereditary basis of almost all aspects of the human psyche was relentless. For Galton, all was nature upon which nurture could have little effect. His first book, *Hereditary Genius* (Galton 1869) was an exposition on the inheritance of intelligence, which he subsequently expanded to take in characteristics as diverse as business acumen, aptitude for hard work, curiosity and the capacity for making moral judgements.

Galton had been an instant convert to his cousin's theory of evolution, and the parallels between natural and artificial selection run by Darwin did not escape him. His conviction of the strong, if not overwhelming, hereditary basis of all psychological characteristics led Galton to the belief that artificial selection could be successfully established amongst humans to drive certain characteristics to extinction and other traits to prominence. The question of which characteristics should be extinguished and which promoted was a moral judgement made by Galton and his followers. The word 'eugenics' was introduced by Galton in the 1880s, and within 20 years the eugenics movement had a strong following on both sides of the Atlantic ocean, including some very influential people.

Eugenics, of course, was the conceptual sibling to the application of evolutionary notions to explain supposed racial differences. This combined with the rampant racialism of the Victorian era to result in racial theories based on the theory of evolution. Legal sterilization of the genetically unfit, which meant those whose behaviour was considered the result of stupidity, insanity (based on judgements across a very broad range of behaviours) or criminal intent and action, was first introduced in Indiana in 1907. By 1934 it had passed into law in 30 states of the USA, as well as in Canada, and four European countries, including Germany. The holocaust let loose upon Europe by the Nazis may be interpreted as the extreme manifestation of the eugenics movement.

Of all the egregious errors of the race theorists and eugenicists, the conceptually most damaging was the assumption that nature and nurture could be causally separated. This was the necessary conceptual precursor to the assertion that one is dominant over the other. Of all the egregious consequences of the unreasoning mantra 'nature not nurture' the worst was the backlash from many social scientists of the equally unreasoning and incorrect maxim of 'nurture not nature'. In the early years of his distinguished career, the anthropologist Franz Boas had been a staunch adherent to pluralistic explanations of human thought and behaviour. However, within a decade, he was advancing the view that it is culture, a form of nurture, that is the overwhelming force in human thought and behaviour (Boas 1911). It was under his stewardship that cultural anthropology was to emerge as the social science with the greatest antipathy to biological explanation.

Gould (1981), Freeman (1983), Degler (1991) and Plotkin (2004) provide somewhat differently nuanced accounts of the rise of the conception that nature and nurture were to be seen as wholly separable causes of the human mind, the supposed dominance of nature over nurture in the early part of the twentieth century, the resultant race theory, and the rise and fall of the eugenics movement.

Curiously unparallel events in experimental psychology led to a similar domination of claims for nurture and environmental causes in psychology itself. Without reference to

the rise of odious Galtonesque doctrines, or indeed initially
to any aspect of the nature–nurture controversy then raging,
John Watson at around the same time attempted to find a
way of positioning a scientific psychology that since its inception had struggled to cope with establishing a science from
what was the essentially solipsistic phenomena of the mind.
His *Psychological Review* paper (Watson 1913) was the start
of behaviourism which ruled over large parts of American
academic psychology for over half a century. What Watson
claimed was that only directly observable events could be
used to explain behaviour, whatever is happening in the
mind/brain being irrelevant and inaccessible. This extreme
form of peripheralism in effect placed psychological explanation firmly in the environment. His subsequent claim
regarding the infinite malleability of humans became one of
early psychology's most famous statements:

> Give me a dozen healthy infants, well-formed and my own
> specified world to bring them up in and I'll guarantee to take
> any one at random and train him to become any type of
> specialist I might select—doctor, lawyer, artist, merchant-chief
> and, yes, even beggar-man and thief, regardless of his talents,
> penchents, tendencies, abilities, vocations, and race of his
> ancestors (Watson 1924, p.104).

Despite a concession to tendencies, abilities and the like,
this assertion was generally taken to be an affirmation of the
tabula rasa in humans.

If what is in the mind/brain is an irrelevance, then so too
is what is in genes and the processes of development; so
too is the history of natural selection. With its penchant for
associationism and rejection of instincts, behaviourism delivered a large part of psychology into the empiricist sphere.
Whilst they came from different conceptual directions,

behaviourism and cultural anthropology were comfortable bed-fellows.

As applied science, by the late 1930s, eugenics had been shown by increased understanding of genetics and embryology to be based on deeply flawed science, and to have aims that were simply unattainable (Paul and Spencer 1995). Add to this the moral outrage deriving from the terrible injustices of forced sterilization and the unprecedented crime perpetrated in Europe as a result of Nazi racial doctrines. The result after the Second World War quite naturally was a revulsion amongst all thinking people to doctrines, scientific or otherwise, which attributed causal significance to genes and selection processes in every form of psychological trait, mechanism or process and every instance of behaviour. It was bogus science that had led to unimaginable evil. A recent review of academic journals has shown that the phrase 'Social Darwinism', the attempted explication of social life by Darwin's theory of evolution, grew exponentially in the 1940s, the great majority of such references being negative and condemnatory (Hodgson 2004).

The major changes to evolutionary theory that resulted from the work of William Hamilton (1964) and G.C. Williams (1966) which added the concept of inclusive fitness to Darwinian individual fitness and subsequently led some theorists to reconfigure evolutionary thinking into replicator theory (Dawkins 1982, 1983; Williams 1992), led to gene-based accounts of some altruistic behaviours that had been observed in many species of animals belonging to different phyla. Had such developments remained confined to explanations of non-human behaviour, the resulting discussions would surely have remained technical and dispassionate. However, when applied to humans from the mid-1970s onwards, the result was one of the more bitter, and personal, controversies within twentieth century science (Segerstrale 2000). The emergence of a more general evolutionary psychology in the 1990s was met with similar resistance, often using similar arguments (Plotkin 2004).

It would be incorrect to assert that hostility to genetic and evolutionary accounts of human psychology and behaviour remains as widespread and strong now as it was in previous decades. If nothing else, the application of evolutionary biological thinking to psychological matters has benefited from lessons learned from the initial round of criticisms directed at evolutionary psychology. There is now less to be critical of. It is possible also that a kind of institutional habituation has occurred, not just to the introduction of evolutionary thinking into psychology, but to accompanying terminology relating to innateness, renewed nature–nurture usage and instinct. However, as Fodor notes, 'Most cognitive scientists still work in a tradition of empiricism and associationism, whose main tenets haven't changed much since Locke and Hume' (Fodor 1998, p. 203), with the result that 'sooner or later political correctness and cognitive science are going to collide. Many tears will be shed and many hands will be wrung in public. So be it. If there is a human nature, and if it is to some interesting extent genetically determined, it is folly for humanists to ignore it' (Fodor 1998, pp. 207–208). Perhaps that reference to 'the enemy' at the London seminar was a part of the hand wringing.

On origins and the significance of the nature–nurture distinction

Few, perhaps no-one, now denies that whatever 'nature' and 'nurture' refer to, they are causally interwoven in determining human thought and behaviour. That is an essential part of any claim for multiple causation. Exactly how they interleave and interact is where the disputes and differences lie, and it is in seeking to understand precisely what their relationship is that it is necessary to understand what each does indeed refer to; and to do that, it is necessary for an initial distinction to be maintained between what is meant by nature on the one hand and nurture on the other.

Recourse to distinctions based on proximity and remoteness of cause, like Mayr's ultimate and proximate causes (Mayr 1961), fails to serve the purpose. All of life, be it of individual organisms, lineages of organisms, and their transformation in time, constitutes a concatenation of proximate causes. What does support an appropriate conceptual framework is one relating to causal origins, previously referred to as causal sources. For the specific case of cognition, it is necessary to consider the question of origins in two stages. The first, and most basic, is the origin of our species. The second are the origins of cognition itself. The next few paragraphs may appear to be absurdly self-evident to some— which, of course, they are. They will appear to be self-evident to all when the day comes that hands are no longer being wrung by die-hard empiricists. Since that day has not yet come, the self-evident must be stated.

There are, with regard to human origins, four possible types of causal explanation. We are either the products of evolution, or the products of some other process knowable by science but not yet known, or we are the accidental outcome of some chaotic and incomprehensible process that falls outside of scientific comprehension or we are the result of special (divine) creation. There are no other possibilities, and there are few serious scientists, not even the hand wringers, who would oppose the first of these and argue in favour of any of the other three. This does not mean that everyone agrees as to how evolution has occurred. It does mean that all do agree that modern humans are the product of the transformation of previous hominin species, and that modern humans are linked to our evolutionary past, **in part**, by our genes.

From this most general of self-evident statements comes the question that brings us closer to hand-wringing territory. How much does this apply to the human mind and the behaviour that it generates? Is it possible that psychological processes and mechanisms are somehow exempt from those causal links to our past evolution that the rest of our bodies are subject to, and hence are not part-caused by genes? Is it possible, in other words, that we should be invoking a form of Cartesian dualism in which 'body stuff' (res extensa) is evolutionarily and hence genetically part-caused, but 'mind stuff' (res cogitans) is not? Since there is, *a priori*, absolutely no reason to invoke such exemption and dualism, it must follow that there should, therefore, be near universal agreement that at least some of the causes of the human mind and behaviour must be rooted in our evolutionary origins. From what is known of the mechanisms within which are embodied the processes of evolution, it then follows that there should also be near universal agreement that those same minds and behaviours must be part-caused by genes. To deny the latter, i.e. the genetic part-causation, is to deny human evolutionary origins.

It should be noted that it is at this point in the self-evident argument that significant room for difference appears in two forms. The one, and this is a frequently held view by hand wringers, is that the evolutionary events in question and the accompanying genetic part-causes are ancient, probably hundreds of millions of years old, and not rooted in immediate human prehistory. As will be seen in a later chapter, the implicit assumption seems to be that there is some kind of proportionality in causal importance between the length of time that has elapsed since some process(es) and mechanism(s) evolved and the force and importance that must be attributed to the other part-causes that enter into the construction and operation of our minds. This is a matter very much at the heart of following chapters.

The other form of difference that enters the argument is the nature of the evolutionary process itself that gives rise to psychological traits. Fodor himself, for instance, has never hidden his doubts about neoDarwinian theory when applied to the mind. '... I'm not actually an adaptationist about the mind: I doubt, that is, that Darwinism is true of the phylogeny of cognition ... I think our kinds of minds are quite likely "hopeful monsters"' (Fodor 1998, p. 190). However, Fodor obviously does not deny evolutionary origins of some kind, even if they are radically different from those postulated by neoDarwinians. This is a matter that will not be pursued much in later chapters. The 'necessary knowledge' of this book owes nothing to the precise form and causes of the transformation of species in time.

Thus, exactly how evolution occurs is irrelevant to the main thrust of the argument. However, what no evolutionist denies, whatever their stamp, is that evolution changes gene forms and frequencies and it is these that constitute the material link between the present and the past. It is this causal force, only ever partial, which is what in this book all references to 'nature' mean. Mameli and Bateson (2006) provide a comprehensive survey and analysis of the notions of 'nature' and innateness.

What then of nurture? From Darwin onwards, evolution has been seen as a two-stage process: the one comprises the effects of the environment on variant forms—selection; the other the transmission of selected variation to subsequent generations. Well, not even the most die-hard of traditional neoDarwinists denies the causal force exerted by the environment on the development of those genes selected in the past in the transformation of genotypes into phenotypes, whether the phenotype has cognitive powers or not. Extreme examples of nurture residing in development would be organisms without nervous systems, such as plants, for whom the environment of development is as much a part-cause of every feature of that organism as the genes that are expressed during development. All such extra-genetic causation is what has traditionally been referred to as 'nurture'. The possibility that development may itself exert causal force on evolution is merely an extension of that traditional Darwinian view that evolution is a two-stage process, and has long been explicitly considered a possibility (Waddington 1959*a* for example). In recent years, the role of development in evolution has been more insistently presented in what is sometimes referred to as developmental systems theory or 'evo–devo' (Jablonka and Lamb 1998; Oyama 2000*b*; Gottlieb 2002; West-Eberhard 2003, to name just a very few of many). However, as stated previously, the precise causal form of evolution is not central to the case for innate knowledge.

What, then, of the more specific question about the origins of cognition. In general terms, cognition in any animal, including humans, is just another phenotypic trait, or set of traits, that is part-caused by selected genes, and part-caused by the environment of development. This means that nature and nurture are both causal forces in cognition itself, the set of psychological traits that most symbolize 'nurture'. Nurture has nature (Plotkin 1994). We are, however, an even more complex species than most that have evolved cognition with regard to two, possibly related, characteristics. Modern humans are a species whose individuals are born altricial, with a significantly greater amount and duration of postnatal brain growth than any other hominid (Coqueugniat *et al.* 2004) (and hence most probably any other animal). This means that our cognitive development is prolonged over a period of years and occurs within a social context of intensive caretaking. For these reasons, developmental effects are likely, *a priori*, to enter powerfully into any causal account of human psychological processes and mechanisms—perhaps more so than any other species that has evolved cognitive traits, including our closest living relatives.

There is, though, one additional factor to consider. Whatever one's views about human cognition and intelligence relative to that of other species of intelligent animal, the intelligence of humans is great, and certainly unique with regard to the form of human culture that it creates and within which it operates (Plotkin 2002*a*, 2003; Tomasello *et al.* 2004).

Thus, much of what we do and know and think is a product of individual intelligences arising from complex developmental experience residing within complex cultures.

There can be no exceptions in any species that has evolved cognitive capacities to the presence of the first two sets of causes (evolution and development) in determining any psychological process and mechanism, including those relating to cognition. In humans, the causation becomes even more complex because of the presence of cultural causation, which is likely to be pervasive, on cognition itself (see Lillard 1998; Siok *et al.* 2004 for examples; see Chapter 6 for others). Thus, for human beings, everything that we do and everything that we are cognitively is a result of some complex causal interaction between our genes, the environment of our development, and the cultures within which our individual cognitive processes and mechanisms function.

These encompass all the traditional domains of nature and nurture within a psychological context. It is nothing more than the conceptual and empirical programmes common to all the biological sciences, but expanded to accommodate the demands of the causal complexity of the human mind. Thus, if science is indeed the pursuit of generative causes woven into general patterns, then the nature–nurture issue is at the heart of psychology. It is not an optional extra. Nor is it resolved or irrelevant. It is the stuff of our daily doings. Psychological science is always the unravelling and understanding of the nature–nurture interaction for every aspect of the human mind, because the nature–nurture interaction is the interleaving of all the causal forces that determine our minds and behaviour. Unravelling that interaction for cognition itself is no less crucial for understanding cognition, though it is an understanding that must be placed within a complex causal architecture.

We are now some 150 years on from the establishment of psychology as a science. It might be thought something of an intellectual scandal for the discipline that the self-evident facts of genetic and evolutionary part-causation need to be spelled out to hand-wringing empiricists. The really important task, though, is for psychology and its related sciences to establish just how far nature extends into nurture, and how great is the influence of nurture on nature. This takes us back in time, not to the beginnings of psychology, but to the beginnings of evolutionary theory.

CHAPTER 2

The advantages of hindsight

If, as Popper declared, the notion of the *tabula rasa* is wrong, it is wrong because of the nature of the relationship between evolution and learning. Exactly what that relationship is, we now understand, is central to a full understanding of learning. It also has something to tell us about how evolution itself might be affected by other processes that promote change, such as early experience and learning itself, and so contributes to a broader understanding of the complexity governing the transformation not only of species in time, but of other forms of change in organisms and how these may be linked to speciation. In the early twenty-first century one can pose the question of how learning is connected to evolution, and evolution to learning, knowing that this is an issue that is both central to a science of cognition and problematic, and knowing too how others fumbled their way to an answer. The earliest of the evolutionary theorists seemed to intuit that learning, memory and thought—those characteristics that distinguish humans and hence presented the greatest challenge to their new ideas—needed to be placed within an evolutionary context. Yet throughout much of the nineteenth and into the twentieth century these pioneering evolutionists either did not want to be seen asking such questions explicitly or, if they did, they often enough gave only partial or contradictory answers. Early learning theorists fared no better. There are, though, lessons to be learned from these early accounts, including how not to approach these matters.

The first evolutionary theorist

It is one of the ironies of evolutionary science that the theorist most derided by contemporary evolutionists offered an account of how evolution occurs which, whilst mostly quite wrong, has elements which in the twenty-first century seem not nearly as outrageous as previously judged.

Jean-Baptiste Lamarck's *Philosophie Zoologique* of 1809 was a 400 page exposition of an evolutionary theory that preceded Darwin's *Origin* by half a century. As Hugh Elliot points out in the introduction to his translation of Lamarck's masterwork, Lamarck's misfortune was to be the author of the first explicit theory of evolution, an idea almost universally condemned at the time, which happened also, as a theory, to be incorrect, and was seen to be incorrect as soon as people read and understood Darwin's own theory 50 years later. So it was that in his own time, Lamarck was either openly damned or simply ignored for having given such strong voice to an idea, evolution, that most of his contemporaries thought a vile and abominable conception at best. Then when Darwin began to convince the majority of scientists that species are indeed transformed in time by a process quite different from that offered by his predecessor, Lamarck's work was denigrated for its being wrong. Now, with that advantage of hindsight, we can see that Lamarck was not as hopelessly wrong as his critics thought. It is also the case that Lamarck was a great deal more courageous than was Darwin, who famously excluded virtually all reference to humans in his *Origin*. Lamarck was not so reticent, there being explicit references to our own species in the *Philosophie*. In a remarkably modern account of human evolution by way of the development of a bipedal gait, opposable thumbs, the consequences of the change in centre of gravity resulting from an upright posture, the consequent dietary and hence dental and jaw changes that bipedalism might entail, all of which he ran together with the consequences of an intense sociality and the resultant demands for more effective communication, he concluded that

> … individuals stood in need of making many signs, in order rapidly to communicate their ideas, which were always becoming more numerous and could no longer be satisfied either with pantomimic signs or with the various possible vocal inflections. For supplying the large quantity of signs which had become necessary, they will by various efforts have achieved the formation of articulate sounds. At first they will only have used a small number, in conjunction with inflexions of the voice; gradually they will have increased, varied and perfected them, in correspondence with the growth in their needs and their gain of practice. In fact, habitual exercise of their throat, tongue and lips in the articulation of sounds will have highly developed that faculty in them.

> Hence would arise for this special race the marvellous faculty of speaking; and seeing that the remote localities to which the individuals of the race would have become distributed, would favour the corruption of the signs agreed upon for the transmission of each idea, languages would arise and everywhere become diversified.

> In this respect, therefore, all will have been achieved by needs alone: they will have given rise to efforts, and the organs adapted to the articulation of sounds will have become developed by habitual use.

> Such are the reflections which might be aroused, if man were distinguished from animals only by his organisation, and if

his origin were not different from theirs. (All are successive paragraphs from p. 173.)

This lengthy quotation makes two points. The first is his frankness in his inclusion of human origins within an evolutionary context, including what many, going back to Descartes, have considered our most exalted characteristic. The second is that they present the essential elements of his theory. Lamarck's evolutionism had two components; one of these is a vision of the ordering of all living creatures, and the other is an explanation of how this order came to be. The former is of little interest and is an account of a *scala naturae* that begins with the continuous spontaneous generation of the most simple life forms—organisms with 'only the rudiments of organization' (p. 237)—which are slowly ('time has no limits and can be drawn upon to any extent' p. 114) and gradually ('it is no longer possible to doubt that nature has done everything little by little and successively', p. 11) transformed into organisms of increasing organizational complexity, and thus ending with human beings. So whilst our origins are the same as those of all other life forms, we nonetheless occupy a lofty position in the great scheme of things.

What is of real interest is how this comes about. Chapter 7 of the *Philosophie* is entitled 'Of the influence of the environment on the activities and habits of animals, and the influence of the activities and habits of these living bodies in modifying their organisation and structure' (p. 106). In this chapter title is Lamarck's theoretical heart, and it was given in the expression of two laws. The first law states: 'In every animal which has now passed the limits of its development, a more frequent and continuous use of any organ gradually strengthens, develops and enlarges that organ, and gives it a power proportional to the length of time it has been so used; while the permanent disuse of any organ imperceptibly weakens and deteriorates it, and progressively diminishes its functional capacity, until it finally disappears' (p. 113). This is usually referred to as the law of use and disuse.

The second law, famously known as the law of inheritance of acquired characters, states: 'All the acquisitions or losses wrought by nature on individuals, through the influence of the environment in which their race has long been placed, and hence through the influence of the predominant use or permanent disuse of any organ; all these are preserved by reproduction to the new individuals which arise, provided that the acquired modifications are common to both sexes, or at least to the individuals which produce the young' (p. 113). As has been pointed out many times, the second law was not original to Lamarck (see Zirkle 1946; Freeman 1974; Mayr 1982 for some examples) but is an element of folk biology that goes back thousands of years. Thus, again as noted by many, it is another of evolutionary biology's ironies that the second law came to be so closely associated with Lamarck, and its incorrectness seen, from Weismann onwards, to be the decisive blow that destroyed Lamarck's theory when Lamarck had merely utilized a commonplace belief. Lamarck's theory was indeed incorrect. Although in several places in the *Philosophie* something akin to natural selection is hinted at, it probably is every reader's conviction as to the importance of natural selection that makes us read these passages as hints of any form. The fact is that Lamarck built on no notion approximating to natural selection, and the inheritance of acquired characters is simply wrong. Nor is it the first law, use and disuse, which is of any great interest, though Darwin himself and others (Mayr 1982) considered it to be of potential significance. It is within the general framework of what Lamarck conjectured leads to use and disuse that can be read in the twenty-first century with some interest.

Lamarck's real contribution was to replace the 'static world picture by a dynamic one in which not only species but the whole chain of being and the entire balance of nature was constantly in flux' (Mayr 1982, p. 352). Darwin added historical causation, selection and a mass of evidence making evolution credible, and as a theory the forerunner of what became the normal understanding of twentieth century science that few things in the universe are constant; everything changes. Lamarck's own understanding of this was faulty because he did not believe that any species ever became extinct, the *scala naturae* being constant in overall form with 'missing' species present somewhere on the planet, even if unknown to us, and anyway being replaced by identical forms as the chain of being transformed in time. Nonetheless, the first half of the *Philosophie* is an account of how every individual organism partakes of a dynamic, changing interaction with its environment because it is the environment which is in constant flux. Lamarck was what later would be come to be called a gradualist uniformitarianist, meaning he believed that the causes of change in the world had always been the same and that this constancy of change led to the gradual—so gradual as to be imperceptible to any one person—transformation of species.

> Now I shall endeavour to show that variations in the environment induce changes in the needs, habits and mode of life of living beings, and especially of animals; and that these changes give rise to modifications or developments in their organs and the shape of their parts. If this is so, it is difficult to deny that the shape or external characters of every living body whatever must vary imperceptibly, although that variation only becomes perceptible after a considerable time (p. 45).

It is in this quotation that a modern evolutionist might find something of interest, but only if it is understood that Lamarck was quite explicit in ruling out any direct effects of the environment on organisms: 'whatever the environment may do, it does not work any direct modification whatever in the shape and organisation of animals' (p. 107). It is the changes in need leading to changes in activity that mediate the effects of environmental change.

Thus it is not his two laws that now should attract attention. It is the causal chain of events that leads to use/disuse alterations in structures and their supposed transmission to offspring wherein lies just a hint of what might be thought significant by evolutionists in the twentieth and twenty-first centuries. The causal chain that Lamarck draws is change in the environment effecting changes in need, and changes in need then resulting in alterations in the organism. If the organism is an animal, then the most important changes being driven by altered needs is activity—behaviour. Behaviour was, for Lamarck, one of the primary causes of evolutionary change. Indeed, in some places in the book, it is behaviour itself that is the engine driving change for the animal, not just changes in the world: '... as the individuals of one of our species change their abode, climate, habits, or manner of life, they become subject to influences which little by little alter the consistency and proportions of their parts, their shape, properties and even their organization; so that in course of time everything in them shares these mutations' (pp. 38–39). What we have here is a glimmer of the idea that change in the environment may originate from within organisms, and that such environmental change in turn reverberates in the structures and functioning of organisms, which latter may in turn feed back to effect further change in the environment—a two-way dynamic interaction of organism and environment in which the origination of initial cause need not of necessity be changes in the environment only, as Lamarck mostly asserted, but might also reside within the organism. It is, perhaps, not reading too much into the *Philosophie* to see here the beginnings of notions such as Waddington's exploitive system (Waddington 1959a) and Odling-Smee's niche construction (Odling-Smee *et al.* 2003).

What is most striking about Lamarck's writings is the eminence given to behaviour in that causal chain leading to use/disuse, and repeated attempts by him to place some kind of cognitive dimension to behaviour—though inexplicably, he made no attempt to link cognition to evolution. He proposes what one might call a *scala cogitans* which begins with irritability in the most 'imperfect animals' which are possessed of no feeling; progresses through the animals that 'are capable of receiving sensations, and possess a very vague inner feeling of their existence' and even 'the faculty of forming ideas'; and which ends with the most perfect animals (humans) being able to combine ideas 'to form judgements and complex ideas' (p. 48). This is a much repeated theme. 'Nature thus succeeds in endowing a living body with the faculty of locomotion, without the impulse of an external force; of perceiving objects external to it; of forming ideas by comparison of impressions received from one object with those received from others; of comparing or combining these ideas which are merely ideas of another order; in short, of thinking' (pp. 48–49).

Right at the end of the book, he made an astonishing extension to this dimension: 'Besides the *individual reason* of which I have been speaking, there is established, in every country and region of the earth, in proportion to the knowledge of the men who live there and to certain other factors, a *public reason*, which is almost universal, and which is upheld until new and sufficient causes operate to change it' (p. 404—italics in the original). What Lamarck is writing about in this brief passage is what a century later would be come to be called culture, culture as shared values and communal knowledge, and almost two centuries later social reality (Searle 1995) and the recognition of the power that human culture has to have been as a causal force in human evolution (Plotkin 2002a). Whatever judgements people make of Lamarck, his thinking truly was ahead of his time.

The whole of Part III of the *Philosophie* is a form of physiological psychology, constituting 'an enquiry into the physical causes of feeling, into the force which produces actions, and lastly into the origin of the acts of intelligence observed in various animals' (p. 283). Intelligence itself is viewed as '... most wonderful, especially when highly developed; and it may then be regarded as the high-water-mark of what nature can achieve by means of organization' (p. 279). It is quite clear that what is referred to here as a *scala cogitans* is implicitely related to Lamarck's *scala naturae*, and hence is a product of evolution. However, Lamarck is never entirely explicit about this, and he never makes the connection between what he describes as 'needs and habits', that crucial part of the causal chain that links changes in the environment to use/disuse, and his conceptions of sensation, emotion, intelligence and inner feeling. Thus he never relates these psychological traits to that dynamic relationship between the environment and organisms.

Lamarck made surprisingly scant observations on instinct, which he seemed to pair with habit as merely unthinking action. 'Hence the origin of (their) habitual actions and special inclinations, which have received the name of instinct', which 'same habits and instinct are handed on from generation to generation' (pp. 352–353). He certainly did not make the explicit link between intelligence and instinct that Herbert Spencer later did using Lamarck's own theory.

In conclusion, and in the absence of his making any linkage between habit, instinct and the *scala cogitans*, what two centuries on seems significant about Lamarck's theory is the overall sense that he imparts of organism and environment in dynamic flux; and of the causal role of behaviour in evolution. For Mayr, 'his recognition of the importance of behaviour' (Mayr 1982, p. 359) is one of Lamarck's important virtues. Just how significant this might have been is attested to by Mayr himself who later in his magisterial 1982 history asserts that 'Many if not most acquisitions of new structures in the course of evolution can be ascribed to selection forces exerted by newly acquired behaviours. Behaviour, thus, plays an important role as the pacemaker of evolutionary change. Most adaptive radiations were apparently caused by behavioural shifts' (Mayr 1982, p. 612). If Mayr is correct, then Lamarck's theory can be judged rather more important than is usually the case.

There is a curious footnote to Lamarck's *Philosophie*. 'I lay down, then, as a fundamental principle and unquestionable truth, the proposition that there are no innate ideas, but that all ideas whatever spring either directly or indirectly from sensations which are felt and noticed' (p. 364). On the previous page, he explicitly acknowledges Locke, adding '*there is nothing in the understanding which was not previously in sensation*' (p. 363—italics in the original). Epistemologically, Lamarck was an empiricist, which may go some way to account for his failure to see any links between innate behaviours, instincts, and intelligence.

Herbert Spencer

As a paradoxical figure in the history of science and philosophy, Spencer can have few rivals. Admired by the likes of

John Stuart Mill during his lifetime, a close friend of T.H. Huxley, revered by the American industrialist Andrew Carnegie and other major financial and industrial figures, Darwin himself altered one of the most famous passages in the final page of the *Origin of Species* in its sixth edition of 1872 to read: 'In the future I see open fields for far more important researches. Psychology will be securely based on the foundation already well laid by Mr. Herbert Spencer, that of the necessary acquirement of each mental power and capacity by gradation' (1872*a*, p. 373). Yet in his autobiography Darwin wrote that 'I am not conscious of having profited in my own work by Spencer's writings. His deductive manner of treating every subject is wholly opposed to my frame of mind. His conclusions never convince me ... his fundamental generalisations ... do not seem to me to be of any strictly scientific use' (p. 64 in the de Beer edition of 1983, first published in 1887 in a volume of collected works edited by Darwin's son Francis).

Similarly contrasting views are to be found long after his death. His work has been referred to with frank contempt by most (Himmelfarb 1968; Freeman 1974; Mayr 1982). Yet in his introduction to a collection of Spencer's writings on social evolution, Peel describes him as 'the first, and probably remains the greatest, person to have written sociology, so-called, in the English language' (Peel 1972, p. vii). Richards, in his wonderful history, judges that 'Spencer's ideas played the sort of role in the development of theories about the evolution of mind and behaviour that can be neither ignored nor denigrated' (Richards 1987, p. 246).

The problem lies partly in his almost wholly deductive methodology intermixed with a scattering of necessarily supportive descriptive biology (and folk psychology and anthropology where necessary), in which it is impossible to judge whether one is reading science or philosophy. Spencer seems to have recognised this himself when, in his autobiography, he tells the following brief tale: 'He (T.H. Huxley) was one of a circle in which tragedy was the topic, when my name came up in connexion with some opinion or other, whereupon he remarked—"Oh! You know, Spencer's idea of a tragedy is a deduction killed by a fact"' (Spencer 1904, vol. 1 p. 403). The other difficulty arises from his insouciance in giving due weight to the scientists whose views and findings he built his ideas on. For example Lamarck, whose theory was absolutely central to Spencer's evolutionism, gets just three casual mentions in his two volume autobiography. In the first edition of his *Principles of Psychology* (1855), Lamarck's name does not appear. This did not change in the second edition of 1870 and 1872, in which he notes in his introduction that the great difference between the reception of the first edition and what he expected for the second would be due to the 'great change of attitude towards the Doctrine of Evolution in general, which has taken place during the last ten years, has made the Doctrine of Mental Evolution seem less unacceptable ...' (p. iv). This is a clear reference to Darwin's work and no-one else's, and the failure to acknowledge this appropriately is a characteristic of Spencer's writing.

It remains the case, however, that no account of the nineteenth century ideas linking evolution with learning can omit Spencer. Unlike Lamarck, he made explicit and direct connections between them, and in doing so he was the first evolutionary epistemologist even though the evolutionary theory that he adopted was wrong. Spencer first came to embrace a theory of evolution after reading a critical account of Lamarck in Lyell's *Principles of Geology* in the early 1840s. He immediately embraced 'the hypothesis that the human race has been developed from some lower race' (Spencer 1904, vol. 1, p. 176) and noted that: 'Its congruity with the course of procedure throughout things at large, gave it an irresistible attraction; and my belief in it never afterwards wavered, much as I was, in after years, ridiculed for entertaining it' (p. 177). Over the next 20 years, Spencer built upon that early conviction that species are indeed transformed in time as the heart of a truly synthetic philosophy that linked all transformations—of species, of individuals during development, of the growth of individual knowledge and of changes in societies—by a marriage of three processes the combined effects of which account for all forms of change in living systems. The first process was largely Lamarckian in character and comprised the dynamic interaction of organisms, or groups of organisms, with environmental change such that living forms remain in a state of equilibrium with the environment. The second borrowed from the conception of a *scala naturae* that proceeds from simple to complex forms and which is clearly stated in Spencer's definition of evolution as 'definable as a change from an incoherent homogeneity to a coherent heterogeneity' (Spencer 1862, p. 291, from Peel 1972)—this was a dimension of complexity and increasing division of labour. The third was Lamarck's second law, the inheritance of acquired characters, adherence to which Spencer never wavered from in spite of the gathering conceptual force behind Darwin's idea of selection as the principal driver of evolution. The outcome of these processes is that change in living systems is always progressive in form, whatever it is that is evolving.

This form of universal progressive transformation resulting from the joint action of those three basic processes extending from the earliest and most 'simple' living forms to the most complex of human societies was not necessarily absurd

as a conception, it being mirrored, though without the progres-
sivism, by what has become known as universal Darwinism in
its different twentieth century forms. The grandeur of
Spencer's system even led some to believe this was a set of
ideas on a par with those of Newton. What should have
seriously damaged his case was that he often resorted to
outrageous analogies in order to support his position. For
example, in an essay entitled *The Social Organism*, Spencer
drew repeated parallels between circulatory systems of single
organisms on the one hand, with travel and communication
systems in human societies on the other.

> Going back once more to those lower animals in which there
> is found nothing but a partial diffusion, not of blood, but
> only of crude, nutritive, fluids, it is to be remarked that the
> channels through which the diffusion takes place, are mere
> excavations through the half-organized substance of the
> body: they have no lining membranes, but are mere *lacunae*
> traversing a rude tissue. Now countries in which civilization is
> but commencing, display a like condition: there are no roads
> properly so called; but the wilderness of vegetal life covering
> the earth's surface, is pierced by tracks, through which the
> distribution of crude commodities takes place' (Spencer 1860,
> p. 66 in the essay collection edited by Peel 1972).

He went on to note the parallels between circulatory
systems in more 'advanced' organisms and the communication and distribution systems of 'advanced' societies; and
also to draw at length similar analogies between nervous
system function in 'primitive' and 'advanced' organisms and
executive functions in societies occupying positions along a
similar dimension.

The parallels drawn by Spencer make the theory appear
ridiculous, but it did have certain virtues. It placed the study
of the human mind and human culture firmly within a

natural science context for the first time, and even if the system was entirely wrong it provided an example that others wielding better theory, like Darwin himself, would later follow. The application of a progressive theory to the transformation of societies also provided an enlightened and optimistic alternative to the natural science accounts of different human societies and cultures that race theorists using Darwinian theory were subsequently to inflict on the social sciences (see Chapter 1). In addition, of course, it also provided the context for Spencer's psychology, which drew specific links between evolution and learning.

Looking back on his life's work, Spencer noted in the second volume of his autobiography that the conceptual backdrop for his *Principles of Psychology* was 'adaptation as a universal principle of bodily life' and 'progressive adaptation became increasingly adjustment of inner subjective relations to outer objective relations' (Spencer 1904, vol. 2, p. 11). In *Principles of Psychology*, he defined life as 'the continuous adjustment of internal relations to external relations' (Spencer 1855, p. 374). Accordingly, in psychological terms, '... all mental phenomena are incidents of the correspondence between the organism and its environment' (p. 584) such correspondence being 'a thing of degree, which passes insensibly from its lowest to its highest forms' (p. 584). Spencer's book is thus the first analysis ever made of the minds of humans and non-humans as changing mental states that in some way match the changing world in which they operate. This was a not insignificant step in developing an evolutionary epistemology.

Spencer was an associationist, who considered the establishment of associations to be part of the process of equilibration by which internal states come to match those external to the organism.

> There is evidence pointing to the inference, that the law in
> virtue of which all psychical states that occur together tend to
> cohere, and cohere the more the more they are repeated
> together, until they become indissoluble—the law in virtue of
> which nervous connections are formed. When a change made
> in one part of an organism is habitually followed by a change
> in another; and when the electrical disturbance thus
> produced in one part, comes to be in constant relation to that
> in another; the frequent restoration of electrical equilibrium
> between the two parts, being always effected through the
> same route, may tend to establish a permanent line of
> conduction—a nerve (Spencer 1855,p. 544).

As was usual in his writing, Spencer had no empirical
support for this neurological 'deduction', but there is here an
anticipation of the likes of Pavlov and Hebb in the twentieth century.

Instincts also play a prominent role in Spencer's psychology.
He distinguished them from reflexes 'in so far as an instinctive action involves the co-ordination of many impressions;
and in so far as the chief ganglion consequently undergoes
complicated changes; and in so far may there be incipient
sensations—a dawning consciousness' (Spencer 1855, p. 540).
Instincts, like all psychological processes and mechanisms,
are subject to progressive development, both within an organism during individual development, and between organisms
as evolution occurs.

> If, as the instincts become higher and higher, the various
> psychical changes of which they are severally composed
> become less and less definitely co-ordinated; there must come
> a time when the co-ordination of them will no longer be
> perfectly regular. If these compound reflex actions, as they
> grow more compound also become less decided; it follows
> that they will eventually become comparatively undecided.
> The actions will begin to lose their distinctively automatic

character. And that which we call instinct will gradually merge into something higher (Spencer 1855, p. 553).

One 'something higher' into which instincts might merge as a means 'of bringing internal relations into harmony with external relations … in consciousness which not only do not include any active adjustment of the organism to its environment, but which often have but a comparatively indefinite reference to external relations' Spencer 1855, p. 554) is memory, which he saw as an internal adjustment to changes in the world which do not necessarily entail an immediate, active response as do instincts. Another 'something higher' is reason, which Spencer considered to be another form of internal adjustment, of adaptation, to the external world, but adjustment in which 'motor changes, and the impressions that must accompany them, simply become nascent—then by the partial excitation of the nervous agents concerned, there is produced an *idea* of such motor changes and impressions; or, as before explained, a *memory* of the motor changes before performed under like circumstances and of the impressions that resulted' (Spencer 1855, p. 566—italics in the original).

Spencer's continuous resort to the notion of changing internal states being in equilibrium with changing external states, together with his insistence on how all psychological states and mechanisms originate in action, in the potency of the response, is also a kind of prescient echo of the cognitive psychology that Piaget would develop some 80 years later. However, what makes Spencer important in the context of this book is his repeated insistence that instinct cannot be separated from these 'somethings higher'. He makes the point many times and in different ways. Thus '… the highest forms of psychical activity arise little by little out of the lowest, and, scientifically considered, cannot be definitely separated from them' (Spencer 1855, p. 564). Thus 'If every instinctive action is an adjustment of inner relations to outer relations—which it is impossible to deny; if every rational action is also an adjustment of inner relations to outer relations—which it is equally impossible to deny; then, any alleged distinction can have no other basis than some difference in the characters of the relations to which the adjustment is made' (Spencer 1855, p. 565), the difference lying along that dimension of simplicity to complexity. 'Thus, the insensible evolution through which instinctive actions pass into rational actions, simultaneously evolves perceptions and rational intuitions out of these complex impressions, by which the higher instincts are guided' (Spencer 1855, p. 571).

Spencer used the second law of Lamarck further to tie instinct, that which is innate, to 'higher' forms of intelligence. 'Thus, the common notion that there is a line of demarcation between reason and instinct, has no foundation whatever in fact' (Spencer 1855, p. 572). Then with explicit reference to differences between Locke and Kant (see Chapter 7) he noted:

> ... the simple universal law that the cohesion of psychical
> states is proportionate to the frequency with which they
> have followed one another in experience, requires but to be
> supplemented by the law that habitual psychical successions
> entail some hereditary tendency to such successions, which,
> under persistent conditions, will become cumulative in
> generation after generation, to supply an explanation of all
> psychological phenomena; and, among others, of the so-called
> 'forms of thought'. Just as we saw that the establishment of
> those compound reflex actions which we call instincts, is
> comprehensible on the principle that inner relations are, by
> perpetual repetition, organized into correspondence with
> outer relations; so, the establishment of those consolidated,

those indissoluble, those *instinctive* mental relations constituting our ideas of Space and Time, is comprehensible on the
same principle (Spencer 1855, p. 579—italics added).

Here again is a faint prescient echo of the evolutionary
Kantianism of Konrad Lorenz a century later, and of the
evolutionary psychology that emerged in the 1980s.

In arguing that 'it is not simply that a modified form of
constitution produced by new habits of life, is bequeathed
to future generations; but it is that the modified nervous
tendencies produced by such new habits of life, are also
bequeathed; and if the new habits of life become permanent, the tendencies become permanent' (Spencer 1855,
p. 526). Spencer was using the notion of the inheritance of
acquired characters to link instincts to learning. Because
what is learned is an adaptive adjustment of internal to
external events, consistent learning of the same thing(s)
becomes, via the inheritance of acquired characters, the
basis of instinct; and instinct forms the inherited behavioural base from which further learning and reasoning
occurs. Thus it was that Spencer made explicit connections
between what is innate and what is learned in a way that
Lamarck did not. Indeed in linking them so tightly again he
anticipated by a century the developments of the 1960s and
1970s, though whether that linkage was of the same kind
that Lorenz and others had made (see Chapter 4) is debateable. The imprecision of Spencer's writings might seem to
allow for an identity with twentieth century theorists that
probably was not there. In any event, on one crucial point
Spencer differed from the stance taken by Lorenz a hundred
years later—Spencer was a Lamarckian wielding soon to
be discredited evolutionary ideas, whereas Lorenz was an
unadulterated Darwinian.

Charles Darwin

Darwin was introduced to the ideas and writings of
Lamarck by one of his Edinburgh mentors, Robert Grant,
when he was a very young student (Desmond and Moore
1991). It was only much later in his life, long after he had
formulated his own theory of evolution, that he came across
the work of Spencer. It is very unlikely that the philosopher
had much effect on any of Darwin's ideas, but the French
biologist certainly did occupy some of Darwin's thoughts
both before, during and after his *Beagle* voyage. One of the
early entries in his *Beagle* journal describes the blindness
of a small mole-like mammal which he came across in
Argentina, noting that 'Lamarck would have been delighted
with this fact, had he known it, when speculating (probably
with more truth than usual with him) on the gradually
acquired blindness of the Aspalax ...' (Darwin 1890, p. 49—
italics in the original). The acerbity may owe something to
his remark being written before Darwin was himself a
convinced evolutionist, and partly to a misunderstanding of
Lamarck, a misunderstanding that was not unique to him.
Richards notes that Darwin had pencilled into the margin
of his copy of Lamarck's *Histoire naturelle* 'Because use
improves an organ, wishing for it, or its use, produces it!!!
Oh—' (Richards 1987, p. 93). As Mayr (1982) points out,
mistranslation of the French 'besoin' as 'want' was widespread and led many to believe quite incorrectly that Lamarck
advocated that it was the will of animals that played a crucial
part in the causal chain that led to evolution, when it was, of
course, 'need' that occupied that role in his *Philosophie* and
elsewhere.

Darwin's theory of evolution was, of course, very different
from that of Lamarck, and not just with regard to the central

role played by variation and natural selection. Darwin drew much closer links between instinct, and learning and habit than did Lamarck. Whilst like Spencer in this regard, he came to this view before Spencer did, and approached it with a subtlety that Spencer never did. Richards notes that another annotation, this time in the margin of a Royal Society publication on animal instinct, read 'important, as showing that instincts probably arise from habit and not structure' (Richards 1987, p. 92). Later entries to his M and N notebooks, written in the period 1838–1839, some of the entries from just before he had conceived of his own theory of evolution and some soon after, read as follows: 'instinct is hereditary knowledge of things which might be /possibly/ acquired by habit' (Gruber 1974, p. 345—the forward slashes enclosing words added by Darwin). A slightly earlier, and more tentative entry reads: 'My father has somewhere heard that pulse of new born babies of labouring classes are slower than those of Gentlefolks, & that peculiarities of forms in trades (as sailor, tailor, blacksmiths?) are likewise hereditary …' (Gruber 1974, p. 274). Much greater certainty is expressed by Darwin more than 30 years later in *The Expression of the Emotions in Man and Animals*: 'Actions, which were at first voluntary, soon become habitual, and at last hereditary, and may then be performed even in opposition to the will (Darwin 1872*b*, p. 356).

There are difficulties in attempting to understand precisely what Darwin was thinking, arising from problems of uncertainty as to exactly what he meant when he used certain words and phrases. For example, the words 'habit', 'habitual' and 'memory' are seldom, if ever, prior to *The Descent of Man* in 1871, placed firmly within what a modern context would be called individual experience and cognition. Sometimes habitual acts seem to be products of individual cognition without any hereditary basis; at other times they are instincts, and hence innate. In the N notebooks dated16 March 1839, for example, Darwin wrote:

> Is not that kind of memory which makes you do a thing properly, even when you cannot remember it, as my father trying to remember the man's Christian name. writing for the surname, analogous to instinctive memory, & consequently instinctive action.—Sir J. Sebright has given the phrase 'hereditary habits' very clearly, all I must do is to generalize it, & see whether applicable at all cases.—& analogize it with ordinary *habits* that is my new part of the view.—let the proof of hereditariness in habits be considered as a grand step if it can be generalized' (Gruber 1974, p. 342—italics in the original).

These were, of course, fragmentary notes to and for himself, and it is unreasonable to expect clarity from them. However, it is difficult to see whether Darwin was simply confused by the complexity of the relationship between what is innate and what is the product of individual experience, or whether he was reaching towards a more complex formulation of how instincts and individual experience and learning interact.

There is also a problem arising, presumably, from the jottings of a man who is slowly settling into a fully materialist stance. Two extracts from the C notebooks of 1838 make the point. 'All structures either direct effect of habit, or hereditary /& combined/ effect of habit'. (Gruber 1974, p. 448). Also 'habits become important element in classification, because structure has tendency to follow it, or it may be hereditary & strictly point out affinities …' (Gruber 1974, p. 450). In the M notebooks, written at around the same period, Darwin also notes that there is a 'strong argument for brain bringing thought, & not merely instinct, a separate thing superadded.—we can thus trace causation of thought.—it is brought within limits of explanation.—obeys same laws as other parts of structure' (Gruber 1974, p. 284). These may be vague notes to himself, but Darwin seems here to have been moving towards a thoroughly physicalist view in which thoughts, habits and instincts are structures in the brain, in some ways comparable with other corporeal structures.

Gruber's view of Darwin's ambiguities is a generous one based on the difference in Darwin's thinking that came with his formulation of natural selection as the principal force of evolutionary change. Prior to that, Darwin was convinced of the non-fixity of species but had no clear notion of how this occurred, but he seemed to accord behaviour considerable significance in the transformation of individual organisms, and hence ultimately in species transformation. According to Gruber:

> For adaptive behavioural change to precede and influence structural change, it is necessary that previously inherited structures do not completely determine behaviour. In other words, instinctive behaviour must be somewhat variable and intelligently guided in ways that depend on the immediate circumstances of life … he believed simply that the fortuitous requirements of a particular situation would evoke an adaptive variation in behaviour, which might then become habitual and finally perhaps instinctual' (Gruber 1974, p. 229–230).

However, after Darwin had taken on the notion of natural selection 'the idea that functional change can precede and influence structural change took on a new force. Those functional changes which were supported by ensuing structural changes would be not only consolidated and preserved, but often enhanced, if natural selection happened to move the course of evolution in the same direction as the initiating functional change' (Gruber 1974, p. 230).

That is a very particular twentieth century view of what Darwin was striving towards, and may well be correct. However, because Darwin famously omitted from *The Origin of Species* almost all mention of what he later called 'mental powers', it is also a view that cannot be confirmed from his more disciplined writings. Another interpretation is 'related to Darwin's lack of a clear distinction between animals' selecting habits because of their usefulness and nature's selecting animals because of their useful habits' (Richards 1987, p. 143).

Wishing to reduce the opposition to his theory of evolution by avoiding mention of humans as much as possible, in *The Origin of Species by Means of Natural Selection* Darwin confined his treatment of behaviour at large to a single chapter on instinct, and with but a fleeting reference to Mozart as a musical prodigy, he concentrated on three specific instincts: egg laying in the cuckoo, 'slave-making' instincts in ants, and egg cell construction in honey bees. Yet even under the rather strict constraints that Darwin placed on his treatment of minds, human or animal, in the *Origins*, there is an ambiguity in the way he presents the notion of instinct:

> An action ... when performed by an animal, more especially by a very young one, without experience, and when performed by many individuals in the same way, without their knowing for what purpose it is performed, is usually said to be instinctive. But I could show that none of these characters are universal. *A little dose of judgement or reason*, as Pierre Huber expresses it, often comes into play, even with animals low in the scale of nature (Darwin 1872a, p. 184— italics added).

His seeming daring in adding a reasoning element to his formulation of instinct appears to confirm the view that he was looking for sources of variation such that instincts would bear the same characteristic of variation as do the corporeal structures that he explicitly likened them to: 'instincts are as important as corporeal structures for the welfare of each species' and further 'it is at least possible that slight modifications of instinct might be profitable to a species; and if it can be shown that instincts do vary ever so little, then I can see no difficulty in natural selection preserving and continually accumulating variations of instinct to any extent that was profitable'. How variations based on the effects of reasoning can be transmitted to offspring is not directly addressed, but the implicit assumption must have been that some form of Lamarckian inheritance of acquired characters was being appealed to by Darwin, even if in that same paragraph he wrote 'I believe that the effects of habit are in many cases of subordinate importance to the effects of natural selection of what may be called spontaneous variations of instincts' (Darwin 1872a, p. 185). So some form of mental power such as reasoning might introduce an element of habit, in the sense of an individually acquired—learned—variation on an inherited behaviour which will slightly change an instinct and, if that variation is beneficial, the habit element may itself become inherited.

In *The Descent of Man*, Darwin continued to consider it likely that what he was by then calling 'intelligent actions' might be inherited and 'converted into instincts' (Darwin 1871, p. 447 in the Modern Library edition). One of the issues that he briefly raised was the relationship between numbers of instincts and amount of intelligence within any one species. He noted with approval Cuvier's avowal that instinct and intelligence stand in inverse relation to one another, but in the next sentence seems equally to approve of Pouchet having demonstrated no such relationship, and concluded a few paragraphs on that 'a high degree of intelligence is certainly compatible with complex instincts, and although actions, at first learned voluntarily can soon through habit be performed with the quickness and certainty of a reflex action, yet it is not improbable that there is a certain amount of *interference* between the development of free intelligence and of instinct—which latter implies some inherited modification of the brain' (Darwin 1871, p. 447 in the Modern Library edition—italics added). So continued the confusion and uncharacteristic lack of clarity as to just what is the relationship between innate instincts, the product of evolution, and intelligence.

Part of that confusion lay in his not asking what intelligence is a product of. That is the telling question that Darwin did not directly address. However, *Descent* is a very different book from his *Origins*. The latter was an account of his theory of evolution with almost no reference to humans, whereas the former was an explicit consideration of humans within an evolutionary framework. Unsurprisingly, Darwin considered 'mental powers' and 'moral faculties' to be the most distinguishing of all human characteristics and those which have made humans 'the most dominant animal that has ever appeared on this earth' Darwin 1871, p. 431 in the Modern Library edition). So three chapters of *Descent* are given over to a comparison, by way of anecdotal material, of the capacity for learning and reasoning in humans and other, usually closely related, animals. What Darwin concluded is unequivocal: it is that across a whole range of powers, including imitation, complex emotions such as revenge and grief, vivid dreaming and hence imagination, reasoning, tool use, abstraction, self-consciousness, communication and language, the differences between humans and other animals is but one of degree, not of kind. What is important to note is that in drawing this conclusion, Darwin thus indirectly answers the question he does not even ask when he considered the relationship between instinct and intelligence in so many other places and in such different ways; intelligence, in its many different forms, is a product of evolution too, just as are instincts.

Had Darwin explicitly noted that instincts and intelligence are both products of evolution, he might have stopped to ask the even more telling question: what does it mean to say that intelligence has evolved? At a minimum he would have had to answer by placing intelligence in its myriad forms alongside all other adaptations, and hence to consider the implications of seeing intelligence as an adaptation. However, that was a question he never did ask, though in a number of places he seemed to come very close to it. The following entry appeared in his M notebook: 'How strange <all> /so many/ birds singing in England, in Tierro del Fuego not one.—now as we know birds learn from each other /though different species/ when in confinement, so they may learn in a state of nature.—singing in birds, not being instinctive, is hereditary knowledge like that of man ...' (Gruber 1974, p. 271). In *Descent* there is this wonderful passage:

> As Horne Tooke, one of the founders of the noble science of philology, observes, language is an art, like brewing or baking; but writing would have been a better simile. It certainly is not a true instinct, for every language has to be learned. It differs, however, widely from all ordinary arts, *for man has an instinctive tendency to speak*, as we see in the babble of our young children; whilst no child has an instinctive tendency to brew, bake, or write' (Darwin 1871, p. 462—italics added).

He goes on to add a sentence later: 'The sounds uttered by birds offer in several respects the nearest analogy to language, for all the members of the same species utter the same instinctive cries expressive of their emotions: and all the kinds which sing, exert their power instinctively; but the actual song, and even the call-notes, are learnt from their parents or foster-parents'. He was here a century ahead of his time.

Nor might he have been far off the same point when in *The Expression of the Emotions in Man and Animals* he wrote: 'When there exists an inherited or instinctive tendency to the performance of an action, or an inherited taste for certain kinds of food, some degree of habit in the individual is often or generally requisite' (Darwin 1872*b*, p. 30).

'Hereditary knowledge', that phrase in his 1838 note, comes closer to a more complete conceptual marriage of evolution and intelligence, the capacity for gaining knowledge, than did the limited and one-dimensional conception of 'intelligence has evolved' that underlies so much of *Descent*. So too does his observation that language learning in humans seems to show a significant difference from certain other kinds of learning. Given the importance of Darwin's evolutionary theory and the astounding mass of his observations and speculations, his failure to work completely through the nature of the linkage between evolution and learning was an entirely understandable oversight, if it could even be called that—but at times he seemed to come very close to the realization that if intelligence in all its forms is indeed the product of evolution and hence are adaptations, then all forms of intelligence must have certain specific characteristics.

There is little for twenty-first century psychology to learn from Darwin's immediate successor, George J. Romanes. As much a Lamarckian as a Darwinian, Romanes' writings drew in equal part from Spencer's psychology on the one hand, and Darwin's view that all mental faculties, including learning and reasoning, are products of evolution on the other. Like both of his predecessors, Romanes, in *Animal Intelligence*, considered instincts and reasoning to meld into one another: 'Whether we look to the growing child or to the ascending scales of animal life, we find that instinct shades into reason by imperceptible degrees ...' (Romanes 1886, p. 15). Just a page later he draws on the same person as did Darwin, Pierre Huber, to state that 'actions in the main instinctive are very commonly tempered by ... "a little dose of judgement or reason", and *vice versa*' (Romanes 1886, p. 16).

Romanes considered the outcomes of both instincts and rational actions to be adaptive in nature but whereas instinctive acts are, he argued, common to all members of a species and involve frequent repetition in the same individual, rational acts in contrast 'are actions which are required to meet circumstances of comparatively rare occurrence in the life-history of the species, and which therefore can only be performed by an intentional effort of adaptation' (Romanes 1886, p. 17). From this he drew the further distinction that whilst instincts occur 'antecedent to individual experience, without necessary knowledge of the relation between means employed and ends attained', 'reason or intelligence is the faculty which is concerned in the intentional adaptation of means to end. It therefore implies the conscious knowledge of the relation between means employed and ends attained, and may be exercised in adaptation to circumstances novel alike to the experience of the individual and to that of the species' (Romanes 1886, p. 17).

In his second book, *Mental Evolution in Animals*, he explicitly stated that acts initially intelligent may, by way of the inheritance of acquired characters, become species-wide instincts. He also, as part of a rather baroque account of mental evolution, considered the way in which what he termed 'secondary instincts' might evolve which are less fixed in form than are primary instincts and may show intelligent variations. Here again are the dullest glimmerings of the notion of directed cognitive mechanisms, deriving, as in Darwin's case, from the understanding that both instincts, whatever these nineteenth century theorists meant by that term, and intelligence are products of evolution.

Lessons to be learned

What sense can be made of the way these great nineteenth century theorists dealt, or failed to deal, with what came to be called the nature–nurture issue? For Lamarck, behaviour mediates the effects of environmental change on the evolution of the 'shape and organization' of animals, but he failed to link any form of cognition to this mediating role, and hence failed to link learning and reasoning to the dynamic interplay between the environment and evolution. He also made no explicit statement that cognition itself is a product of evolution and adopted an openly empiricist stance in his denial of innate knowledge. Spencer's position, in contrast, was an uninhibited and clear naturalization of the human mind and human culture. For him the mind was a continuous adjustment of internal to external relations. Intelligence precedes instinct and, by way of the inheritance of acquired characters, is causal in the form that instincts take. Intelligence gives rise to instinct, and these inherited traits 'gradually merge' with memory and reason. Thus did Spencer make connections between nature and nurture, between instinct and intelligence, but his argument was unconvincing at best, incoherent at worst, and built upon an incorrect theory of evolution. It is easy to dismiss Spencer now, but his appeal in the latter part of the nineteenth and for some way into the twentieth century rested precisely on the way he married nature with nurture and hence made evolutionary biology acceptable, even frankly appealing, to those who sought for a scientific understanding of human affairs when the social sciences had little to offer.

Empirical observation of many kinds formed the fertile ground from which Darwin's reading of Malthus led to a potent theory of species transformation. In the *Origin*, Darwin's consistent theme is selection acting on variation leading to evolution by way of 'better adapting (individuals) to their altered conditions, (which) would tend to be preserved' (Darwin 1872*a*, p. 63). The notion of adaptation is pervasive throughout his first book as well as in *Descent*, in the latter within a comparative framework. However, Darwin did not examine the idea of what an adaptation is with any depth beyond that it is a feature which is 'useful'. However much the notion of adaptation as a product of variation and selection makes Darwin's ideas incomparably superior to that of Spencer, what 'useful' actually means for any particular adaptation in terms of it having a function was generally subordinated in *Origin* to the much more important generic role for Darwin that adaptations play in increasing what would later be termed fitness. Where he examined specific instances of behavioural adaptations, in the chapter on instincts, learning or intelligence play no part in the instincts described. In *Descent* no single form of 'mental power', which corresponds to what one today would be some form or other of cognition, is considered in detail beyond an anecdotal comparative framework.

So Darwin never really considered the relationship between instinct and learning beyond some vague Spencerian musings about voluntary acts being transmuted first into habits and then into instincts, and a flirtation with the conception that 'a little dose of judgement and reason' may enter into instinctive acts. With the phrase 'hereditary knowledge' and in his musings on the learning of birdsong and human language, he may have come closer to what he did not otherwise do; considered what it must mean for 'mental powers' if they are indeed products of the evolutionary process having specific functions 'useful' to the creatures possessing them.

Such are the advantages of hindsight. Had Darwin focused more on the implications of mental powers as adaptations, he might have been better able to draw that clear distinction that Richards points to: the selection of intelligence in animals by the process of evolution, and the selection of specific skills, habits, thoughts or ideas by those animals so evolved. There is universal scientific acceptance that Darwin provided the correct explanation for the appearance of design in living beings. Such design must include cognition. Yet it was some decades after Darwin's death before someone was explicitly to ask what it meant to think of traits such as learning and reasoning as being products of natural design. We will return to this theme in Chapter 4. First, though, we need briefly to consider the work of two other early theorists whose ideas on the relationship between evolution and learning had a surprisingly modern ring.

CHAPTER 3

Moving on

Conway Lloyd Morgan in Britain and James Mark Baldwin in the USA, near contemporaries of one another, shared several other characteristics. Each had a philosophical sophistication unusual amongst the evolutionists and most psychologists of their day. Each was a pioneer, if in different ways. Morgan was one of the first experimental comparative psychologists; Baldwin made seminal contributions in developmental psychology, being the first to understand that human cognitive development proceeds through a series of stages, each of which is qualitatively different from those preceding it. Both wrote a form of memetics, the notion that ideas are the cultural analogues of genes that evolve by way of selection, some 70 and more years before Dawkins' *The Selfish Gene* (1976a). Also, both anticipated major ways of advancing thinking as to how evolution and learning may be linked to one another. It is the latter, of course, which is the primary concern of this chapter.

Conway Lloyd Morgan

The lineage of the application of evolutionary theory to the minds of humans, and other animals, runs from Darwin through Romanes and then on to Morgan. However, whereas Romanes had merely extended Darwin's anecdotal method by which observers sent in unconfirmable reports of behaviours in animals from which the observers or Romanes then

drew mostly unsupportable conclusions as to the psychological powers of the creatures concerned, Morgan was made of
much sterner stuff analytically. He wrote of 'the little gratu-
itous, unwarrantable, human touch which is so often filled
in, no doubt in perfect good faith, by the narrators of anec-
dotes. Against such interpolations we must always be on our
guard. It is so difficult not to introduce a little dose of reason'
(Morgan 1891, p. 367). Later in the same work, *Animal Life
and Intelligence*, he warned of the distorting effects of anthro-
pomorphizing:

> Remembering this, it is always well to look narrowly at every
> anecdote of animal intelligence and emotion, and endeavour
> *to distinguish observed fact from observer's inference*. If we take
> the great number of stories illustrative of revenge, conscious-
> ness of guilt, an idea of caste, deceitfulness, cruelty, and so
> forth, in the higher mammalia, we shall find but few that do
> not admit of a different interpretation from that given by the
> narrator (Morgan 1891, p. 399—italics in the original).

Thus, for example, while Morgan did not question Romanes'
account of his sister's monkey being able to unscrew a variety of objects, he doubted very much that this indicated that
the animal understood the principle of the screw as a means
of binding objects together, which was the interpretation
made by Romanes.

This caution, psychology's version of Ockham's razor, eventually found formal statement by Morgan which he expressed
as follows: 'In no case may we interpret an action as the
outcome of the exercise of a higher psychical faculty, if it can
be interpreted as the outcome of the exercise of one which
stands lower in the psychological scale' (Morgan 1894, p. 53).
As a principle of parsimony, Morgan provided an evolutionary justification for what became known as Morgan's canon:
if some simple psychological mechanism can arrive at an

adequately adaptive behaviour, then the processes of evolution could not be so wasteful as to give rise to a more complex and correspondingly costly mechanism to achieve the same end.

Morgan was not just a philosophically principled psychological theorist, he was an avowed monist: 'the so-called connection between the molecular changes in the brain and the concomitant states of consciousness is assumed to be identity' (Morgan 1891, p. 465). He was also an experimenter on animal behaviour, even if he did use unrefined and makeshift equipment.

> I kept some young chicks in my study in an improvised pen floored with newspaper, the edges of which were turned up and supported, to form frail but sufficient retaining walls. One of the little birds, a week old, stood near the corner of the pen, pecking vigorously and persistently at something, which proved to be the number on the page of the turned-up newspaper. He then transferred his attention and his efforts to the corner of the paper just within his reach. Seizing this, he pulled at it, bending the newspaper down, and thus making a breach in the wall of the pen. Through this he stepped forth into the wider world of my study. I restored the paper as before, caught the bird, and replaced him near the scene of his former efforts. He again pecked at the corner of the paper, pulled it down, and escaped. I then put him back as far as possible from the spot. Presently he came round to the same corner, repeated his previous behaviour, and again made his escape (Morgan 1900, p. 55).

The parallels with the experiments on cats that Edward Thorndike was performing at about the same time in the USA is clear, and like Thorndike, Morgan provided a minimalist interpretation of his observations. Under the discipline of his own canon, he argued that just two psychological elements explained the chicks' behaviour. The one was an instinctive tendency to peck at small visual stimuli. The second was learning an association between an act and its consequences; or to be more precise, between the neural basis of an act and the neural basis of the sensory consequences of the action. Another form of association that Morgan recognized was between two forms of perception, i.e. between sensory events. Drawing on other experiments he had performed with chicks exposed to caterpillars of differing appearances and tastes, and observing how the young birds ceased to peck at the distasteful insects with their prominently displayed visual appearance, he assumed the existence of associative neural connections being established between neural centres subserving the perception of visual and gustatory stimuli. These two forms of association would, of course, in subsequent years be transformed into classical conditioning and instrumental, trial-and-error learning or operant conditioning.

Morgan was too well read not to know that his explanations owed much to the pleasure–pain principles which Spencer and Alexander Bain had developed decades earlier. However, they differed in two important respects from those of his predecessors. The one was that he was observing behaviour within an experimental context, albeit a crude one. The second was that principle of parsimony. Morgan had realized that a significant amount of the animal behaviour that he was observing, mostly in mammals and birds, was the product of learning processes. However, as far as animal learning was concerned, he was an entirely different kind of comparative psychologist to Romanes and Darwin, writing in the simplest of possible terms about his chicks:

> We have seen the nature of the elements (sensory data, including as essential those supplied by the behaviour itself, with a pleasurable or painful tone) which enter into such a situation; we have seen that they owe their primary origin

to direct presentation, but that they may be subsequently
introduced indirectly in re-presentative form; we have seen
that the situation as a whole results from the coalescence of
the data. There only remains the question how the felt situation takes effect on behaviour. And to this question, unfortunately, we can give but a meagre and incomplete reply.
All we can say is, that connections seem to be in some
way established between the centres of conscious control
and the centres of congenital response; and that through
these channels the responsive behaviour may be either
checked or augmented (as a whole or in part), according
to the tone, disagreeable or pleasant, that suffuses the
situation. How this is effected, we do not fully know (Morgan
1900, p. 56).

The congenital response(s) referred to in the previous
paragraph were, broadly speaking, for Morgan of two kinds.
There are innate responses elicited by specific stimuli, such as
his chicks pecking at small objects. Also there are emotions,
which divide along lines of pleasure or pain 'that are to a
large extent instinctive' (Morgan 1891, p. 390). For an explanation of the behaviour of non-humans, this was a relatively
small conceptual toolbag compared with his predecessors.
He understood implicitly that learning carries on from
evolution; that in some sense it takes up a task that completes
the evolutionary processes. All that he envisaged were evolved
instincts and emotions around which relatively simple learning processes would act to scaffold together innate elements,
be they emotional or motivational propensities or instinctive
behaviours together with novel behavioural forms, in such a
way that the resultant action is adaptive. 'The utilization of
chance experience, without the framing and application of
an organized scheme of knowledge, appears to be the
predominant method of animal intelligence' (Morgan 1900,
p. 153). In his mature formulations he would have no truck

with the inheritance of acquired characters as the means by which instincts derived from learning. There were instincts at birth or hatching which set the direction of learning, and then a relatively simple set of associative learning mechanisms to weave together adaptive behaviours. In many respects, this was a position very close to that presented by late twentieth century developmental empiricists (see Chapter 5).

His canon, of course, required a scale of psychological faculties. Morgan was fairly certain that for most non-human animals, perhaps all of them, that scale ended at associative learning. Human intelligence, however, goes beyond associative learning. In *Animal Behaviour*, he considered what exactly might be 'in the mind' of one of his chicks when acquiring new behaviours, and concluded that his canon required that we need not think beyond some form of consciousness of simple stimuli and the capacity for forming links between them. However, humans present a 'later phase in mental development: there can be no doubt that they are capable of framing, with definite intention, and of set purpose, both general and abstract conceptions' (Morgan 1900, p. 58). He went on to describe human intelligence as being 'character-ized by a new purpose or end of consciousness, namely, to explain the situations hitherto merely accepted as they are given in presentation or re-presentation; they require delib-erate attention to the relationships which hold good among the several elements of successive situations; and they involve, so far as behaviour is concerned, the intentional application of an ideal scheme with the object of rational guidance' (Morgan 1900, p. 59). Humans too, of course, are capable of acquiring simple associations. However, what we are also capable of is the perception and application of abstract rules of relationship, which is what he believed underpins human conceptualization and insight.

What then of the relationship between learning and intelligence on the one hand and instinct on the other? Like so many biologists of the nineteenth century, including Darwin himself, Morgan in his earliest writings considered the evolutionary origins of behaviours characteristic of species as both Darwinian and Lamarckian in origin. However, he was persuaded by the work of Weismann that a Spencerian vision of instincts as originating in individual intelligence was quite untenable, and he also discarded the Romanes notion of consciousness as a necessary part of instinctive behaviour. However, he was always alert to the possibility that the relationship between what is innate and what is learned is complex. He understood that both instinct and habit 'are based upon innate capacity. But whereas habitual activities always require some learning and practice, and very often some intelligence, on the part of the individual, instinctive activities are performed without instruction or training, through the exercise of no intelligent adaptation on the part of the performer, and either at once and without practice (perfect instincts) or by self-suggested trial and practice (incomplete instincts)' (Morgan 1891, p. 422). Morgan would have had no difficulties with the idea presented half a century on that innate behaviours of a species can be sharpened and focused by learning (e.g. Hailman 1967). He also wrote of 'deferred instincts' to describe behaviours that appeared to be innate, in the sense that they require no practice and are species-general, but which appear at a time remote from birth or hatching. However, in every case,

> Weismann's theory of the origins of instincts necessarily altogether excludes intelligence as a co-operating factor. The essential point on which that theory is absolutely insistent is that what is handed on through inheritance is *an innate, and not an individually acquired, character*. Now since intelligent

actions are characteristically individual, and performed in special adaptation to special circumstances, it would seem, at first sight, that an intelligent modification of an instinct could not, on Professor Weismann's view, be handed on (Morgan 1891, p. 440—italics in the original).

Thus while Morgan certainly considered the likelihood that many innate behaviours could be modified by individual experience, what he considered untenable was that such modifications could be passed on to offspring.

Morgan's thinking, however, was not closed to another possible link between nature in the form of instincts, and nurture as represented by individual intelligence, even though the realization that instincts could be modified by intelligence forms a connection that rather blurs any real distinction at the outset. One should not deny

> ... all connection of any sort between accommodation and adaptation. When we remember that plastic modification and germinal variation have been working together, in close association, all along the line of organic evolution to reach the common goal of adjustment to the circumstances of life it is difficult to believe that they have been throughout the whole process altogether independent of each other. Granted that acquired modifications, as such, are not directly inherited, they may none the less afford the conditions under which *coincident variations* escape elimination. By coincident variations I mean those the direction of which coincides with that taken by modification (Morgan 1900, p. 37—italics in the original).

Morgan provides this passage with a footnote which refers the reader to the work of Baldwin and Osborn. What he was referring to as coincident variation much later came to be known as the Baldwin effect and, since the association of the idea with the name of Baldwin is so strong, discussion of it will be deferred until the second part of this chapter.

In the final pages of *Animal Life and Intelligence*, Morgan advanced a line of thought which he explicitly associated with Alfred Wallace, co-creator along with Darwin of the concept of natural selection as causal in the transformation of species, as to the extent to which the evolution of intelligence in humans has reached a point where natural selection may no longer operate on the human mind. '... we may note', he wrote 'that there are sundry activities of man, the outcome of his conceptual thought and emotion, which are also, under the conditions of social life, to a large extent beyond the pale of elimination. I refer to the aesthetic activities—music, painting, sculpture, and the like; in a word, the activities associated with art, literature, and pure science. These, in the main, take rank alongside the ideas of which they are the outward expression. Natural selection, which deals with practical, life-preserving, and life-continuing activities, has little to say to them' (p. 484).

He developed his argument with the general principle that '*the environment of an idea is the system of ideas among which it is introduced*' (p. 485—italics in the original) and noted that the environment of a hypothesis is other hypotheses, that of a moral ideal other moral ideals, and that of a religious conception other religious conceptions. In arguing that as the neural processes which intervene between a stimulus and activity become so complex and indirect, they become progressively removed from the effects of natural selection, there is some ambiguity as to whether he was arguing both for a form of within-brain evolution, i.e. ideas or ideals already present in a person's mind form the context for other ideas and ideals within that same person's mind—selection 'in a somewhat metaphorical, or at least extended sense' (p. 488), or whether his phrase 'interneural evolution' also applies to between-brain evolution in a social species such as

Homo sapiens. That he was intending at least to include the latter, that is to extend evolution to the social–cultural sphere, seems certain, however, when his examples are considered: 'Slavery would never have been abolished through natural selection; by this means the modest behaviour of a chaste woman could not have been developed. To natural selection neither the Factory Acts nor the artistic products in this year's academy were due; by this were determined neither the conduct of John Howard nor that of Florence Nightingale' (p. 489). Yet in the few remaining pages of the book he continues to argue for interneural evolution and 'elimination through incongruity'. What Morgan seems to be articulating is a nineteenth century form of memetics, where evolution occurs through the interaction of many brains, where the processes may be similar to biological evolution and the trans- formation of species, but the selection filters and the entities evolving are different. It does, though, also seem clear that he was also meaning to extend evolution as a process into the workings of single minds, as William James had done a decade earlier (James 1880).

For Morgan, then, nature, evolution, seemed to have a less intrusive causal role in nurture, individual intelligence and culture, than was the case for Darwin, and certainly very much less than in the writings of Spencer. His learning and reasoning processes appear to be much more general process in form, both for animals and for humans. And while he never abandoned a Darwinian stance in the most general sense, he certainly drew firm limits to the power of natural selection, though not necessarily of other forms of selection. His was a highly disciplined originality of thought that set the tone for later general process theories of learning, but which he always maintained within a strictly evolutionary approach. As a child of his time, his adherence to the centrality of evolution made him very different from most later learning theorists, whose general process approach seemed to cut them adrift from most biological theory.

James Mark Baldwin

There is nobody else in the history of scientific, academic, psychology whose reputation is as uncertain and disputed as that of Baldwin. To most undergraduate students, his name would mean nothing. It is a name that does not even appear in Leahey's (1987) near 500 page history; in that of Brennan (1994) it is mentioned twice, in each case merely as his being co-founder of the *Psychological Review*; Boring's classic *A History of Experimental Psychology* (1957) does devote four pages out of more than 700 to him, and he is mentioned in about a dozen other places in the work; in his magisterial account of evolutionary theories of mind and behaviour Richards (1987) devotes an entire chapter to Baldwin; and it can, and has been, argued that Baldwin anticipated by close to a century the establishment of a true evolutionary psychology in which the theory of evolution draws some of the essential conceptual lines onto which an adequate psychology must be mapped (Plotkin 2004). Broughton and Freeman-Moir (1982) edited a volume on Baldwin's cognitive–developmental psychology; and, most recently, Weber and Depew (2003) edited a book on the Baldwin Effect. This resurgence of interest is owed to the rise of evolutionary psychology from the late 1980s onwards and to the somewhat earlier emergence of an evolutionary epistemology under the principal guidance of Donald Campbell. While psychology, apart perhaps from its developmentalists, might have largely forgotten Baldwin, it was his consistent insistence on the importance of evolution to the understanding of the mind, and of the mind to evolution, that is responsible for any renaissance of his ideas in the present.

Given that the relationship between evolution and learning is central to understanding the necessary knowledge in the title of this book, Baldwin's work provides at least five notable foci of ideas, all contributing in some way to how we must see that relationship. It is not accurate to place them in separate conceptual parcels but it does provide clarity to what was a veritable storm of different ideas. Already mentioned, the first and most pervasive of these was Baldwin's core notion that cognition of any and every kind simply could not be properly understood away from evolutionary considerations. In his most approachable book, *Darwin and the Humanities* (1909), written as part of the American Philosophical Society's 50th anniversary celebrations of the publication of *The Origin of Species*, Baldwin wrote

> I must admit that the result of my labours for twenty-five years, the net result, that is, of my scientific work until now, is a contribution, whatever it may turn out to be worth, to the theory of Darwinism in the sciences of life and mind. I call it a 'confession', but 'claim' would be a better word; for who would not consider it an honor to be allowed to 'claim' that he had done something to carry Darwin's great and illuminating conception into those fields of more general philosophical interest, in which in the end its value for human thought must be estimated?' (p. ix).

No other psychologist was to write in that way for another 80 years. It should be noted that Baldwin was a Darwinian in the sense of his being, as he noted in the same preface to *Darwin in the Humanities*, a 'Wallaceist'. (Alfred Russel Wallace was the co-discoverer of natural selection who, unlike Darwin, would have no truck at all with Lamarck's principles of evolution—see Chapter 2.) In this way, Baldwin emphasized his absolute rejection of Lamarckian theory, even more

so than Darwin himself, and his adherence to an evolutionary theory based solely on the processes that generate variation, the selection of limited numbers of variants and the
propagation of the selected variants.

In his earliest book, his *Handbook of Psychology: Senses
and Intellect* published in 1890, Baldwin noted the importance of both evolution and individual development: '… the
determination of the barest woof and warp of thought itself,
is a matter of origins, as the evolutionists claim, and the problem should be approached as well from the side of infant and
comparative psychology, as from the side of developed
reason' (p. 14). In the preface to his *Mental Development in the
Child and Race* (1895), he wrote of the need for a 'synthesis
of the current biological theory of organic adaptation with
the doctrine of the infant's development' (p. vii) and of 'a
basis in the natural history of man as a social being' (p. x).
No other philosopher or psychologist of that time, including
the great William James, was more explicit in their acceptance of evolutionary theory and the need to see it at the core
of any theory of mind and knowledge. In that same 1895
book, Baldwin expanded on the scope of his 'genetic' theory—
genetic in the sense of 'origins', since the science of genetics
had yet to be born and Baldwin had no more conception of
the physical basis of inheritance than did anyone else in the
1890s—within the broadest possible context of a 'biological
theory of adaptation' thus:

> It is clear that we are led to two relatively distinct questions:
> questions which are now familiar to us when put in the terms
> covered by the words 'phylogenesis' and 'ontogenesis'. First,
> how has the development of organic life proceeded, showing
> constantly, as it does, forms of greater complexity and higher
> adaptation? This is the phylogenetic question; and as we
> should expect, this is the question over which biologists have
> had their most earnest and lasting controversy. This is also

the question that has mainly interested biologists. But the second question, the ontogenetic question, is of equal importance: the question, how does the individual organism manage to adjust itself better and better to its environment? How is it that we, or the brute, or the amoeba, can *learn to do anything*? (Baldwin 1895, p. 171—italics in the original).

Here Baldwin makes a clear distinction between evolution and learning. He was never in doubt that the latter is a product of the former, but in separating them into two conceptual domains, in order better to analyse each, he missed the vital connection that Lorenz was later to make (see Chapter 4). Yet, as will become clear over the next few pages, he certainly did also make a very strong linkage between evolution and learning of two other kinds. Before we consider these, two other, if less important, foci of his thinking on the relationship between evolution and learning must be mentioned.

Baldwin's own efforts at empirical science were limited. Boring disapprovingly quotes Baldwin as inveighing against 'that most vicious and Philistine attempt, in some quarters, to put psychology in the strait-jacket of barren observation, to draw the life-blood of all science, speculative advance, into the secrets of things—this ultra-positivistic cry has come here as everywhere else and put a ban upon theory. On the contrary, give us theories, theories, always theories. Let every man who has a theory pronounce his theory' (Boring 1957, p. 529). However, when his daughters were born Baldwin observed them closely and made the discovery that was to underpin much of twentieth century cognitive developmental science. This is that cognitive development proceeds through a series of stages, each qualitatively different from, though built upon, the stages that preceded it.

Prior to the birth of his children, Baldwin had adhered to what today would be described as a nativist position, what

Wozniak (1982) calls a coordinative epistemology, in which he considered learning and thought about the world to be the product of evolution in the sense that all the processes and mechanisms of mind by which we come to have knowledge of the world are the result of phylogenesis. It was the experience of his children that led him to understand the importance of individual cognitive development, as a phenomenon to be understood in its own right, perhaps independent of phylogenesis—'perhaps' because as an evolutionist through and through he understood the necessity of *some* linkage of ontogenesis to evolution, but the independence arose from his sense, in the earlier stages of his career, that cognitive development is a process *sui generis*.

In a number of ways, Baldwin anticipated the theory of Piaget by decades. He postulated a central role for what he called the law of dynamogenesis: 'Every organic stimulus brings about changes in movement' (Baldwin 1895, p. 161), and movement, action of some kind, became central to his account of cognitive development. As Gruber (1982) put it, 'One of the ideas that Baldwin pioneered was the constructive function of repetitive activity' (p. xviii). He defined imitation as the process whereby 'the stimulus starts a motor process which tends to reproduce the stimulus and through it, the motor process again' (Baldwin 1895, p. 126). He combined this notion of the centrality of repetitive actions with a developing trajectory of suggestibility in the infant to result in a sequence of stages which leads from something very like Piaget's sensorimotor schemas to a stage of persistent imitation where the child consciously strives to match the actions of a model. Even his use of the words accommodation and assimilation anticipate Piaget and, given that Baldwin lived the last 20 years of his life in France associating with the likes of Janet and Claparade who were mentors and tutors to the young Piaget, it is hard to accept Piaget's assertion that Baldwin had little influence on his own intellectual development (Piaget 1979/1982).

Another focus of Baldwin's thinking is again present at the outset of the 1895 book on mental development, where in the preface he wrote that 'it is in genetic theory that social or collective psychology must find both its root and its ripe fruitage. We have no social psychology, because we have had no doctrine of the *socius*. We have had theories of the *ego* and the *alter*; but that they did not reveal the *socius* is just their condemnation' (Baldwin 1895, p. ix). Baldwin believed that central to the child's growing cognitive capacity is that imitation, in all its stages, occurs overwhelmingly within a social world. While in the early stages of development imitation is largely concerned with the behaviour of others, it progresses to the ideas and knowledge of others, and hence to the *socius*.

> In the qualities of the socius or socialized individual, we have the type of personal fitness upon which the qualifications of the group for survival will depend. Only so far as the individuals of the group are 'socii', members capable of cooperation and willing to cooperate with their fellows, will the group 'hold together' effectively, in competition with other groups (Baldwin 1909, p. 43).

Here are the beginnings of a social psychology based on evolutionary principles. Furthermore, in a manner much more explicit and less ambiguous than Morgan, Baldwin extended evolution into what a century later would be called memetics:

> But when we come to ask for a full account of the propagation of mental acquisitions from generation to generation, we find it necessary to recognize another form of handing down or real transmission. Once admit that the intelligence,

even in its simplest forms, as seen in imitation, play and
the resulting accommodative actions, can be applied to the
learning of anything, and that variations in plasticity are
selected to allow of its development—this once admitted,
we have the possibility of a continuous handing down from
generation to generation, a 'social heredity', which is no
longer subject to the limitations set upon physical heredity
(Baldwin 1895, p. 28).

Successive cognitive developmental stages were postulated
for the acquisition of socially acquired knowledge. In the first,
projective consciousness, the child comes to differentiate
between people and all other objects in the world. Subjective
consciousness then follows as the child becomes aware of its
own subjective states of feeling and knowledge. In the final
stage, ejective consciousness, the developing child comes to
the understanding that others have such subjective states as
well, which is essential for understanding the community of
shared knowledge and feelings in order fully to enter into a
culture. Once again Baldwin had understood the importance
of, and anticipated by close on a century, what in the 1980s
came to be called theory of mind, the attribution of intentional mental states to others.

The notion of cultural evolution was new neither to
Baldwin nor to Morgan, Wallace having considered such a
process an essential part of the human species. What was
novel was the extent to which Baldwin used the unifying
concept of organic selection to knit these various layers of
evolution and learning together, organic selection being the
fourth and fifth foci of his attempt to relate evolution and
learning—or the phylogenesis and ontogenesis of mind,
nature and nurture. The phrase organic selection was first
used by Baldwin to account for how organisms respond to
what in the 1895 book he called the 'law of excess' and the

principle of 'over-production', notions he freely acknowledged were present in the writings of Spencer and Bain. That
same phrase, organic selection, he later used to refer to what
on first publication was called 'a new factor in evolution'
(Baldwin 1896). Richards suggests that this was intentional,
Baldwin being eager to establish his priority in thinking of
the 'new factor'. Conceptually, though, they are really two
different ideas.

Organic selection in its 'law of excess' form Baldwin
frankly owned to being part of a long line of thought beginning with Wallace, who in the 1860s had suggested that the
production of excessive numbers of variants, the selection of
a small subset of these and the propagation of those selected
variants occurred in human culture, the same processes as he
and Darwin had offered for species transformation—indeed
Wallace suggested that once human cultural evolution came
into force, the biological evolution of humans ceased. Not
long after Wallace made this assertion, T.H. Huxley wrote a
letter to Darwin suggesting that the evolutionary processes
might operate within organisms, what Darwin in his reply, in
which he rejected the idea, called 'natural selection amongst
the molecules'. Spencer, of course, had also envisaged evolution as occurring as a within-organism process, but had
employed Lamarck's form of evolutionary processes.
William James (1880), reacting against Spencer's whole position, used as his argument the internalization of Darwinian
evolution to account for creativity:

> ... new conceptions, emotions and active tendencies which
> evolve are originally **produced** in the shape of random
> images, fancies, accidental outbirths (sic) of spontaneous
> variation in the functional activity of the excessively unstable
> human brain, which the outer environment simply confirms
> or refutes, adopts or rejects, preserves or destroys—**selects**, in

short, just as it selects morphological and social variations
due to molecular accidents of an analogous sort (James 1880,
p. 456—emphasis in the original).

James' is as clear a statement of Baldwin's 'law of excess'—
what might be better stated as the law of 'the reduction of
excess by limited selection'—as one can find in the writings
of that era. In 1881 Roux had a book published which was
an account of individual development in the same terms,
a work with which Baldwin was familiar.

In *Darwin and the Humanities*, Baldwin expounded on the
same theme that he had developed more fully in *Development
and Evolution* (1902), which was that there is exactly the
same internal selectionist process underlying all forms of
learning in all species that can learn:

> The problem of 'educability', of 'profiting by experience', has
> been attacked throughout the entire range of organic forms,
> with striking harmony of results, summed up by the phrase
> 'trial and error'. From the infusoria's limited modification
> of behaviour to the child's extended education, it is found
> that all learning is by a process of strenuous, excessive, and
> varied discharges. Through such discharges adjustive modifi-
> cations occur in the mass of earlier habits; pleasure and pain,
> and in the higher animals, attention, being the regulating
> functions. It takes place in a manner to which the Darwinian
> conception is strictly applied. Quite apart, then, from the
> details of the analysis in particular cases, and from the prob-
> lem of isolating the psychic and organic factors involved, we
> may record this result as a striking application of Darwinism
> (Baldwin 1909, p. 16).

For Baldwin, all forms of learning or intelligence occur by
way of an internalized Darwinian algorithm. It was to this
internalized Darwinian process that Baldwin first applied
the phrase 'organic selection'. And it is this form of organic

selection that a number of twentieth century theorists, including Karl Popper and Donald Campbell, adopted in what became known as evolutionary epistemology or selection theory (Plotkin 1982, 1994).

There was a somewhat different usage of the phrase organic selection that Baldwin employed, and this is the fifth and final focus Baldwin had on the relationship between phylogeny and ontogeny. It was what he himself described as 'a new factor in evolution' (Baldwin 1896), and which he considered to be a significant causal force in evolution. It will be remembered from the previous section of this chapter that Morgan had written about 'coincident variations' and it was a matter of considerable surprise that Baldwin and Morgan gave back-to-back talks at the same New York Academy of Sciences meeting in 1895 in which they each expressed an idea of coincident variation identical to that of the other. Richards (1987) considers this to have been the result of each being influenced to think along similar lines by the same set of writings of Romanes. It might be noted that a Lamarckian palaeontologist, Henry Fairfield Osborn, had also come up with the same idea at about the same time. Given that the new factor was used by Baldwin to counter the Lamarckian explanation for complex co-adaptations which Osborn was seeking to explain, the coincidence of three individuals coming up with the same idea at almost the same time is not that great a coincidence as it might first seem. In any event, Morgan considered the idea to be owed to others, notably Romanes and Weismann, and Osborn simply did not have Baldwin's standing in matters relating to behaviour. Baldwin himself considered the concept of sufficient importance that he peddled the idea repeatedly, and increasingly wrapped it so close to his original usage of organic selection that for readers it must have seemed as if the one implied the other and so it soon came to be seen as Baldwin's idea and no one else's—indeed some decades later it came to be known as the Baldwin effect.

The 'new factor', Baldwin argued, had two components. The first are sets of ontogenetic variations, a very important number of which he termed psycho-genetic, which are processes 'all classed broadly under the terms 'intelligent', i.e. imitation, gregarious influences, maternal instruction, the lessons of pleasure and pain, and of experience generally, and reasoning from means to ends' (Baldwin 1896, p. 443). Under certain circumstances, such ontogenetic variations will be, by the process of organic selection, 'undergo(ing) modifications of their congenital functions or of the structures which they get congenitally—these creatures will live; while those that cannot, will not' (Baldwin 1896, p. 445). (Parenthetically, it might be noted that Baldwin's conception of evolution was different in emphasis from Darwin, and very different from that which followed the modern synthesis some 30 or so years beyond 1896. In more modern evolutionary parlance, learned behavioural adaptations may increase the fitness of intelligent organisms. For Baldwin, selection meant elimination.)

Inherent in the new factor is an element that Baldwin mentions, but does not concentrate on much. 'By this means those congenital or phylogenetic variations are kept in existence, which lend themselves to intelligent, imitative, adaptive, and mechanical modification during the lifetime of the creatures which have them. **Other congenital variations are not thus kept in existence**' (Baldwin 1896, p. 445—emphasis added). What is implied by the sentence emphasized in this quotation is that it is not just learning generically which is the product of evolution, and not learning as a general process, which both Morgan and Baldwin took almost for granted; what is implied is that some forms of learning are different from others; some congenital variations of learning itself, are kept in existence, or as potential variants of learning, whereas others are not. In short, that learning may come in different forms. Here we have Baldwin close to Lorenz's insight (Chapter 4), but he never really seemed to see where that idea might go.

The second component of the new factor is the appearance and selection of 'phylogenetic variation' which complements ontogenetic variation and ultimately makes the latter unnecessary. (Baldwin was writing this in the years before a science of genetics was born. Neither he nor anyone else then knew anything about the physical basis of biological inheritance. For 'phylogenetic variations' read genes, though Baldwin would not have known this. Thus what he was envisaging was learned behaviours, behaviours necessary for survival, being superceded in time by innate behaviours, part-caused by selected genes, which increase fitness in the same way and to the same extent as those behaviours that had been learned.) 'Thus kept alive, the species has all the time necessary to perfect the variations required by a complete instinct' (Baldwin 1896, p. 447) and so 'congenital variations, on the one hand, are kept alive and made effective by their use for adaptations in the life of the individual; and, on the other hand, adaptations become congenital by further progress and refinement of variation in the same lines of function of those which their acquisition by the individual called into play' (Baldwin 1896, p. 447). Hence Morgan's phrase 'coincident variations'. Ontogenetic (learned) variations are replaced by phylogenetic (genetic) variations. It must be stressed that the ontogenetic adaptations need not be learned, but might be different physiology as in muscle strength, or anatomical, for example, callosities. However, there is no doubt that for Baldwin himself it was learned adaptations that presented the most dramatic and potent form of the new factor. Given the subject matter of this book, it is the only form of ontogenetic variation of relevance.

Baldwin's new factor is **not** the Lamarckian inheritance of acquired characters reinvented. It is a purely Darwinian process because the replacement of ontogenetic with phylogenetic variants is not one which is connected or directed, but occurs purely by chance. If the ontogenetic variants improve fitness and maintain survival for long enough, then, by chance, genetic variants will arise which will fill the same role as the former and so learned adaptations would have been superseded by innate behavioural adaptations. Later, in the same 1896 *American Naturalist* paper, he explicitly includes human social learning, the 'extra-organic transmission from generation to generation' (Baldwin 1896, p. 537) within the general framework of the 'new factor', thus bringing social learning as a causal force into biological evolution. Baldwin was repeatedly insistent that what he was positing was not a form of Lamarckianism, and in that he was correct. However, it went some way to solving the problem of co-adapted complexes which was thought by some, including Osborn, to be explicable only through the workings of a Lamarckian form of evolution. For example, complex courtship rituals in creatures such as fish are a set of co-adapted behaviours, and people doubted that the chance variation of Darwin, acting on its own, could achieve the fine interleaving of such behavioural chains; what the new factor did was provide for an interleaving of ontogenetic and genetic variation such that the possibility of such unlikely complex behaviours evolving is much increased.

Thus it was that in *Darwin and the Humanities* Baldwin provided the following account for the origin of instincts which answers the criticisms of Romanes and other Lamarckians that only Lamarckian evolution could account for the early stages in the evolution of instincts and the necessary correlations of their components:

> It appeared evident that if Darwin's principle of variation with selection, on the one hand, and Weismann's principle of 'intra-selection', taken with the psychologist's 'functional selection', on the other hand—if these principles were true, then a further result followed of itself. If, that is, a selection of processes and habits goes on within the organism— a functional selection resulting in a real molding of the individual—there would be at every stage of growth *a combination of congenital characters with acquired modifications*; natural selection would fall in each case upon *this joint or correlated result*; and the organisms showing the most effective combinations would survive. *Variation plus modification*, the joint product actually present at the time the struggle comes on, *this is what selection proceeds upon*, and not, as strict neo-Darwinism or Weismannism supposes, upon the congenital variations taken alone (Baldwin 1909, pp. 17–18—italics in the original).

It is quite clear from Baldwin's writings in the period from 1900 to 1909 that he believed that his new factor was a force in evolutionary change which went beyond Darwin's original theory. The new factor, a co-ordinative force combining sources of variation deriving from individual development and learning on the one hand, and genetic sources of variation on the other hand, was an entirely new conception of the relationship between nature and nurture—the new factor envisages nature and nurture locked together as joint causes of evolution.

If the new factor had been presented in just this simple form, with learning creating the necessary behavioural adaptations until chance genetic variants with results coincident with those of learning arose, with the resulting instinctive actions making the learning of the behaviour redundant, there would have been less cause for concern by some that Baldwin was merely introducing another form of the inheritance of acquired characters. Baldwin certainly was not. However, it was, perhaps, going unnecessarily beyond such a simple exposition and to write about the way in which the ontogenetic and congenital characters interact in a particular manner that roused suspicions. For example, in *Darwin and the Humanities* he asserted that 'the result is that variation would tell most *when in the direction in which the accommodations were being made and found useful*; and on the other hand, accommodations would be made *where the variations best permitted*' (Baldwin 1909, p. 18—italics in the original) The first part of the sentence, whilst not invoking some direct causal interaction, nonetheless is close enough to cause some unease. There is some sense in which ontogenetic variants are guiding the selection and fixation of genetic variants, even though the latter arise purely by chance. In this regard, Baldwin did his cause no good.

Scandal resulted in Baldwin leaving the USA in 1909 and he spent almost all the rest of his life in France, very little of which was devoted to developing his psychological theory. Towards the end of his life, he wrote an academic/intellectual autobiography (Baldwin 1930), one of the most significant features of which is the paucity of reference either to organic selection or the new factor in evolution. Out of some 30 pages, evolution accounts for less than one page, which stands in stark contrast to the shape and emphasis of his work through much of the 1890s until 1909. One possible explanation for this is simply that as an old man looking back on a lifetime's work his perspective had changed and so had the pride and prominence that he gave to the different threads of that work. Another is that he had become aware of a major problem with the idea of the new factor, and simply had no answer for it.

The problem lies in the question concerning what the advantages might be for a trait that is genetically part-caused over that same trait which originally was acquired by ontogenetic plasticity such as learning. In short, if learning is supplying adequate behavioural adaptations, what is the advantage of innate instincts that achieve the same end? If there are none, the new factor would never come into play. There are two possible related answers. One concerns the relative costs of maintaining the information, in genetic or neural network form, upon which a behaviour is built. The difficulty for this line of argument is that, as argued in Chapter 1, learning of every form must itself be a product of evolution, and hence genetically part-caused. We do not, however, yet know how any form of cognition is part-caused genetically, and hence how much might be the costs; equally, we do not yet know much about the neurological basis of cognition and hence what those costs might be. This argument then is currently mere handwaving as a defence of the new factor. The second line of argument concerns the relative reliability or unreliability of learning as opposed to instinct. This is an idea that Ancel (1999) built on when she modelled the Baldwin effect in environments of varying degrees of volatility. In environments of low to middling fluctuation of conditions, the effect is much more likely to play a significant evolutionary role; in environments of high volatility, the effect is much less likely to occur, with learning, or other forms of plasticity, being retained as the more effective means of surviving the conditions. Ancel's work is perhaps the most interesting and important of the modern revival of interest in the Baldwin effect. However, such cost: benefit considerations and quantitative modelling were not available to Baldwin. On the face of it, the sense might have drained from an evolutionary idea when no advantage could be posited for its occurrence, and this is what might have changed Baldwin's own view of the importance of the new factor.

Whatever change came over Baldwin's regard for the idea, the new factor was much discussed at the time as a plausible causal force that should be added to Darwin's natural selection. Huxley (1942) was a particular enthusiast of the idea. Others were not. Simpson (1953), who coined the phrase 'The Baldwin Effect', thought it an entirely plausible notion, and an evolutionary force 'that probably has occurred'. His doubts concerned the frequency with which the effect might have been significant. This is because the chances of the appropriate genetic changes arising, which underlie the replacing instincts and which map onto the equivalent learned behaviours, must be very small indeed. He also noted the complete lack of evidence more than 50 years after it had first been put forward for the Baldwin effect ever having occurred. One criticism made by Simpson, however, was plain nonsense. Considering the Baldwin effect in the context of the idea of reaction range (i.e. that genetical systems do not rigidly dictate phenotypic characters but set up a range of possibilities which is importantly determined by the environment of development), he asserted that the Baldwin effect might be considered to be a shift from determination of a genetical system of broad range, which is what learning is, to one of much more limited range, the innate instinct. 'Narrowing of the reaction range thus exchanges short-term and more plastic for long-term and more rigid adaptation' (Simpson 1953, p. 116). However, this is nonsense because nothing in Baldwin's writing on his new factor suggested that the capacity for learning somehow disappears when genetically generated variants replace ontogenetic plasticity. The learning capacity remains and may operate further within the context of the instincts that the new factor has created.

Mayr (1963) was also hostile, partly because he argued that since the ontogenetic plasticity that the Baldwin effect required was itself a product of evolution, there was nothing new about Baldwin's new factor. This, however, is a weak argument. Evolution has resulted in many traits which are themselves further forces in the process of evolution. Sexual reproduction, for example, is widely recognized as significantly altering rates of evolutionary change, and the fact that such reproduction was itself a product of evolution, changes nobody's view on that. Maynard-Smith (1987), on the other hand, showed some enthusiasm for the Baldwin effect following the modelling of Hinton and Nowlan (1987) who were able to demonstrate that 'This effect allows learning organisms to evolve *much* faster than their nonlearning equivalents' (p. 495—italics in the original).

It is worth noting that the Baldwin effect has often been equated with other ideas in the evolutionary literature which revolve around the processes of development (e.g. Gottlieb 1992). One of the most frequently drawn parallels has been with Waddington's notion of genetic assimilation (see Waddington 1975 for a number of his papers on this issue). Waddington maintained that the genotypes of most multicellular organisms contain greater genetic variability than is normally expressed in the phenotype. He also argued for the existence of buffered developmental pathways which protect against environmental and intra-genomic perturbation, thus ensuring the development of relatively fixed phenotypic forms, which he called canalization. However, under conditions of considerable developmental stress, such as marked changes in temperature, some of the previously unexpressed genetic variation may find phenotypic expression in novel phenotypic traits and, if selection for the new phenotypic form occurs, then through canalization the novel trait might become fixed in expression and occur even in the absence of the initiating environmental event. Waddington had firm empirical evidence for genetic assimilation which, on the surface, looks to be similar to the Baldwin effect, but actually it is quite different as a hypothesized process in evolutionary change. The Baldwin effect is dependent upon new genetic variants arising independently of any ontogenetic variation—though their selection may not be independent—whereas genetic assimilation is the product of selection for already existing genetic variants. Waddington's is thus a much more plausible possible evolutionary force than is the Baldwin effect. Others (Matsuda 1987; Schmalhausen 1949) have also invoked genetic assimilation kinds of developmental destabilization as preludes to the expression of previously unexpressed genetic variation, which are closer to Waddington than to Baldwin.

None of these developmentally weighted accounts of how development may enter into evolution are of direct relevance to a more specific approach on the relationship between evolution and learning. As Richards (1987) notes repeatedly, part of the significance, perhaps all of the significance, for Baldwin of his new factor was that it brought some aspect of mind into the process of evolution—the most powerful force in biology was not wholly blind; in at least some organisms, and presumably certainly in the case of humans, consciousness and cognition have a role to play in evolutionary transformation. In a sense, the recent resurgence, small as it is, in the use of Baldwin's new factor is as much owed to the need to bring some aspects of psychology into mainstream biology as it is to the understanding of Baldwin's original conception that an adequate psychology must have some form of evolutionary content at its heart.

The philosopher Daniel Dennett, in his account of the evolution of the human mind (Dennett 1991), uses the Baldwin effect in a very broad, generic manner to achieve both ends. For Dennett, the Baldwin effect is the means by which 'postnatal design fixing' (p. 183) can become hard-wired. He adopts the Baldwinian position virtually in its entirety, with the modern writer's advantage of more recent work, like that of Hinton and Nowlan, that quantitatively models Baldwin's idea. First, he advances the view that cognition should be understood within the general perspective of the constant need for adaptive design. His second view is that cognitive adaptations of every kind, be they the result of simple associative learning or more complex hypothesis formation, occur by way of selection within the individual—Baldwin's original conception of organic selection:

> ... one way or another, the plastic brain is capable of reorganizing itself adaptively in response to the particular novelties encountered in the organism's environment, and the process by which the brain does this is almost certainly a mechanical process strongly analogous to natural selection. This is the first new medium of evolution: postnatal design-fixing in individual brains (Dennett 1991, p. 184).

Dennett then offers an example using Hinton and Nowlan's modelling that is based not on the simple Baldwin effect by which ontogenetic plasticity ensures survival until genetic variation *purely by chance* results in such behavioural forms becoming innate, but the rather more complex, and to some suspect, interplay between ontogenetic and genetic variants. This is because what is posited is change in selection pressures that results in evolution more speedily arriving at a behavioural adaptation that no longer is wholly caused by a general form of ontogenetic variation and adaptation.

> Thanks to the Baldwin Effect, species can be said to pretest the efficacy of particular different designs by phenotypic (individual) exploration of the space of nearby possibilities. If a particularly winning setting is thereby discovered, this discovery will create a new selection pressure: organisms that are closer in the adaptive landscape to that discovery will have a clear advantage over those more distant. This means that species with plasticity will tend to evolve faster (and more 'clearsightedly') than those without it. So evolution in the second medium, phenotypic plasticity, can enhance evolution in the first medium, genetic variation (Dennett 1991, p. 186–187).

Apart from the claim for speeding up evolution, the interaction between ontogenetic and genetic variation, via the creation of new selection pressures, is very close to the kind of position Baldwin adopted in his later writings, as quoted earlier from *Darwin and the Humanities*, where a kind of interactive guidance mimics an inheritance of acquired characters—the only difference is in that speeding up, but it is a speeding up that matters.

In a more recent defence of his position, Dennett defended himself against some of his critics, notably against the view that the Baldwin effect adds nothing new to thinking about evolution: 'design explorations by phenotypic trial and error are just as mechanical and nonmiraculous as explorations by genetic natural selection; they just occur more swiftly and at less cost, and once design improvements are thereby discovered, genetic assimilation can incorporate them gradually into the genome' (Dennett 2003, p. 72).

Well, they certainly occur more swiftly, but whether at less cost is an assertion that can be challenged, as Ancel (1999) demonstrated, even if non-empirically. In that same riposte Dennett offered some form of language acquisition device as just the kind of mechanism, or set of mechanisms, which might have come into being only through the operation of such ontogenetic–genetic co-evolution, because 'a practice that is both learnable (with effort) and highly advantageous once learned *can* become more and more easily learned, can move gradually into the status of not needing to be learned at all' (Dennett 2003, p. 73—italics in the original).

It is in the realm of the evolution of language that the most notable attempt to use the Baldwin effect, or something like it, has occurred. The evolution of language presents a host of problems, not least because language is not a simple trait but a conglomerate of known capacities and mechanisms, such as working memory, the discrimination of temporal order of auditory input and recursion. Some of these component processes and mechanisms must have evolved for reasons apart from their eventual incorporation into language competence. Language, then, is really an exaptation built out of multiple components, some of which, like working memory, originally evolved for different functions. Whether language is truly a trait unique to humans amongst living species remains debateable (see Lloyd 2004, for example). Most, however, would judge it to be so, in which event human language must have at least one component that is human specific, or perhaps a structuring of components that is unique to our species. How language could have evolved is psychology's puzzle equivalent to the much older question of how something as complex as the eye could have evolved, but on a much larger scale of complexity. It is an issue well suited to some form of solution by way of the Baldwin effect.

Deacon (1997, 2003) has tried to do just that. Deacon's is a very complex and wide-ranging argument about the way we might begin to understand language within a biological, specifically evolutionary, framework. He provides a distinctively different approach from that of the likes of Pinker (1994) or Hauser, Chomsky and Fitch (2002), all of whom rely on relatively conventional accounts of the evolution by natural selection of an innate organ of the human mind that allows for language competence. Deacon is different because, among other things, he presents an account in which co-evolution within a multilevel evolutionary landscape allows the transformations occurring at one level to have a causal influence at other levels. That, of course, is what Baldwin's new factor is: selectional processes acting at an ontogenetic level become replaced, and in his stronger formulations, influence, evolution at a genetic, phylogenetic level. As he came to emphasize social evolution, a two-tier conception was broadened to a three-tier conception: social evolution between individuals within a social group, ontogenetic evolution occurring within the brain/mind of the individual and biological evolution as conventionally understood. Deacon's analysis adds at least one further level, that of the 'purely semiotic realm' (Deacon 2003, p. 100). Of course, what such multilevel theorizing does is cast out simplistic dichotomies such as nature and nurture. 'I believe that many structural features of language are derived from sources of "information" other than nature or nurture. The demands of symbol learning can ultimately be construed as selection pressures over and above those that are contributed by genetic, neural, social or ecological sources' (Deacon 2003, p. 101).

For Deacon, none of these evolutionary levels are independent of the others but, most importantly, it is semiotics that increases these multiple interactions:

> ... the very nature of symbolic reference, and its unusual cognitive demands when compared to nonsymbolic forms of reference, is a selection force working on those neurological resources most critical to supporting it. In the context of a society heavily dependent on symbol use—as is any conceivable human society, but no nonhuman societies—brains would have been under intense selection to adapt to these needs. This, then, is a case of selection pressures affecting the evolution of a biological substrate (the brain) and yet which is imposed, not by the physical environment, but ultimately from a purely semiotic realm (Deacon 2003, p. 100).

Deacon's concern is not to raise the Baldwin effect as the major force that conventional evolutionists such as Simpson and Mayr rejected. He simply appeals to it as a historically prior, if for his purposes, oversimplified, idea by which evolutionary forces operate across levels. It might also be noted that while he did not use the phrase 'niche construction' in his 1997 book, the conception was intrinsic to his argument, and he freely acknowledges its importance in his later writing, by which time the work of Odling-Smee and his colleagues (Odling-Smee et al. 2003) had become much more widely known. In his review of the 2003 book, Kevin Laland (2003) suggests that the Baldwin effect is actually a special case of the more encompassing idea of niche construction. Whether this is correct or not, or whether it is only in Deacon's hands that this is so, is not important. What does matter is that Laland and Deacon are tying the Baldwin effect to an evolutionary idea that many consider to be one of the most important advances in evolutionary theory for decades (see Chapter 6). There can be little doubt

that, despite his relative neglect of the topic in his autobio-
graphical notes, Baldwin would have been delighted.

A footnote to a chapter, so much of which concerns
the Baldwin effect, is that contemporary developmental/
evolutionary systems theorists, those advancing the cause of
understanding of how development enters causally into
biological evolution, find a natural place for Baldwin's new
factor, just as they do for Waddington's genetic assimilation.
West-Eberhard (2003), for example, sees the idea as a
broader conception than that of Waddington and one for
which 'there is good reason to resurrect a modern expanded
version' (West-Eberhard 2003, p. 25).

In conclusion, Baldwin and Morgan were both major
figures in developing understanding of how evolution and
learning are to be understood in relation to each other. Both
leaned towards general process theory; both were aware of
the importance of seeing learning in a social context; yet
both were also convinced of the necessity of seeing learning
as a product of evolution and, in the case of the Baldwin
effect, as a force for evolution in its own right.

CHAPTER 4

Towards a solution: constraints on learning

In his *Descent of Man*, Darwin considered intelligence to be a product of evolution, and so compared the 'mental powers' of humans with those of other mammals. However, as argued in Chapter 2, the clear acceptance that human mental powers as well as those of other animals, what now would be labelled as forms of intelligence or cognition, have evolved and hence are likely to be adaptations, was never pursued by Darwin in terms of the implications for cognition when understood as an adaptation or set of adaptations—and this despite seeming to come so close with phrases such as 'hereditary knowledge' when writing in his notebooks about birdsong and human language, and despite Gruber's assertion about Darwin's conceptual closeness to psychology. It was also seen in the previous chapter that both Morgan and Baldwin extended understanding on the relationship between evolution on the one hand and intelligence and learning on the other. In the case of Morgan, it was with the remarkably modern minimalist position with regard to that relationship; for Baldwin, apart from the 'new factor', it was by internalizing selection, his notion of 'organic selection', as a part of the process essential to how learning occurs. Yet neither, as in the case of Darwin, considered what might be the conceptual consequences for understanding intelligence were it considered to be an adaptation. It was the ethologist Konrad Lorenz who was to do this, but in order to understand how he came to this view it is necessary to see Lorenz within the context of the discipline, ethology, that he himself founded; the critical responses, especially from north America, to his theory; and how such criticism led him to revise his ideas about how learning and evolution relate to one another.

The principles of classical ethology

There are numerous accounts by historians on the origins of ethology generally as a scientific discipline (see Durant 1981; Burkhardt 1983 for examples) and the specific role of Lorenz (Kalikow 1975, 1976; Burkhardt 2005). The phrase 'classical ethology' is used to distinguish the early formulations, chiefly by European zoologists, from the expanded discipline that developed from it. Lorenz was by far the most important figure in the early stages of ethology, and it is from his early writings and lectures that one can get the best sense of what kind of science he was attempting to establish.

Early in the twentieth century some psychologists had succumbed to an extraordinarily weak extension into their subject of the unfolding evolutionary biology of the day by declaring almost any disposition shared by more than one individual to be an instinct. Literally thousands of instincts were described, many so absurdly localized and manifestly parochial social beliefs (Boakes 1984 provides choice examples) that instinct theory of that day contributed significantly to the decline of serious biological foundations for psychology for decades (Plotkin 2004) and was effectively banned from mainstream psychological study by the rise of behaviourism. Lorenz was as contemptuous of this form of instinct theory as the psychologists who ousted such thinking, but for different reasons. For Lorenz, the notion of instinct was absolutely central to the science of behaviour that he was founding, but it was, at that time, a very different kind of science from that which psychologists of any kind were attempting to establish.

Lorenz was a dedicated evolutionist convinced of the necessity for understanding behaviour within a materialist, mechanistic framework; and, very importantly, that understanding could not be divorced from the context of any animal's natural environment. In his first major publication, he expressly dismisses premature experimental work, declaring that '... unless we know the natural behaviour of a species, experiments are largely worthless. In my opinion comparative psychology must be regarded and pursued as a biological science ... We must have at least a rough idea of the over-all system of instinctive actions in a species, and know how it functions in the natural conditions where it evolved' (Lorenz 1935, p. 91). Thus it was that he dismissed the kind of experimental work of the likes of Morgan and Thorndike. However, he also dismissed the notions of instinct that psychology had earlier offered, focusing his critical attention especially upon what he considered to be the pervasively vitalist ideas of those such as the social psychologist William McDougall, whose work on instinct, he asserted, was entirely devoid of an evolutionary perspective and was essentially abiological (Lorenz 1937).

At a major symposium after the Second World War, Lorenz, whose pre-war writings were relatively unknown, introduced ethology as a new science based on the 'discovery of a new *particulate* process' (Lorenz 1950, p. 221—italics in the original), a particulate process, he thought, comparable with genetics, conceptually, if not also in terms of general biological importance:

> The distinct and particulate physiological process whose discovery may be identified with the origin of comparative ethology as an independent branch of science is represented by a certain type of innate, genetically determined behaviour patterns (sic). Charles Otis Whitman, who was the first to discover them, called them simply 'Instincts'; Oskar Heinroth, who, ten years later, independently rediscovered them, spoke of 'arteigene Triebhandlungen'; I myself have called them 'Instinkthandlungen'... (Lorenz 1950, p. 219).

He suggested in the next sentence that they be termed 'endogenous movements'. Heinroth's German phrase means 'species-specific drive action' (Lorenz 1937, p. 130), which implies behaviour that is highly end directed, and of course, unique to a species. The rest of the world quickly came to refer to them by the traditional word instinct, as Whitman had originally suggested.

Lorenz's original conception was that instincts constitute chains of reflexes. Through the influence of van Holst, he dropped this idea and moved to a different view: an instinct is the behavioural manifestation of a complex central nervous system unit (hence the notion of a particulate process) with specific genetic origins. The activity of such a particulate unit is initiated by a specific sensory event known as a sign stimulus or releaser which in turn activates an 'innate releasing mechanism' that results in a stereotyped behavioural sequence called a fixed action pattern. All instincts, argued Lorenz, have specific fitness-enhancing (not a phrase that Lorenz would have used, but this is certainly what he meant) biological functions and are products of evolution. It follows, then, that all instincts must be part-caused by genes as products of a history of selection. Some, such as those that come to have a communicative role through a process called ritualization, are instincts which 'acquire a new function' and hence 'an entirely new instinct may be born' (Lorenz 1966, p. 278) through the appropriation or co-option of already existing instincts with different functions— a process that fits well with Gould's later notion of exaptation as the correct basis for understanding the mind and behaviour in evolutionary terms (Gould 1991), though Gould himself did not make the connection.

It is not the concern of this chapter to provide a complete account of the science of ethology developed by Lorenz and his colleagues, notably Niko Tinbergen. There are, however, certain features that are relevant to Lorenz's later writings about learning. The first concerns Lorenz's argument that behaviour, specifically instincts, is to be seen within a comparative framework. This was an absolutely central and crucial part of Lorenz's thinking and warrants a lengthy quotation:

> Comparative anatomy and systematics, using a broad base of induction gained by observation and description, brought order into the chaotic multiplicity of living species and prepared the way for the recognition of the common origin of all living creatures. Once this basic evolutionary fact was established, it was an unavoidable conclusion that a historical explanation is needed for practically every detail of structure and function observed in living creatures. Such historical explanation is indeed also a *causal* one: if we ask why man has auditory organs at the sides of his head, with auditory canals connecting them with the pharynx, one of the causal explanations of this state of affairs is that all this is so, because man is descended from water-breathing vertebrates which had a gill-opening in that part of their anatomy. Thus research into the phyletic history of an organ or function becomes an indispensable part of its scientific study. The application to behaviour of the comparative method which

reconstructs the phyletic history of organisms by studying the
similarity and dissimilarity of their characters is indeed one
of the most important procedures of ethological research
(Lorenz 1966, p. 273).

Whilst this is as clear an exposition as there is of how
important Lorenz thought the comparative perspective is to
the study of instincts, it did not come as a revelation to him
in the 1960s. His earlier writings, including those of the
1930s, are soaked in the same idea. For example, in a 1937
paper, he wrote that 'all innate behaviour patterns that could
be followed up over a larger or smaller section of the zoolog-
ical system can serve as taxonomic characters, exactly as the
outward form of any skeletal element or other organ can'
(Lorenz 1937, p. 148). Later, in the same paper, he reiterates
the point that 'innate motor patterns behave exactly the
same as organs in their phyletic variability, and that, like
organs, they can and must be approached with comparative
methods' (Lorenz 1937, p. 174). Darwin himself had made
exactly the same point in the chapter on instinct in his
Origin of Species, and what Lorenz was doing was resuscitat-
ing a Darwinian idea that had been largely forgotten. Lorenz
laid great store by it; when he was awarded the Nobel Prize
in 1973, he stated that the comparative method applied to
behaviour was his most significant achievement.

It was almost certainly this particular view of the instincts
and their importance for comparative study that led him to
the position that he initially took on the relationship
between evolved behavioural traits, instincts, and learning.
During his time as a prisoner of war in the Soviet Union,
Lorenz wrote what has become known as his Russian manuscript, part of which Griffiths (2004) quotes as follows:
'Such innate, species-specific motor patterns represent characters *that must have behaved like morphological characters in*

the course of evolution. Indeed they must have behaved like *particularly conservative characters* (Lorenz 1996 p. 237—italics in the original). This, for Lorenz, was how to make a real biological science out of behaviour; instincts should stand alongside any other phenotypic trait both as comparative markers within a homology-based comparative evolutionary framework, and as adaptive particulate structures having fitness-enhancing properties, again within an evolutionary context. Waiting around the scientific corner, of course, would be the inevitable links to the suites of genes that, in this view, must be the part-causes of such instincts, and hence cementing the status of the new science with links to genetics, one of the most successful branches of all twentieth century science. As Kingsland (2005) notes in her review of Burkhardt (2005), Lorenz was a visionary thinker. He was also ambitious, with all of his 1930 papers bearing testament to his belief that he was the founder of a new science in which instincts, properly defined and placed within the context of evolutionary biology, would be the central empirical and conceptual entity. For these reasons, Lorenz's early formulations lay out instincts as wholly separate from learned behaviours and hence, by implication, from learning itself. He needed an enduring unit, not one whose very essence is change—a view not far from that expressed by Williams (1966) as to why the gene, not the phenotype or the group, should be seen as the unit of selection.

In the 1935 paper, one of his criticisms of Morgan was his failure to recognize 'a phenomenon which I have called "instinct–training interlocking"'... This is the singular fact that in numerous behaviour patterns of birds and other animals, innate and acquired links alternate directly in a functional unit of behaviour. If the inserted acquired components are overlooked, a variability wholly foreign to its nature is attributed to the purely instinctive behaviour pattern' (p. 97).

In a paper of 2 years later, Lorenz slightly expanded the point, and in a manner that contains a faint harbinger of the stance he would later adopt on learning:

> Instinctively innate and individually acquired links often succeed each other directly in the functionally uniform action chains of higher animals. I have termed this phenomenon 'instinct–training interlocking', and emphasized that similar interlockings also occur between instinctive and insightful behaviour. Here, where we are dealing with the effects of experience, we must first discuss the interlocking of instinct and training. Its essence lies in the fact that a conditioned action is inserted in an innate chain of acts at a certain, also innately determined point. This action must be acquired by each individual in the course of his ontogenetic development. In such a case the innate action chain has a *gap*, into which, instead of an instinctive act, a 'faculty to acquire' is inserted. This faculty is sometimes a very specific one. It may apply to changeable living conditions; it may even be an adaptation to an inconstancy of this sort. I would recall the adaptiveness of bees which, as von Frisch was able to show, may be called an adjustment to the blossoming of various plants (Lorenz 1937, p. 137—italics in the original).

It is worth noting the sentence 'This faculty is sometimes a very specific one'. Another example that he gave was the fetching of nest material and its incorporation into nest structures by Corvidae. Twenty years later, he was making the same point that if instincts change they do so only slowly and only as a consequence of evolution—they 'stubbornly resist learning in the individual' (Lorenz 1958, p. 51).

Thus we see him asserting again and again that instinctive behaviour and learned behaviour are entirely separate, even though they may be linked together to form complex behavioural chains of mixed origins. It seems that he had to take this stand if he were to maintain the argument that these particulate structures or processes are sufficiently invariant in form to stand as species markers. His vision of ethology as a new science, it must have seemed to him at the time, absolutely dictated this stance. Learning would have provided too much variability.

Lorenz added one further point to this distinction that classical ethology had to make:

> It is an *essential* quality of instinctive behaviour that it copes with tasks to which the mental faculties of a species are not equal. For this reason alone, it seems impossible that an animal should be able to improve upon its own instinctive actions through learning or insight. Strictly speaking, we cannot really decide whether in principle instinctive behaviour can or cannot be modified by learning and insight. We can only say that no such adaptation occurs, because the tasks which an animal's environment sets and which it solves instinctively *always* goes far beyond the mental capacity of the species. The ability to solve a task of this kind by learning or insight evidently never exists *side by side* with an instinctive motor pattern which fits the same task. The reason is probably that *once* the ability to solve a task by learning or insight appears in the phylogenesis of a species, this solution, with its adaptive plasticity, must have far higher survival value than any mastering of the same task by rigid instinctive actions' (Lorenz 1937, p. 154).

This is a strange statement; one may also infer from the lack of reference that Lorenz, curiously, knew nothing of the Baldwin effect, and had he done so he would have thought it incorrect.

An example of Lorenz's early thinking about the relationship between instinct and learning concerns the phenomenon imprinting. The English naturalist Douglas Spalding in the early 1870s undertook a series of observations and experiments on newly hatched chicks and was one of the first to describe what he called the 'following reaction'. Heinroth, who had a significant effect on Lorenz's thinking, had also written about the tendency of young birds of certain species to follow animals, usually their parents, to whom they are exposed soon after hatching. It is no surprise, therefore, that Lorenz, much of whose observations were made upon nidifugous birds such as ducks and geese, should have had something to say on the phenomenon, for which he coined the word imprinting. Lorenz's own 'studies' of imprinting were rather cursory when compared with the wealth of systematic observation and experimentation on the phenomenon which occurred during the period from around 1960 to 1985 (see Fabricius 1964; Salzen 1970; Green 1982 for examples of studies and reviews of studies that covered a wide range of the principal features of imprinting), and its extension from parental imprinting to sexual imprinting (Bateson 1978) and beyond the class *Aves* to include certain species of mammal, fish and even some invertebrates. What is important, however, was not Lorenz's 'data', such as they were, but his thoughts as to how to explain imprinting.

In the 1935 paper, he wrote of imprinting as a developmental process quite different from any form of learning: 'In complex behaviour patterns, consisting of innate and acquired elements, the object of an instinctive act is often the acquired component ... As a rule, the object is acquired by something very much like training. However, in a certain group of instinctive acts—those relative to fellow members of the species—where the motor response is innate while the releaser is not, the acquiring process is basically different and cannot, to my mind, be identified with learning' (Lorenz 1935, p. 102). Imprinting is just such an instance of an innate response relative to fellow members of a species.

'The process of imprinting differs radically from the acquisition of the objects of other instinctive acts whose releasing
mechanism is not innate. Whereas in the latter case the
object seems always to be acquired by self-training, or learning, imprinting has a number of features which distinguish
it fundamentally from a learning process. It has no equal in
the psychology of any other animal, least of all a mammal'
(Lorenz 1935, p. 104).

Lorenz singled out two specific features of imprinting
which he argued meant that learning could not be involved
in whatever process is occurring. The first is that it can only
occur 'within a brief critical period in the life of an individual' (Lorenz 1935, p. 104); the second is that 'once the phys-
iologically critical period is over, the animal knows the
imprinted object of its innate reactions to a fellow member
of the species exactly as though this knowledge were innate.
It cannot be forgotten!' (Lorenz 1935, p. 105). In his 1937
review, he added another reason for asserting that imprinting does not involve learning: 'The animal does not act
according to the principle of trial and error, as it does when
acquiring an instinct–training interlocking, nor is it led by
reward and punishment' (p. 145).

Again, it must be stressed that all of Lorenz's 1930s
notions on imprinting have subsequently been shown empirically to be incorrect. Imprinting certainly is a form of learning; it is not wholly confined to a 'critical' period, though it
certainly does occur more readily within a 'sensitive' period;
and it can be reversed. However, again that is not the point.
What is the point is that clearly believing, on the basis of
what he knew at the time, that imprinting does not involve a
form of learning, he turned this belief into a further claim
for the fundamental nature of instincts. He did this by pointing to 'a striking analogy between the origin of the system of

instinctive behaviour patterns and processes familiar from developmental morphology' (Lorenz 1935, p. 105). Using the work of major figures in experimental embryology and their work on embryonic induction by which tissue transplanted early enough in development in some species is shown to have a prospective potency determined by the area of the embryo into which it is transplanted, Lorenz argued that the notions of regulative embryos and mosaic embryos might be used to understand instincts. 'Similarly, we might well distinguish between mosaic and regulative systems of instincts, and apply the idea of inductive determination to instinctive reactions whose object is not innately known to an animal, but is molded by the environment, especially by a fellow member of the species. There are a great many analogies between the functional plan of an animal's instincts and the functional plan of its organic structure' (Lorenz 1935, p. 106). Not only is imprinting explained, argued Lorenz, by a process analogous to prospective potency in embryonic development, but once again an identity is established for instincts as fundamental biological units whose development is on a par with any other organ system.

Critical arguments

Lorenz's classical ethological ideas did not go unchallenged, the principal arguments being directed against his notion of instinct and his use of the word 'innate'. In his classic *The Organization of Behaviour*, Hebb (1949) was sympathetic to the general thrust of Lorenz's analysis: 'The term "instinctive" will be used here to refer to behaviour, other than reflex, in which innate factors play a *predominant* part. Empirically, this is behaviour in which the motor pattern is variable but with an end result that is predictable from a knowledge of the species, without knowing the history of the individual animal. This class of behaviour must be recognized' (Hebb 1949, p. 166). Clearly Hebb was asserting the Lorenzian notion of the importance of seeing a certain 'class' of behaviour within a phylogenetic perspective. In a later paper (Hebb 1953), his declaration that asking about the relative importance of innate versus learning factors made no more sense than asking whether it is length or breadth that contributes more to the area of a surface, rather changed his earlier stance on the predominance of innate factors in such behaviours. In his 1949 book, Hebb also was clear, in flat contradiction to Lorenz's early views on the absolute distinction that must be drawn between instinctive and innate behaviours, that '"instinct" may fundamentally involve some learning even at "lower" phylogenetic levels, if the kind of learning involved is strictly limited and if it may occur in a matter of seconds' (Hebb 1949, pp. 168–169), and that 'there is no evidence to justify the *a priori* assumption that the control of learned and the control of instinctive behaviour are quite separate processes' (p. 169).

Over half a century later, Marler (2004) observed on the basis of the wealth of evidence from birdsong studies which were not available in the 1940s and 1950s that 'we do indeed speak readily of bird songs as innate or learned' (p. 195). Earlier in the same review, Marler lamented that 'if only Hebb's temperate views had prevailed over the more inflammatory approach of Lehrman, the history of the innateness concept might have proceeded very differently' (Marler 2004, p. 193). It is likely that the tone of Lehrman's writing (Lehrman 1953) was due in part to Lorenz's known association with Nazi doctrine (Nisbett 1976; Plotkin 2004). However, whatever the causes, Lehrman's review was clever, vituperative and highly influential.

Lehrman's criticisms were many, and for convenience will be grouped into just two kinds. First, using specific documented examples of behaviour that classical ethology would have labelled instinctive, such as pecking at grain in chicks, Lehrman pointed to strong evidence of the role of associative learning in the early experience of the chick. Later investigations, such as Hailman's studies of feeding behaviour in sea gull chicks (1967, 1969), showed without doubt that Lehrman had been correct in his general point that behaviours which classical ethologists would have classified as instincts have significant experiential causes, including learned components. In the case of begging behaviour in gull chicks, Hailman's findings were especially persuasive in showing how even a relatively simple behaviour is differentially affected by both non-learning and learning developmental events, including the strong possibility of the social influences of other chicks in the nest.

A further point of criticism concerning the evidence for so-called instincts came from the often labelled 'deprivation' experiments where animals reared in conditions which prevented them from practising a particular behaviour or observing it performed by others would, when the opportunity offered itself, perform that behaviour. Lehrman did not dispute the basic finding, though it might be noted that the resultant 'normality' of the behaviour concerned had often been overstated. What Lehrman correctly observed was that the logic of such experiments merely demonstrated what conditions were not essential for the development of a specific behaviour, and spoke not at all to what conditions were causal in its ontogeny.

Lehrman's second argument was theoretical, but as equally important as the evidence-based criticism. It was that 'instinctive' behaviours, like all other behaviours, do not emerge simply, invariantly and inevitably. All behaviour is a product of a complex cascade of developmental processes, some of which might include learning: 'analysis of the developmental process involved shows that the behaviour patterns concerned are not unitary, autonomously developing things, but rather that they emerge ontogenetically in complex ways from the previously developed organization of the organism in a given setting' (Lehrman 1953, p. 343). Lehrman was especially strong on this point and deserves lengthy quotation:

> The 'instinct' is obviously not present in the zygote. Just as obviously, it is present in the behaviour of the animal after the appropriate age. The problem for the investigator who wishes to make a causal analysis of behaviour is: How did this behaviour come about? The use of 'explanatory' categories such as 'innate' and 'genically (sic) fixed' obscures the necessity of investigating developmental *processes* in order to gain insight into the actual mechanisms of behaviour and their inter-relations. The problem of development is the problem of the development of new structures and activity patterns from the resolution of the interaction of *existing* structures and patterns, within the organism and its internal environment, and between the organism and its outer environment. At any stage of development, the new features emerge from the interactions within the *current* stage and between the *current* stage and the environment. The interaction out of which the organism develops is *not* one, as is so often said, between heredity and environment. It is between *organism* and environment. And the organism is different at each different stage of its development (Lehrman 1953, p. 345— italics in the original),

This short-sightedness of conceptualization, Lehrman argued, was a gross oversimplification and led to a number of additional mistakes. One is the egregious error of Lorenz having adopted what was, in essence, the developmental notion of preformism—the long discredited idea that the fertilized egg contains in microscopic miniature all the organization and structure of the developed adult (see Chapter 5). 'The development of an "instinctive" act inevitably appears to Lorenz to be the self-differentiation of a preformed, autonomous thing. Thus Lorenz sees the developing behaviour of the animal as progressing *toward* the full-blown 'instinct' rather than as developing *out* of interactions among processes present at that stage' (Lehrman 1953, p. 352).

Another grave error which originated in a lack of understanding of the complexity of development lay in Lorenz conflating levels of organization phylogenetically, developmentally, behaviourally and neurologically. One consequence of this was that the classical ethologists, whilst claiming to operate primarily within the context of an analysis of homology (common descent), frequently wrote and thought within the much less rigorous framework of analogy (convergent evolution). Thus it was that so-called instincts of, say, protection of young by mothers was compared between humans and birds, who, of course, are evolved from a remote common ancestor in stem reptiles some 280 million years ago and so any such comparisons are worthless since it is highly unlikely that parental behaviour patterns in such relatively unrelated animals would be similar because of common ancestry. The approach, concluded Lehrman, 'becomes profoundly anti-evolutionary' (Lehrman 1953, p. 357).

This, to put it mildly, was strong stuff, published, what was more, in a highly respected scientific journal. It should be added that some 15 or so years after Lehrman's original critique, he wrote a chapter for a volume commemorating the work of T.C. Schneirla in which he, almost, apologized, at least for the tone of the 1953 piece: '… when I look over

my 1953 critique of his theory, I perceive elements of hostility to which its target would have been bound to react.
My critique does not now read to me like an analysis of a
scientific problem, with an evaluation of the contribution of
a particular point of view, but rather like an assault upon a
theoretical point of view, the writer of which assault was not
interested in pointing out what positive contributions that
point of view had made' (Lehrman 1970, p. 22). He went on
to say that, in terms of formulating the issues of the evolution and function of behaviour, Lorenz's contribution had
been massive; and so too had been his work which 'created
a school based upon the conception of species-specific
behaviour as a part of the animal's adaptation to its natural
environment' (Lehrman 1970, p. 22). Yet he then added that
'I do not now disagree with any of the basic ideas expressed
in my critique!'

Before considering Lorenz's response to such criticism, no
account of it would be complete without including some of
Lehrman's mentor, T.C. Schneirla's, views. Unsurprisingly,
given the relationship between Lehrman and Schneirla, the
latter's appraisal of classical ethology is, in its theoretical
points, mostly indistinguishable from that of the former,
though Schneirla offers a much wider database to support
his claims. In one respect, that of open acceptance of the
importance of species-typical behaviour, Schneirla is closer
to Lorenz than his pupil. 'Undeniably, the influence of
genetic constitution is expressed somehow in the functions
and behaviour of every animal. Raccoons, for instance, could
not readily be brought to peck at their food as do chicks. The
"instinct problem" therefore centers around the occurrence
of behaviour that may be termed species-stereotyped or
species-specific, species-characteristic or species-typical'
(Schneirla 1956, pp. 133–134). Instinct, however, as defined

by classical ethology, 'is not a real and demonstrated agency in the causation of behaviour, but a word for the problem of species-typical behaviour at all phyletic levels' (Schneirla 1956, p. 136).

In all other respects, though, Schneirla's position is indistinguishable from that of Lehrman. Lorenz's stance, he argued, was a form of preformism; genetic effects are only ever indirect, mediated by the complexity of interacting developmental processes and mechanisms; that any distinction between what Schneirla called the 'native' and 'acquired' is highly ambiguous; and finally that 'the 'instinct' problem is one of development, different for each phyletic level' (Schneirla 1956, p. 136). His concluding statement, comprising three points, was indistinguishable from the developmental biology of half a century later (see Chapter 5):

> (1) In the development of any animal, systems of intervening variables mediate between genic (sic) influences and processes in ontogeny through which adaptive behaviour appears. The range of these variables, from biochemical and physical conditions to the effects of experience, depends basically upon limitations imposed by the genic constitution of the species. (2) On all phyletic levels, behavioural organization arises in development through the interrelationships of intrinsic and extrinsic factors influencing growth and differentiation. Only in a misleading sense can the genic constitution be said to determine the organization of behaviour patterns, even in phyla characterized by the most rigid lines of development. (3) In a strict theoretical sense the terms 'innate' and 'acquired' cannot therefore be applied validly to behaviour or to the organization of behaviour. Accordingly, it is suggested that the term 'instinct' be retired from scientific usage, except to designate a developmental process resulting in species-typical behaviour (Schneirla 1956, p. 177).

Earlier in the same paper, he was entirely consistent in noting that 'indirectly, all learning is somehow influenced by

genes' (p. 136), though he did not draw any specific implications from that observation.

Lorenz's response

A striking feature of both Lehrman's and Schneirla's critical
reviews of Lorenz's conception of instincts as products of
evolution and hence as innate, genetically determined behaviours, is how much they both focused on developmental
issues and how little attention was paid to the evolutionary
considerations so central to Lorenz's thinking, as Lehrman
admitted in his 1970 paper. Schneirla clearly understood the
problem as centring upon species-specific behaviours, but
considered this to be a matter to be resolved by developmental study. Lehrman thought Lorenz's work on the evolution of behaviour important insofar as it might provide the
basis for understanding species-specific behaviour within the
context of its natural environment. Yet neither really seemed
to understand the scientific importance that Lorenz attributed to 'particulate behaviours' *as products of histories of natural selection*. It was as if all the attention of his critics had been
focused on the former, the notion of particulate behaviours,
and none upon what in a number of places subsequently
Lorenz emphasized as the need to understand the function or
functions of those behaviours whose 'survival values' have
exerted the selection pressures which have *caused* the behaviour to evolve. His critics, Lorenz complained, simply did not
understand the thrust of his argument.

The principal response came in a monograph (Lorenz
1965) published surprisingly late following the 1950s writings of Lehrman, Schneirla, Hebb and others, and which was
subsequently expanded upon in later work (Lorenz 1969,
1977). The overwhelmingly important part of that response
concerned learning. Less important were two other general

points regarding development and the deprivation experiment, whose relevance to the notion of the necessary knowledge of the title of this book is very small, and so which will be dealt with here first and in a summary manner.

Just as his critics never seemed to appreciate his main point, so Lorenz equally failed to understand theirs. 'What rules ontogeny, in bodily as well as in behavioural development, is *obviously* the hereditary blueprint contained in the genome and *not* the environmental circumstances indispensable to its realization.' (Lorenz 1965 p. 42—italics added). The 'indispensable' was a clever concession to his critics, but the assertion of the dominating importance of genes, quite apart from the now (though not then) rather outmoded notion of the genome as a blueprint (see Chapter 5), points to his simply not submitting to, perhaps not understanding, the developmentalists' point of view of the importance of cascading and very complex developmental processes finely in tune to the environments within which those processes occur. In part, much depends upon what is meant by 'information' deriving from 'experience'. Lehrman had made much of the work of Kuo (1932*a,b,c,d*) on the pre-hatching occurrence of head movements in the embryonic chick caused initially by heartbeat and amnion contractions and how this might be an important part of the development of the chick's post-hatching pecking behaviour—might, because Lehrman had rather stretched his point from Kuo's work on chicks to Coghill's earlier observations (Coghill 1929) on animals of an entirely different vertebrate class. However tenuous Lehrman's point may have been, in Lorenz's view Kuo's and Lehrman's interpretation of the developmental importance of this passive movement forced on the chick's head 'vastly overrates' its importance to visually guided pecking behaviour. In the company of the many, many evolutionists (see Dawkins 1982; Pinker 1997 for more recent and prominent examples) whose emphasis has been on the evolutionary origins of adaptations, Lorenz argued that 'no biologist in his right senses will forget that the blueprint contained in the genome requires innumerable environmental factors in order to be realized in the phenogeny (sic) of structures and functions' (Lorenz 1965, p. 37), including such basics as nutrition and the development of other organ systems necessary to sustain neural and behavioural function. 'Whatever wonders phenogeny may perform, however, it cannot extract from these factors information which is not contained in them' (Lorenz 1965, p. 37), for example that male stickleback fish have a red underbelly. Yet he conceded that among processes and mechanisms of many kinds, be they functions of sensory or motor competence, 'among these functions there may be some that require ontogenetically acquired information for their development' (Lorenz 1965, p. 38). Yet 'if one assesses, even ever so roughly, the amount of information which quite undubitably is transmitted by way of the genome and compares it with what (even conceding the most unlikely possibilities) could have been acquired in individual life, the proportion is astounding' (Lorenz 1965, p. 26) when one is explaining the causes of species-typical behaviour, be it male sticklebacks fighting other males that intrude into their territory or the integrated sensory–motor coordination necessary for birds of prey to hunt successfully. It might be noted that any claim about 'proportion' and comparison of information is merely declamatory. Such information could not have been measured then, and cannot be measured now. We simply do not know how to do so.

Thus did Lorenz in his 1965 monograph provide the routine concession to the necessity and importance of ontogeny, a concession that developmentalists to this day consider inadequate (see Chapter 5). His general point, however, was that the arguments of developmentalists provided no adequate explanation of adaptive behaviours and their underlying mechanisms and processes. For adequate explanation there is an absolute necessity for the notion of the innate, and this is what the monograph set about rescuing and enlarging upon. His closing summary statement said it all: 'The primary aim of this book is to prevent the discrediting of a concept which, though it has been used occasionally in an imprecise manner, is indispensable to an ethological approach. This concept is that of the innate' (Lorenz 1965, p. 101). Lorenz set about this in two ways. The first was to correct the imprecision of his, and others', usage. The second was to provide an explicit account of ethology as a comparative science of behavioural adaptations, and, to the crucial point of this book, to extend the concept of adaptation to learning itself.

Lorenz immediately and implicitly accepted that his earlier use of the word innate had been unintentionally preformistic. The opening paragraph to the monograph states: 'What is preformed in the genome and inherited by the individual is not any 'character', such as we can see and describe in a living organism, but a limited range of possible forms in which an identical genetic blueprint can find expression in phenogeny ... The term "innate" should never, on principle, be applied to organs or behaviour patterns, even if their modifiability should be negligible' (Lorenz 1965, p. 1). What is innate, argued Lorenz, and what is essential to the causal explanation of all behaviour and its underlying processes and mechanisms, is whatever it is in the genome, what Lorenz called genetic information, that (1) is essential for the development of species-typical behaviour; (2) is the result of a history of natural selection; and hence (3) that the behaviour or its underlying processes and mechanisms be adaptive in the full evolutionary sense of that word (see next section); and (4) be genetically part-caused.

In the 1965 monograph, Lorenz spends little time on the first of these points. Nor, as already noted, was this anything on which Schneirla at least disagreed with him. Species-typical does not mean species-specific, since behaviours (and cognitive functioning), like other phenotypic attributes, may be shared with other species within even quite wide taxonomic categories such as families or classes. However, it does imply species-universal in the sense that, pathology aside, all members of a species will have the behavioural attribute, albeit often within a range of variability—again like any other phenotypic trait, be it facial configuration, opposable thumbs, or any other structural character.

Nor, unlike his previous hard stand on the absolute dichotomy between innate behaviours (instincts) and those that are learned, was he in 1965 and later insisting on such an absolute distinction. Thus 'it is practically never possible to state that all the information underlying the adaptedness of a whole functional unit is phylogenetically acquired' (Lorenz 1965, p. 25). And in defence of his view that he had never asserted that studying the development of behaviour is unnecessary for the causal understanding of its adult form, in more than one part of the monograph Lorenz argues for the existence of very rapid learning being a part of the development of species typical behaviours. For example, '... as far as receptor patterns (in other words, releasing mechanisms) are concerned ... there is hardly one which, indubitably based on innate information, is not rendered more selective by additional learning. A flashlike conditioning can take place at the very first function of a releasing mechanism and has to be taken into consideration in order to avoid the danger of mistaking what had actually been learned in the first experiment for innate information in later ones' (Lorenz 1965, p. 35). Later he noted that 'the "decoding" of genome-bound information is ... first, by means of morphological ontogeny producing structure; and second, by means of trial-and-error behaviour exploiting structure as a teaching apparatus' (Lorenz 1965, p. 79).

However much he may have softened his position on these issues, he was absolute in his maintaining the necessity, the scientific necessity framed within a causal explanation, of continuing to distinguish between the notion of the innate and the individually acquired, even, as will become evident, when he considered the latter to be a product of the former. The vehicle he used for the distinction was his information metaphor and the centre of his argument was a particular notion of adaptation: '"Adaptation" is the process which moulds the organism so that it fits its environment in a way achieving survival. Adaptedness is always the irrefutable proof that this process has taken place. Any moulding of the organism to its environment is a process so closely akin to that of forming, within organic structure, an image of the environment that it is completely correct to speak of information concerning environment being acquired by the organism' (Lorenz 1965, p. 7). This is the core of his argument because he asserts that there are two ways by which that information can be gained. The one is by way of population-level or species evolution entailing changes in gene frequencies and gene forms within breeding populations. This is information carried in the genome and is the link each living organism has to the evolution of the species of which it is a member. The other is by way of the interaction of the individual organism with its environment. In many, perhaps most, organisms that interaction does not involve changes within neural networks; when neural change does occur (memory, in effect) we refer to it usually as learning. Lorenz's point is that the latter, the information gained by the individual interacting with its environment, whether learned or non-learned, does not directly result in changes in the genome and hence is not heritable.

Stripped down to this most basic level of his argument, Lorenz is clearly taking a stand that any evolutionist of that day would take who was brought up to swim conceptually within the modern synthesis of Darwinian natural selection and genetics. In that sense his argument is almost prosaic—some forms of biological information can be passed on to offspring and other forms cannot (with the exception, of course, of animals that have evolved culture, more of which in Chapter 6) and all that Lorenz was doing was maintaining that hard-won distinction that emerged in the late nineteenth century from the work of Weismann and others. It echoes faithfully the writings of Morgan quoted in Chapter 3 of this book: 'The essential point on which that theory (Wesmann's) is absolutely insistent is that what is handed on through inheritance is *an innate, and not an individually acquired, character*' (Morgan 1891). So Lorenz's stand in this respect was utterly ordinary and wholly uncontroversial, except that he was subjecting naturally occurring behaviour to theoretical scrutiny of a kind; and as became clear in his later writings of 1969 and 1977, his use of the information metaphor, gained phylogenetically or ontogenetically, had taken him squarely into the area that was known as evolutionary epistemology (Campbell 1974; Plotkin 1982). However, his principal case for the importance of maintaining the notion of the innate boiled down to such basic and well accepted arguments that it is hard to understand what point his critics had ever had in this specific regard.

In summary, then, Lorenz was trenchant and entirely non-revolutionary in maintaining the concept of the innate, and in distinguishing it from traits that are individually acquired. However, in the 1965 monograph he did indeed take a revolutionary step forward, and that, rather curiously, was in his treatment of learning.

It was noted earlier in this chapter that some 30 years before, Lorenz had, when writing about 'instinct–training interlocking', noted that the 'faculty to acquire' in the case of the training component of the behavioural chain may be a 'very specific one'. Hebb (1949) too had indicated his belief in some form of directed learning as part of his casting cold water on the instinct–learning distinction: '… instinct is not a separate process from intelligence or insight. It is intelligence, or insight, that is innately limited in variety' (p. 169). It is impossible to know whether Lorenz's own earlier thoughts, or those of Hebb, directed him towards the conceptual epiphany with regard to learning that he had undergone in writing his monograph—and conceptual epiphany is a phrase that does not overstate the importance of his revised thoughts on learning. However, some hint of where his ideas originated from may be found in an earlier paper which considered the light that modern biology throws on the epistemological position of Kant. Lorenz was as convinced a Kantian as he was an evolutionist, and in 1941 had published a paper in which he questioned whether Kant's *a priori* categories and intuitions, despite these being the means by which we make sense of the world, nonetheless are not related in any meaningful way to the real properties of the world (see Chapter 7). As an evolutionist, Lorenz had argued that Kant had been wrong to assert that there is no necessary relationship between our, or any other animal's, *a priori* categories and intuitions and the nature of the world in which we live. Such innate features of mind, for that is precisely what Kant's *a priori* are, have to be products of long histories of natural selection, and as such had to be directly connected with what is out there in the world. 'Is it at all probable', asked Lorenz, 'that the laws of our cognitive apparatus should be disconnected with those of the real world?' (Lorenz 1941, p. 122 in the 1982 reprinted English translation). His answer was an emphatic no. The cognition of any creature able to acquire knowledge of the world has to bear a positive relationship to that experienced world.

The 1941 paper had been a rather general and unfocused one, which did not dwell at any length on the cognitive implications. Not so the 1965 monograph. Countering the standard interactionist position that all behaviour is an inextricable mix of the innate and the acquired, Lorenz noted something general about learning that, as far as is known, had passed unnoticed in the previous 60 and more years when the study of learning as a serious science had attempted to formulate general learning laws, almost always within an associationistic framework. (It should though be noted that the many previous attempts to relate reinforcement to biological needs might be seen as a similar move to the one Lorenz took.)

> The more complicated an adapted process, the less chance there is that a random change will improve its adaptedness. There are no life processes more complicated than those which take place in the central nervous system and control behaviour. Randon change must, with an overpowering probability, result in their disintegration ... The amazing and never-to-be-forgotten fact is that learning does, in the majority of cases, increase the survival value of the behaviour mechanisms which it modifies (Lorenz 1965, p. 12).

He went on to assert that the reason why comparative psychologists had failed to notice this was because of the unnatural circumstances of the laboratory learning experiments, but to an evolutionist and a naturalist who observed the behaviour of animals in their natural environments, i.e. anyone 'tolerably versed in biological thought' (Lorenz 1965, p. 13), it is obvious that learning is the product of processes and mechanisms of high differentiation and fitness-enhancing properties that can only be the products of evolution. Like all other adaptive behaviours, those that are learned are part-caused by information carried in the genome. Put crudely, learning is an instinct or, more probably, different forms of learning are different forms of instinct. In more acceptable biological terms, learning is an adaptation, a product of evolution, and hence genetically part-caused.

In part, Lorenz's argument was a defence against his critics who had accused him of spuriously separating learning from instinct. However, it seems equally correct, because the monograph is awash with repeated unpacking of his argument, that at least in the pre-1965 sense, any absolute separation of information coming from phylogenetic and ontogenetic sources is an incorrect conceptualization (though this does not deny the importance of the distinction drawn in terms of what can and cannot be inherited). Some kind of new causal architecture is needed to encompass the innate and the learned. 'The central problem of all reinforcing and/or extinguishing mechanisms lies in their content of innate information telling them what is "good" and what is "bad" for the organism' (Lorenz 1965, p. 17). Also 'the notion that learning or any other change of behaviour achieving survival value could possibly be the function of a non-specifically organized and programmed aggregation of neural elements, is absolutely untenable' (Lorenz 1965, pp. 30–31). There are many other such statements throughout the monograph.

In answering his critics, Lorenz had conceptually married learning, and all forms of cognition, to evolution. The connection conceptually established meant that new forms of connectedness and causal relations need to be recognized. In doing so, he at times placed his own earlier writings within the realm of the condemned.

> An amazing number of scientists, otherwise biologically minded people among them, seem unable to grasp the fact that the stratified structure of the whole world of organisms absolutely forbids the conceptualization of living systems or life processes in terms of 'disjunctive'—that is to say, mutually exclusive—concepts. It is nonsense to oppose to each other 'animal' and 'man', 'nature' and 'culture', 'innate programming' and 'learning', as if the old logical diagram of alpha and nonalpha were applicable to them. Man, as I have just said, is still an animal; human nature persists in and is the basis of culture; *and all learning is very specifically innately programmed*' (Lorenz 1969, pp. 20–21—italics added).

Thus can be seen how Lorenz had moved on from his monograph to a much grander evolutionary epistemological position, but at the heart of it was the same conceptual breakthrough of the 1965 book.

The explicit recognition of learning as an adaptation has explicit implications. Chapter 2 had indicated the prescient echoes in the writings of both Spencer and Darwin of Lorenz's insight. Darwin especially, with his phrase 'hereditary knowledge' when referring to learned birdsong, or his observation that language learning in children is the product of an 'instinctive tendency to speak' which is quite different from other acquired skills such as baking or writing came very close to the Lorenzian notion of the innate bases of learning.

Lorenz called these innate bases 'innate teaching mechanisms' or 'innate school marms'. In much of the monograph,

Lorenz gropes towards some kind of identification of what these innate teaching mechanisms might be which are variously, but always speculatively, considered as links between reinforcement and specific stimuli or responses, complex response chains within specific environmental circumstances, perceptual configurations and attentional mechanisms. What is implicit in his ideas is that there are different kinds of teaching mechanisms attaching to different kinds of learning, both within and between species. What is also implicit is that learning is almost never open-ended. It is constrained, and the result of constrained learning is that it is always targeted upon specific features of the world.

The argument presented here, in short, is that while others may have come close to the same insight that Lorenz had, and Tinbergen (1951) certainly did, in chasing down its implications, all of which centre on learning as constrained because it is a set of evolved adaptations, Lorenz delivered an entirely new way of thinking about cognition. One of the less edifying features of these events were the responses of his old critics. Lehrman's 1970 reply to Lorenz's monograph completely misses the novel way in which the notion of learning as constrained adaptation changes the way cognition should be thought of. Schneirla (1966) does mention the Lorenzian notion of the innate school marm. However, in an especially vituperative and negative review of the monograph he notes that 'the implication that the genes rigidly "program" the animal's learning is opposed by the results of many experiments, as well as by evidence from animal training' (p. 194). However, Lorenz had never stated nor meant that learning is 'rigid', whatever that might mean, when arguing that learning is an evolved adaptation. As to evidence, contrast Schneirla's comment with Lorenz's confident 'all observational and experimental evidence goes to confirm this assumption' (Lorenz 1965, p. 18). As will become clear from the last section of this chapter, neither Schneirla nor Lorenz were correct when writing about the evidence. The data supporting Lorenz began to accumulate after the monograph had been published and Schneirla had reviewed it. Before we review some of this evidence, however, it is as well to consider Lorenz's notion of learning as an adaptation within the current view of just what an adaptation is.

How strong is the claim that learning is an adaptation?

Lorenz's adoption of the notion that learning is an adaptation was a clever response to the, largely, correct accusations of his critics that he had previously driven an absolute distinction between instincts and learning. Lorenz's 1965 retort was that no such distinction is possible if learning itself is an instinct; and if this could be shown with certainty to be correct then it alters in quite fundamental ways how learning should be understood and investigated. On the other hand, the concept of adaptation is itself fraught with difficulties, both conceptual and empirical. In one of the most influential evolutionary monographs of the second half of the twentieth century, adaptation was described as 'a special and onerous concept that should be used only where it is really necessary' (Williams 1966, p. 4). Williams argued, correctly, that adaptations are what make organisms different from non-living entities and irreducible to chemistry and physics. This is because a temporal dimension comprising a history of selection has to be brought into a causal account of the adaptive features of organisms. The problems 'arise from the current absence of rigorous criteria for deciding whether a given character is adaptive, and if so, to precisely what is it an adaptation' (Williams 1966, p. 4). Four decades on these problems have not been resolved, especially when the concept of adaptation is applied to learning.

The argument Lorenz used in the monograph and in subsequent publications was that learning fulfils a specific function that cannot be carried out by the main evolutionary programme because the latter gains information at too slow a pace relative to rates of certain forms of environmental change. This function, Lorenz asserted, has significant 'survival value' and hence has been selected for by constant selection pressures exerted by persistent environmental change of certain kinds and the inherent temporal sampling limitations of evolution driven by selection acting on variant forms of genotypes and phenotypes.

Natural selection, variation and function are the principal causal features in any discussion of adaptation. The consequence is design; indeed, design is the most common attribute of adaptation in virtually all evolutionary texts. Ridley (1996), for example, writes that 'adaptation refers to "design" in life—those properties of living things that enable them to survive and reproduce in nature' (p. 5). One of the odd features of Darwin's *Origin of Species* is that the word adaptation does not appear in the index, though it is a key component of Darwin's thesis. Indeed it was its centrality to almost every aspect of his theory that resulted in its not being separated out in the index. Evolution for Darwin was inseparable from adaptation. In the Introduction, he had argued that a theory that accounted for the transformation of species in time would be an inadequate theory unless that theory could also show how so many species have acquired that 'perfection of structure and coadaptation which justly excites our admiration' (p. 28). Famously, in one of the chapters in which he considered potential difficulties for the theory, a section was subheaded 'organs of extreme perfection' where he briefly discussed the evolution of eyes. The power of Darwin's theory was that it provided a scientific account of design when the only other explanation was that of a Creator (Dawkins 1986). Indeed, design in living forms remains the central argument for modern-day creationism, so called intelligent design. Nor is it a modern conception. Some acknowledgement of design is present in ancient philosophical writings which noted the seeming harmony of living things with their surroundings. Prominent in Aristotle's analysis of causes were those he referred to as 'final' causes. Final cause is that for which a thing exists, and implies a goal or end-directedness; a relationship of fit between living creatures and the world in which they exist. The conception of natural harmony was easily subsumed under creationist religious precepts, as just noted. So, unlike diversity and species change, something akin to adaptation had been noted for millennia. It was not surprising that Darwin considered it one of the challenges, perhaps *the* challenge, for any adequate theory of biology.

No biologist, whatever their theoretical orientation or area of expertise, now denies that adaptations exist. There is some disagreement about how they arise, though almost everyone accepts that selection acting on variation is the main cause; for most biologists, even those with a radically different view of speciation from neoDarwinism, it is considered to be the only cause. Where the real difficulties lie is in knowing what are adaptations and how they can be distinguished from non-adaptive characteristics of the phenotype, how they can be measured and what the burden of proof must be for the usually intuitive claim that an attribute of an organism is indeed an adaptation. Even in the most seemingly clear-cut cases, questions have been raised. Coloration and camouflage have been favourite targets for claims of adaptedness but, as in the case of perhaps the most celebrated of all avowed instances of adaptation, namely the case of melanism in the moth *Biston betularia* in industrializing areas of midland England through the nineteenth century, scepticism continues to be voiced as to the adequacy of the claimed demonstrations that the change in colour of these moths was indeed an adaptation to changes in the general background coloration of vegetation in Victorian England (e.g. Lees 1981; Hailman 1982). The declaration, for that was all that it was, that it was an adaptation was initially made by the lepidopterist J.W. Tutt in the 1890s. It speaks volumes for the insouciant acceptance of claims for adaptedness that empirical evidence as to whether the melanism was indeed an adaptation were only attempted some 50 years later (Kettlewell 1955), and then the evidence that the darkened colours of the moths did measurably improve fitness was far from strong. It might be overstating the case to argue that the importance of adaptation to evolutionary theory is inversely related to the certainty that empirical measurement has bestowed on the notion at large—that it just seems so *obvious* that certain traits *must* be adaptations. It is difficult to deny, however, that at least certain disciplines within evolutionary biology at large have not observed Williams' warning as to the onerous nature of the concept and the absence of rigorous criteria for making the absolute scientific case that something is indeed an adaptation.

In part, the problem has arisen through the supposed slowness of the process by which adaptations evolve—the vertebrate eye, for example, is properly assumed to have evolved over hundreds of millions of years. For over a century following the publication of the *Origin* it was widely assumed that direct observation of the evolution of adaptations simply could not occur. In the last couple of decades, however, there have been increasing numbers of reports of adaptive change observed in just a relatively few generations over a period of 10 years or less, sometimes much less. John Endler, for example, observed changes in coloration of freshwater fish in less than 10 generations and was able to measure the fitness differences that correlated with the changes in colour (Endler 1986; Weiner 1995). Over a period of less than a decade, changes have been reported in the morphology of the limbs of *Anolis* lizards on some small Carribean islands, such change complying with predictions based on changes in density of vegetation in their natural habitat (Losos *et al.* 1997). Perhaps most satisfying of all have been reports on changes in beak form amongst Darwin's Galapagos finches as a consequence of weather change and dietary shifts, such alterations again showing co-relations between form and fitness (Grant 1991).

An early attempt to provide empirical data showing real fitness effects of a behaviour that was assumed to be an adaptation were those of Tinbergen and his colleagues with regard to egg shell removal by black-headed gulls (Tinbergen *et al.* 1962), which demonstrated that predation on the nests of these birds was much reduced by this behaviour. Subsequent behavioural studies, for example those by Zach (1979) on whelk shell opening in crows by dropping the whelks onto rocky surfaces which demonstrated that the actual height of the drop was optimal relative to the energy expenditure of flying to different heights, the calorific value of the whelks and the number of drops needed to smash the shells, have demonstrated a satisfying fit between the behaviour in question and the function that it serves. In general, the modelling of optimization has gone some way to redeeming the concept of adaptation in terms of design that can be empirically tested and measured (Maynard Smith 1978; Parker and Maynard Smith 1990). Another successful approach has been the comparative method for explaining adaptations. 'One reason that the comparative method has proved so important is that many evolutionary explanations are not open to experimentation. We cannot physically rerun the evolutionary sequences' (Harvey and Purvis 1991, p. 619), but what nature provides in abundance is a form of natural experimentation that comparative study takes advantage of. Testis size and the number of sperm per ejaculate, for example, have been demonstrated to vary in predictable fashion with mating patterns in dozens of species of primates and other mammals (Smith 1984).

All of this is good news and shows us how a science of evolutionary adaptation can and should be done. The less good news is that there remain difficulties with the very idea of what an adaptation is and the overemphasis on adaptation as the cause of phenotypic characters (Ghiselin 1966; Gould and Lewontin 1978; Lewontin 1978, 1980, 1982; Gould and Vrba 1982); and there are still many instances of evolutionary explanations, especially as they apply to cognition, both human and non-human, where claims of adaptiveness remain easy to make but very difficult to be certain of. This, alas, is especially the case for evolutionary psychology (Lloyd 1999; Laland and Brown 2002; Plotkin 2004).

In most general terms, the criticisms made of the notion of adaptation, or rather of the exponents of the concept of adaptation, fall into one of two kinds. The first is one of theoretical impoverishment strangely reminiscent of events surrounding the young William James, the American philosopher, who, as the historian Robert Richards (1987) describes, came close to a despairing madness, in part at least because of the awful vision presented to the young James by Spencerian evolutionary theory and its application to human thought. James was enraged by the passivity of the organism in the evolutionary process, including the thinking human organism, and its absolute determination by the external world that was implicit in Spencer's theory. For Spencer, the world moulded the forms of life by *stamping* itself upon life. Spencer's was an instructionist theory of evolution. Organisms, Spencer believed, were instructed by environmental forces and had no autonomous causal powers that contributed to their own development, individual intelligence or evolution. According to Richards, Darwin's theory in which variation, indeterminate, chance-like and internally driven, is selected by the world—a theory in which autogenously generated forces are equal to those being imposed by the environment—provided James with a vision of life in which internally generated causes are at least equal to those coming from the outside. Apart from the beneficial effects for James' mental well-being, the result was that seminal paper in evolutionary epistemology by James, briefly described in Chapter 3, in which he drew strong parallels between Darwin's theory of evolution and how to account for creative thought in humans (James 1880).

Lewontin may not have been the despairing young thinker that James was 100 years before, but his central objection to standard neoDarwinian accounts of adaptation was that the organism is seen as passive, 'alienated' and, at best, a second-class citizen in the causal forces of evolution—a view not at all unlike that taken of Spencerian evolution by James. This one-sided form of theory Lewontin believed applied at the level of both evolution and individual development. He considered the same failings applied also to selectionist theories of learning: 'The fundamental error of evolutionary epistemologies as they now exist is their failure to understand how much of what is "out there" is the product of what is "in here". Organism and environment are co-determined' (Lewontin 1982, p. 169). Thus did Lewontin hold in this most general form that adaptation is a *'bad organizing concept* for biological research. The adaptationist's exemplars do not represent nature in general, and even in the paradigm cases (like industrial melanism) the adaptationist framework misdescribes, to some extent, the causal structure. Further, Lewontin does not just think that adaptation is a bad organizing concept for biology: he thinks the concept has a larger negative role, in reinforcing an erroneous general picture of the place of humans within our environment, both biological and cultural' (Godfrey-Smith 1999, p. 181—italics in the original).

This criticism of theoretical impoverishment or inadequacy and its urging towards a more active, constructivist approach has some interesting echoes in the work of a number of theorists of cognitive development that will be described in the next chapter. The notion of niche construction of Odling-Smee and his colleagues was strongly stimulated in its initial formulation by Lewontin's ideas, and will be considered in Chapter 6. The main point for this chapter is that the classical 'concept of adaptation implies a preexisting world that poses a problem to which an adaptation is the solution' (Lewontin 1978, p. 157). This, he argues again and again, is simply wrong. 'This view of environment as causally prior to, and ontologically independent of, organisms is the surfacing in evolutionary theory of the underlying Cartesian structure of our world view' (Lewontin 1982, p. 159). It is a powerful criticism and greatly reduces the importance and utility of the more formal approaches to quantifiable analyses of adaptation, such as those by Sommerhoff (1950, 1969) and the systems theory accounts of Bok and Wahlert (1965) and Bok (1980). It should be noted, though, that Bok too was sceptical about certain features of classical adaptation theory based in part on 'the fact that the organism modifies noticeably many or most aspects of its umwelt in its interaction with it' (Bok 1980, pp. 219–220).

Lewontin drew out a number of additional shortcomings of the conventional view of adaptations, all of which follow from that basic failure to take into account the 'interpenetration of organism and environment' (1982, p. 159). These include the idea that niches exist prior to organisms inhabiting them, the failure to understand that organisms change niches, and the inability of theories that consider adaptations merely to track environments to account for organic diversity.

The second form of criticism of conventional approaches to adaptation relates to the more practical matter of overattributing adaptiveness and hence the inability of such theories properly to describe and dissect apart adaptations from other attributes, both adaptive and non-adaptive. The random fixation of alleles, pleiotrophy and allometry were presented by Gould and Lewontin (1978) in their spandrels paper as three of the principal sources of alternative explanations for phenotypic features. Furthermore, the criticism goes, adaptationists are inclined to pay insufficient attention to factors that will detract from phenotypic features as 'organs of perfection'. These will include necessary cost–benefit payoffs as phenotypic attributes interact with one another, genetic and developmental constraints, and changes of function termed exaptation by Gould and Vrba (1982). Any one of these factors, if not some combination of several of them, will drive adaptations away from being the best engineered 'solutions' to the supposed problems framed by the environment.

How, in the light of these criticisms, might the quest for understanding learning as an adaptation fare? Not especially well at present, is the brief response. As products of histories of selection pressures which benefit fitness, adaptations must be part-caused by genes. Apart from the most fragmentary evidence for genes which might play a role in learning in its more generic or general process sense (Morrison and van der Kooy 2001; Egan *et al.* 2003; Hobert 2003; Goldberg and Weinberger 2004), or slender evidence for genetic involvement in a specific form of human learning of language (Lai *et al.* 2001), there is simply nothing that ties learning of any kind with any certainty to genes of any kind. This may not place the notion of learning as adaptation on too different a basis to claims for other adaptive traits, such as webbed feet in swimming birds, most of which have genetic origins which remain uninvestigated and unknown. What makes the position of adaptive claims for learning harder to defend though is that, of course, almost nothing is known about the neurological bases of learning.

Lack of any substantial neuroscientific understanding of learning also means that the cost of neural network functioning is wholly unknown. It is well understood that nervous systems are energetically extremely costly relative to other types of tissues and organs. However, how much of the brain of a learner is involved in learning is simply unknown. There is another aspect of costs about which we have no clear understanding. As will be seen in the next section of this chapter, learning does seem to be directed in many cases, and hence less error prone than learning that is unguided. However, no learning process is perfect. Some level of error must surely characterize any learning process. Yet we know nothing of the costs of such errors in natural environments.

So we have no knowledge of the neurological costs of learning or the costs of its inherent error rates. There is not a single study in the literature that records the effects of the removal of the capacity to learn on fitness levels in animals that normally do learn. In summary, cost–benefit analyses and all other forms of optimality modelling are simply not available at present for learning; comparative studies have been fragmentary and at times biologically illiterate (Hodos and Campbell 1969); and no empirical demonstrations of fitness effects have ever been undertaken.

There is another difficulty for any claims about the adaptive nature of learning relating to the issue of design. Waddington once observed that 'the systematic exploration of the evolutionary strategies in facing an unknown, but usually not wholly unforecastable, future ... take(s) us into a realm of thought which is the most challenging ... of the basic problems of biology. The main issue in evolution is how populations deal with uncertain futures' (Waddington 1969*b*, p. 122). This is a wider framing of the generalized function of learning that Lorenz argued for, i.e. that learning is an adaptation to rates of change in the world that exceed the information sampling rates of the main evolutionary programme. In most general terms, those neural networks that house learning along with the immune system are organs whose function is to adapt to uncertain futures, uncertain futures that span internal chemical and external physical and social worlds (Plotkin and Odling-Smee 1979; Plotkin 1994). In generic terms, all learning is most probably an adaptation to the uncertain futures problem. This is not, however, the intuition of design that comes to both biologist and non-biologist alike from looking at a phenotypic character such as coloration and declaring that this 'obviously' has the function of camouflage. The notion of the uncertain futures problem emerges from careful argument and analysis; but it is so abstract a notion of function as to leave one floundering for any more concrete and specific notion of what good design for dealing with an uncertain future must look like or how it should be specified and measured.

There is, however, an additional argument that bolsters the case for learning being an adaptation and for which empirical support may be presented. It is built on an argument that contrasts two ideas. The one has already been presented. If learning has a generic function, it is to provide adaptive behaviours on the basis of information gain which is unavailable to the main evolutionary programme because of evolution's sampling limitations. If evolution be conceived as a machine that gathers knowledge, then its weakness deriving from the rate at which this occurs, which is a function of the interval of time that lapses between conception and the time at which each individual animal can enter reproduction, is offset by forms of individual information gain by individual learners (Plotkin 1994, 2002b). Information gain by the individual learner is, by definition, a relatively rapid process. It has to be because that is its function. All forms of cognition must be relatively fast if they are to serve any function at all.

The second point was nicely made by Edelman when pondering what any newborn organism must first experience: '... the world is initially an unlabeled place. The number of partitions of potential "objects" or "events" in an econiche is enormous if not infinite' (Edelman 1987, p. 3). This is correct. If the world can indeed be partitioned in a virtually infinitely large number of ways, then any *undirected* learning process would be slow and clumsy. The chances of such an undirected process rapidly supplying information that is necessary for the learner to know would be remote. For learning to work, then, it must be directed to the specific places in the world about which learning has to occur if it is to have biological utility. Learning *must* be constrained and directed. The evidence for constrained learning is currently the only empirical support for the claim that learning is an adaptation.

Evidence for constraints on learning

As already noted, Lorenz's assertion as to the evidence for the existence of innate teaching mechanisms was simply incorrect factually. More importantly, it went wholly against the theoretical grain of all learning theory then current, and all learning theory as it had developed from the experiments of Thorndike in the USA and Pavlov in Russia. Despite occasionally voiced misgivings about the paucity of the range of data generated in learning laboratories (Beach 1950) and the poverty of the theoretical base of comparative learning studies (Hodos and Campbell 1969), the great majority of the learning literature, both human and non-human, assumed the existence of a general learning process—a process of such generality that it can learn anything and hence could learn everything. Usually this was cast within some form of associationism and, when multiple forms of learning were considered, they were invariably thought of as variant forms of what is associated with what, most commonly in terms of the classical–instrumental (operant) conditioning dichotomy. Habituation and problem-solving were occasionally considered, but usually in the context of studies of learning in animals different from the commonly used laboratory species. The reasons for this careless acceptance of general process theory is the subject for a historian of science but must owe something to associative learning being wide-spread across species. It might also indicate the attractive-ness of minimalist learning principles of the kind that Morgan pioneered. A third possible reason may lie in associ-ationism being an important part of empiricist philosophy. It might also have been influenced by a form of what-connects-with-what folk psychological belief about learning. Whatever the reasons, any examination of the writings of major learning theorists of the first half of the twentieth century, be it Pavlov, Spencer, Hull, Skinner or anyone else, shows so unthinking an acceptance of a single process called 'learning' which is universal across those species that can learn, including humans, that it is no exaggeration to say that 'learning' seemed widely to be seen as something with the same generality as 'movement', and hence that it mattered little what species or what information gain was being studied. Yet while no serious thinking scientist would assume that study-ing locomotion in the horse could be of use in understand-ing that of the pigeon, there was widespread acceptance that language learning in humans could be understood within the same general associationist framework as classical or instrumental conditioning in dogs or rats. The famous example, of course, was Skinner's *Verbal Behaviour* (Skinner 1957). That almost nobody seemed to be thinking of the possibility of entirely different forms of learning processes in different species, or indeed in the same species acquiring different forms of information, casts real doubts on the conceptual capabilities of the twentieth century psychologists responsible for learning theory. It certainly beggars early twenty-first century belief.

The important point, though, is that at the time Lorenz's monograph was published there was no empirical support for its central claim, despite a well known paper (Breland and Breland 1961) which poured scorn on the doctrine of the 'American "learning labs"' and urged that more attention be paid to 'ethological facts and attitudes'. The breaking of the mould came with the 'cue to consequence' reports by Garcia and his colleagues which showed that the equipotentiality assumption of general process theory, i.e. that all stimuli, responses and reinforcements are equally associable, is incorrect (Garcia and Koelling 1966; Garcia *et al.* 1966). Specifically, Garcia demonstrated that conditioned aversion to nausea in rats occurred to olfactory or gustatory cues over exceptionally long conditioned stimulus (CS)–unconditioned stimulus (US) intervals, and that such aversive conditioning could not occur to place cues. A few years later, a paper comparing such aversive conditioning in rats and quails showed that the cue to consequence effect in the latter was the opposite to that of the former, and invited the conclusion that the cues to consequence effects were adaptive constraints on the aversive conditioning of species with quite different diets (Wilcoxon *et al.* 1971). Famously, Garcia had had considerable difficulty in getting his original observations published in mainstream journals whose editors and referees were steeped in general process doctrine. It was no surprise later to learn that Lorenz's impact on Garcia's work and thought was 'enormous' (Garcia 1991), though in those early papers, as well as in the subsequent publications of Seligman and Bolles and others which marked the beginnings of a significant shift away from the notions of equipotentiality specifically and general process theory generally, neither Lorenz nor Tinbergen were cited—though it may have been prudent omission of the authors hoping not to alienate journal referees further.

Within a relatively short time after the publication of Garcia's findings, notions such as preparedness (Seligman 1970), species-specific defence reactions (Bolles 1970), salience (Kalat and Rozin 1970) and 'adaptive specializations of learning' (Rozin and Kalat 1971) began to appear in psychology's most prestigious journals, all redolent of the concept of innate teaching mechanisms. Shortly after that, the phrase 'constraints on learning' became prominent in important publications (Shettleworth 1972; Hinde and Stevenson-Hinde 1973) in which clear references to ethological ideas were present. By the 1980s, volumes, conference proceedings and textbooks relating to the constraints on learning were being published (Marler and Terrace 1984; Bolles and Beecher 1988; Davey 1989) and an article entitled 'Learning by instinct' appeared in *Scientific American* (Gould and Marler 1987). The Lorenzian connection between learning and evolution was established. The variety of empirical studies supporting that connection came in many different forms and continue to appear (for recent reviews, see Shettleworth 1998, 2000). This is no place for an exhaustive review, and only three areas of research representative of this literature will be considered.

The first is the learning of song in songbirds. There are thousands of species of Passerine (song) birds most of which have to learn their song and, as any biologist would expect, the findings on just how much such learning is constrained is variable, as is the exact nature of the constraints (Logan 1983; Marler and Slabberkoorn 2004). Marler (2004), one of the pioneers of birdsong learning and its understanding within the theoretical framework of constraints on learning, warns that a number of earlier beliefs about the learning of birdsong are proving to be wrong, including the supposed immutability of adult birdsong: 'fully crystallized adult song turns out to be more subject to modification than had ever been suspected' (p. 198). Nonetheless, what is clear and unchanged is the repeated observation of a sensitive period for song learning in newly hatched male songbirds; and in some species, exposure to conspecific song is essential for the acquisition of normal song by young adults (Marler 1997), including the acquisition of local dialects in species such as the white-crowned sparrow. In such species, even though they might be limited in numbers, these are animals that even in the absence of the experience of adult song will develop abnormal song that is recognizably different from the abnormal song of other species of bird also deprived of exposure to normal adult song. In such species, then, some of the motor component of their song repertoire is indeed innate. These same species, in terms of what must be learned, nonetheless must hear conspecific song if they are to sing normally, and in the white-crowned sparrow the precise acoustic cues for normal learning of white-crown sparrow song are known (Soha and Marler 2000). That means that such birds at hatching know what song they must learn. They are emphatically not *tabula rasa* learners; and the empirical findings point to the learning constraints being some form of representational knowledge of fragments of their own species song.

It must be stressed again that such findings do not prove such learning constraints to be adaptations, either through optimization modelling of some kind, or through any direct observation of fitness gains by showing that sparrows deprived of the ability to recognize and learn conspecific song have significantly reduced numbers of offspring. However, the evidence for constrained learning is as clear in such studies as it could be. In Edelman's terms, the numbers of ways the world of sounds can be partitioned by white-crowned sparrows is hugely reduced. They are pointed to quite specific features of the world in terms of what they must learn and hence they are able to learn rapidly and with greatly reduced likelihood of error. There is also the intuitive, but strong, argument that such learning constraint probably is indeed an adaptation, because many species of songbird live in communities where different species overlap and, since birdsong as an integral part of their mating systems, a failure to limit song output to those of a bird's own species might mean highly wasteful mating behaviour.

The complex nature of birdsong as a signalling system has drawn a number of comparisons with human language and speech (for example Doupe and Kuhl 1999; Brainard and Doupe 2002). One of the parallels between birdsong and language learning have been arguments as to the extent to which either needs highly specific innate knowledge, or whether a much more minimalist account will suffice. A recent study modelling white-crowned sparrow song, supported by empirical findings in young birds of what can be learned on the basis of heard sequences, showed that a minimal representation of white-crown sparrow song suffices for the tutoring of song in these birds: '… complex song structure can emerge from sparse sequence information acquired during tutoring' (Rose et al. 2004, p. 753). While the modelling was based on the assumption that the birds reproduce heard song using auditory feedback, the reasoning can easily be extended to an analysis of what innate tuning of neural networks will yield in terms of learned song from hearing conspecifics. The implication is that the amount of information might be very minimal indeed. Be that as it may, it is beside the point. Constraints are likely to be minimal. That detracts in no way from them being evolved adaptations of learning.

The second line of evidence for constraints on learning also comes from birds, but in this case foraging behaviour with the emphasis of the investigators being to place learning in an appropriate ecological context. Foraging behaviour has been one of the favoured areas for testing optimality modelling (Krebs and McCleery 1984), but the role of learning in such behaviour is unclear (and not to be confused with studies of memory in food-caching species). In the two studies to be cited, optimality modelling was not undertaken, but the role of learning is prominent. The initial study was entirely observational. Kamil (1978) recorded the foraging behaviour of a nectar-feeding species of honeycreeper. The temporal distributions of visits to flower clusters showed that birds were less likely to return to flower clusters that had already been foraged from within a certain time period, and the intervals recorded accorded well with the observed rate of nectar generation by the plants. That is, the payoff for birds was greater if they avoided returning to flower clusters which they had recently visited.

The second paper by Kamil and his colleagues was an extension of the observation on honeycreepers and had Cole *et al.* (1982) testing three species of hummingbirds in controlled laboratory conditions to see whether they were more inclined to learn a win–shift strategy than a win–stay strategy. The latter strategy derives directly from expectations of reinforcement theory. A response that has been reinforced should have a strengthened probability of reoccurrence. A win–shift strategy, insofar as it runs counter to expectations from reinforcement theory, might be taken as particularly strong evidence for a constraint on learning. Cole *et al.* found hummingbirds to behave in accordance with Kamil's earlier observations on foraging honeycreepers and to acquire a win–shift strategy more readily than a win–stay strategy. Here again, the learning is weighted, and weighted in favour of expectations based on efficiency of foraging.

An often voiced criticism of cross-species comparisons of learning is that any dissimilarity observed may arise from sensory or motor differences rather than differences in learning processes and mechanisms. The third example of constraints on learning avoided this problem by using within-species comparisons. Gaulin and Fitzgerald's (1989) study was outstanding not only because it got around this difficulty, but also because it was unusually well grounded in theory and previous empirical findings and showed how developmental factors could enter into the constraints on learning story. It has long been known that spatial abilities are marked by significant sex differences in a number of mammalian species (Potegal 1982), with strong experimental evidence showing that androgen levels are one of the potent proximate causes of such differences. Gaulin and Fitzgerald also based their work on sexual selection theory which holds that the strength of disruptive selection is proportionate to the ratio of male to female reproductive success. The closer to one that ratio is, the weaker is disruptive selection; the further from one that ratio is, the stronger is disruptive selection. Thus it follows that in species which display predominantly monogamous mating systems, disruptive selection will be weakest because the reproductive variance ratio is closer to unity; in polygynous species, where the ratio departs significantly from unity, disruptive selection will be greater. Putting these together, i.e. the theoretical line on sexual selection and the previous empirical findings on sex differences, they predicted that strong sex differences in spatial ability, specifically spatial learning ability, will be found in a polygynous species where the males range widely and the females are relatively sedentary, whereas in monogamous species where ranging behaviour is small and equal in both males and females, they predicted that no such spatial learning differences will be present.

Gaulin and Fitzgerald tested their prediction on two congeneric species of vole, one of which is polygynous (meadow voles) and the other monogamous (prairie voles). Radiotelemetric field studies confirmed that the males of the polygynous species expand by up to an order of magnitude their spatial ranging areas during the breeding season, whereas neither the females of that species nor either sex of the monogamous species do so. Laboratory experiments using seven mazes of different degrees of complexity then showed that while no consistent sex differences in spatial learning was present in the monogamous voles, the polygynous species' males performed significantly better at learning mazes than did the females.

Again, the precise adaptive significance of such sex-difference based constraint on spatial learning is unproven, though Gaulin and Fitzgerald reasonably conjecture that 'any surplus ranging behaviour presumably entails energetic (and perhaps risk) costs that should be avoided in the absence of compensatory benefits. Sexual selection theory suggests a possible compensatory fitness benefit from additional matings, but this compensatory benefit would typically be limited to reproductively active males of polygynous species' (pp. 328–329). More certain is the conclusion that such learning differences cannot be accounted for by sensory or motor effects.

Sex differences, of course, arise from different developmental trajectories originating in the genetic differences that determine sex. All constraints must of necessity entail development causes, and the Gaulin and Fitzgerald study is an especially stark demonstration of this. However, many developmental causes themselves have their origins in genes.

Evidence for constraints on learning in humans

In an echo of Lorenz's rejection of the disconnection between Kant's *a prioris* (see Chapter 7) and the 'real' nature of the world, Shepard has developed a particularly powerful form of evolutionary Kantianism: 'When formalized at a sufficient level of abstraction, mental principles that have evolved as adaptations to principles that have long held throughout the universe might be found to partake of some of the generality of those prior principles—perhaps even attaining the kind of universality, invariance and formal elegance (if not the quantitative precision) accorded only to the laws of physics and mathematics' (Shepard 2001*a*, pp. 581–582). In other words, repeating in that *Behavioural and Brain Sciences* article words he had written 20 years before, 'the world appears the way it does because we are the way we are, and we are the way we are because we have evolved in a world the way it is' (Shepard 2001*b*, p. 738). Shepard's argument is pitched at a highly abstract level of perceptual functioning and seeks a form of perceptual and cognitive generality that transcends some, perhaps many, species' boundaries. However, he is not arguing for a general process position along the lines of empiricist *tabula rasa* associationism of the kind that behaviourists attempted to foist on psychology. Shepard is aware that the generality is confined to animals that share certain characteristics, such as 'advanced visual and locomotor capabilities'. So he is arguing that the way an animal interacts with the world determines at a deep and abstract level the way that that world is perceived and cognitively processed. Steeped in a fundamental evolutionary premise that *all* cognition is a set of adaptations to the experienced world, Shepard provides a starting point for any argument that cognition is constrained both by the experienced world of the present and the experienced world that formed the selection pressures of the past. This, of course, includes the kinds of human perception and cognition that Shepard explicitly addresses.

Shepard's is an account of evolutionary constraint in the broadest possible way. What, then, of narrower possible constraints on human cognition of the kind found in non-human animals? Some of the experiments and observations of constraints on learning in non-humans derived from accidental observations which did not accord with the widely accepted idea of learning as a general process. Such was the case for Garcia. However, once the idea of constraints had entered the conceptual landscape of the late 1960s and 1970s, most were determined by what was known of the behaviour of particular species (like foraging patterns in nectar-feeding birds, or whether they are monogamous or polygamous as in the case of the voles) or of the particular kinds of problems they confront (such as having to learn species-specific song in a world where the song of other species of songbird is to be heard). Humans, however, do not provide the same narrowing of behavioural or biological space which experimenters could exploit. This is because as a species we are so behaviourally diverse and able to live in an astonishingly wide range of ecologies and climates.

We are left then with three ways of deciding where to look for learning constraints in humans. The one is to concentrate on behaviours, or psychological processes and mechanisms postulated to exist on the basis of those behaviours, which appear to be unique to our species. The reasoning behind doing so is not that species-specificity absolutely requires constrained learning, but rather that unique behaviours simply form a focus for observation. The second is to look for forms of cognition that would facilitate the ability to adapt to such environmental diversity in the form of thought and problem solving. The third is to accept in a general way the kind of universal adaptation stance of Shepard and see whether evidence for evolved cognition is available when the effects of prior experience are minimal—in short, studies of cognitive development.

Before conducting a very brief survey of the literature to see whether constraints on human learning do exist, two points need to be made. The first has already been touched on; constraints on learning do not mean total differences of process or mechanism in learning, though it might do so. However, as in the case of nausea conditioning in rats and quail, the constraints might act on a computationally identical process of association. What is different is the stimuli that are able to enter into the associations, and the temporal parameters of the pairing of those stimuli. On the other hand, the constraints may indeed arise from learning processes and mechanisms that are fundamentally different. What constraints signal, whatever kind they may be, is that the learning is a product of a history of natural selection that points the learner to what must be learned.

The second point is basically one of terminology. The comparative literature has a long history of confining itself, until relatively recently, to the word 'learning' when applied to the acquisition of information or knowledge by animals. The more generic word 'cognition' has been habitually used in recent years for human information or knowledge gain, and learning has tended to have a more limited usage. For our purposes, it is the generic word for gaining information or knowledge that is the more appropriate, so 'cognition' will be freely used when applied to our own species. Obviously there is no difference intended when using either word.

Returning to the issue of cognitive constraints in humans, a very brief survey begins with cognitive constraints which direct learning towards particular behaviours or specific psychological events which are unique to ourselves. There are two obvious candidates; language and theory of mind. Despite continuing claims for the existence of language in a small number of bonobo (pygmy) chimpanzees (Lloyd 2004; Savage-Rumbaugh *et al.* 2004), language of any sort comparable with that which humans have has never been observed under natural conditions in any other species. It may be that a small number of exceptional bonobos, raised under very unusual conditions, acquire language. However, as a naturally occurring trait, it remains the overwhelming opinion of primatologists, linguists and psycholinguists that language is a human-specific characteristic (Pinker 1994; Calvin and Bickerton 2000; Hauser *et al.* 2002; Jackendoff 2004, which represents a very small selection of such publications). That uniqueness itself speaks volumes. Whilst a figure of 98 per cent plus is frequently bandied about as the number of genes that humans and chimpanzees have in common, initial sequencing of the chimpanzee genome and a comparison with that of humans (Mikkelsen *et al.* 2005; Ze Cheng *et al.* 2005) reveals that the differences that have accumulated between the human and chimpanzee genome since each diverged from a common ancestor constitutes 'approximately thirty-five million single-nucleotide changes, five million insertion/deletion events, and various chromosomal rearrangements' (Mikkelsen *et al.* 2005, p. 69). Some part of these genetic differences must be the genetic part-cause of human language. A trait cannot be confined to a single species and be caused only by common developmental experience of all the members of that species, a common experience that separates them from other species acting on a general learning process common to all species. Species-specificity demands genetic part-cause unique to that species.

Until the late 1950s the majority of psychologists believed that language is acquired using cognitive mechanisms shared with other forms of learning. The general process accounts of Skinner, Piaget and others were then put to rout by the generative grammar approach of Chomsky and his colleagues, using conceptual tools such as the poverty of the stimulus argument, which still retains wide support from theorists of very different backgrounds (Crain and Pietroski 2001; Laurence and Margolis 2001), together with the remarkable identity of the features and patterns of acquisition no matter what native language is being acquired. The Chomskian notion of language as an innate organ of mind became widespread. Whilst the details have changed over the decades, at its most general, the claim is that language learning, whilst it must share certain mechanisms, such as working memory, with other forms of human cognition, occurs by way of an as yet unknown number of specialist learning devices. These are what are responsible for the relatively fixed features of language learning in the child, irrespective of what language is being learned, including sign language. The notion of a universal grammar remains prominent (for example, Novak *et al.* 2002; Yang 2004) though how it is characterized varies. Also prominent is the recent suggestion that computational mechanisms that allow for recursion are central to language (Chomsky 2000; Hauser *et al.* 2002) though, as in so many issues relating to language, even more recent analyses challenge (Jackendoff and Pinker 2005; Pinker and Jackendoff 2005) and defend (Fitch *et al.* 2005) this claim.

Few topics in cognition and neuroscience are more fascinating and more contentious than language. Recent carefully controlled studies showing that infants as young as 8 weeks of age are especially attentive to speech sounds (Vouloumanos and Werker 2004) and that deaf children in Nicaragua have spontaneously created a new form of sign language (Senghas *et al.* 2004) are just two examples of the extraordinary, and different, nature of language learning. Nonetheless, language learning and its evolution remains highly controversial (Christiansen and Kirby 2003). Just how much of the necessary cognitive apparatus is shared with other species is unknown, but there have been clear demonstrations of forms of learning that must enter into language competence that are present in at least one other species, and a not especially phylogenetically close one at that (Ramus *et al.* 2000). It also remains the case that a modern form of general process theory continues to claim that language learning does not need special learning mechanisms (see Chapter 5). Nonetheless, the overwhelming weight of evidence remains that learning of language is an evolved trait unique to humans, that it is an innate cognitive disposition, and hence that it is constrained by its genetic part-causation to learn about a very specific and narrow feature of the world of humans.

The evidence for theory of mind as being an innate cognitive predisposition is less strong, because there is evidence for something approximating to this complex cognitive mechanism existing in other species, notably chimpanzees, but perhaps other species as well. This does not mean that theory of mind does not, or cannot, constitute evidence for cognitive constraint evolved through a history of selection pressures that are common to a number of species that share characteristics such as a high degree of sociality and certain already existing cognitive skills. It just makes the case harder to be certain of. The attribution of intentional mental states to others was identified as a crucial component of cognitive development in the human child in the 1980s (Perner *et al.* 1987; Perner 1991). However, a recent series of studies has indicated that chimpanzees, if tested under conditions close to the competitive form of natural chimpanzee behaviour where dominance rank is a pervasive influence, do show significant signs of being able to behave in ways that indicate that chimpanzees can make inferences about what another animal knows as a function of what it knows that the other animal has seen (Hare *et al.* 2000, 2001; Call *et al.* 2004; Hauser 2005; Melis *et al.* 2006). Indeed, dogs too seem able to infer where in space to pay attention on the basis of direction of gaze (Hare and Tomasello 2005). Another intriguing part of the puzzle is that the recent implication of mirror cells in the ventral premotor cortex of macaque monkeys in several aspects of social cognition (Rizzolatti *et al.* 1996) has now been extended to the existence of mirror cells in humans and their implication in human social cognition (Frith and Frith 2001, 2004; Gallese *et al.* 2004). So it is likely that if theory of mind is an example of constrained cognition, the constraints may be spread quite widely across mammalian species, particularly those for whom eye contact and direction of gaze is important.

Eye contact and direction of gaze may be crucial to the development of theory of mind (Baron-Cohen and Cross 1992; Baron-Cohen 1995). Human infants have a tendency to pay more visual attention to the human face than any other visual object (see below)—a tendency according to Johnson and Morton (1991) that is present immediately after birth. A recent study (Farroni *et al.* 2002) shows that 2-day-old infants prefer to look at faces that engage them in mutual gaze. Baron-Cohen postulated the existence of an 'intentionality detector', based on an earlier idea of Premack that the human infant is born with the innate tendency to perceive intention in any self-propelled object that appears to change motion unaided by any other object (Premack and Premack 2003 provide a lucid review of this and other ideas about social cognition within this general framework), this intentionality detector acting in concert with an innate eye-direction detector. These interlocking innate tendencies to pay attention to eyes and direction of gaze are the start, according to Baron-Cohen, of the developmental sequence that involves the move from dyadic to triadic representations, proto-declarative pointing, pretend play and the understanding that others have beliefs including false beliefs. As far as is known, this developmental sequence that extends over the first 4 years of life is invariant and not restricted to any specific culture.

Thus whilst both humans and some other species may share an innate tendency to look at faces, specifically eyes, and to be sensitive to gaze direction, and whilst chimpanzees may have a very limited form of mental state attribution to others, the complexity of mental state attribution in humans almost certainly exceeds that of any other species. Nonetheless, whatever its complexity, the whole complex developmental sequence in normally sighted individuals begins with a specific innate attentional predisposition. Even if nothing else is constrained about theory of mind, and that is debateable, the very start of the postnatal developmental process is in this way constrained by a very specific innate attentional mechanism. The issue of modularity as innate versus modularization by way of a developmental sequence will be touched upon in the next chapter. Suffice it to say here that just as language presents a clear case of cognitive modularity, however it comes to be so, so too, it has been argued, does theory of mind represent the functioning of a domain-specific learning module (Leslie *et al.* 2004; Leslie 2005).

What then of constraints on cognition that might be adaptive in a diversity of environments by restricting thought to a relatively limited number of problem-solving heuristics that have fast and effective application in a wide range of circumstances? 'How can anyone be rational in a world where knowledge is limited, time is pressing, and deep thought is often an unattainable luxury?' (Todd and Gigerenzer 2000, p. 727). Fast and frugal heuristics is the answer that Gigerenzer and his colleagues offer. They argue that traditional approaches to rationality are effectively unbounded, slow and clumsy, whereas, as argued earlier in this chapter, the whole point of cognition is to provide adaptive behaviours to environments that change more rapidly than the main evolutionary programme can deal with: 'the function of heuristics is not to be coherent. Rather, their function is to make reasonable, adaptive inferences about the real social and physical world given limited time and knowledge' (Todd and Gigerenzer 2000, p. 737) Heuristics are 'strategies that guide information search and modify problem representations to facilitate solutions' (Goldstein and Gigerenzer 2002, p. 75), one such being the 'recognition heuristic' which operates by making effective use of a combination of missing knowledge and the power of recognition memory in reasoning about a range of problems. Heuristics for Gigerenzer are constraints on human cognition that allow it to focus on specific and limited parts of the total number of rational solutions to a problem. Since 'cognition is the art of focussing on the relevant and deliberately ignoring the rest' (Todd and Gigerenzer 2000, p. 737), heuristics embody one of the means by which this is effected. Gigerenzer's approach is an exemplar of the view that 'emphasize(s) that the mind uses a collection of many specifically designed adaptive strategies rather than a few general-purpose power tools' (Todd and Gigerenzer 2000, p. 740), a metaphor that he uses to separate himself from the more rigid Swiss army knife metaphor of some evolutionary psychologists because his approach 'puts more emphasis on the possibility of recombining tools and building blocks and the nesting of heuristics' (Todd and Gigerenzer 2000, p. 740).

Fast and frugal heuristics are an example of Simon's notion of 'satisficing', whereby evolution acts not to optimize but to provide a satisfactory adaptation: 'no one in his right mind will satisfice if he can equally well optimize; no one will settle for good or better if he can have best. But that is not the way the problem usually presents itself in actual design situations' (Simon 1982, p. 138).

Another example of cognition that can be turned to satisficing account in diverse environments for the solution of many different forms of problem solving is numerical competence, which has been demonstrated repeatedly, and in carefully controlled studies, in infants as young as 5 months of age (Wynne 1998; Wynn et al. 2002). It should be noted that the capacity for processing numbers has also been demonstrated in at least two species of monkey (Brannon and Terrace 1998; Hauser and Carey 2003), though exactly what such processing involves is subject to some dispute (Cohen and Marks 2002). Thus if numerical processing has its origins in some innate cognitive capacity, as has been claimed (Geary 1994; Pinker 1996; Butterworth 1999; Dehaene et al. 2006), it may be somewhat more like cognitive processing in the attribution of intentional mental states than language in one specific respect, namely the extent to which it is a uniquely human cognitive trait. This should not be taken to mean that numerical processing is dependent on, or necessarily shares mechanisms with, other forms of constrained cognitive processing. Indeed, Gelman and

Butterworth (2005) argue that numerical concepts and capacity are quite independent of language.

It is likely, however, that while humans might share some numerical processing capacity with other primates, we have numerical capacities that far exceed those of other animals. Feigenson *et al.* (2004) theorize that this is because there are two 'core' systems for representing and processing numbers. The one, which we share with at least some other primates, deals with large and approximate numerical magnitudes; the other computes precise representations of small numbers and is human-specific. Functional imaging studies tend to support this distinction in terms of where these computations occur. The main thrust of the argument, then, is that if Feigenson and her colleagues are correct, the argument for considering number cognition as constrained comes from two directions. The one is the processing ability for large and approximate number processing as a core cognitive capacity set off from other cognitive processes, with cognitive constraints shared with other species. The second is the human-specific core of numerical processing, where the argument for constraint is exactly the same as that presented above for language learning as a form of innate, genetically part-determined cognition.

Finally, what do developmental studies in general tell us about the extent to which one can conclude that human cognition, at least in part, is constrained in the same way as that of non-human animals by being directed into specific search spaces, such as species-specific song in songbirds? If they tell us that constraint is universal in cognition, then that of humans should appear to be innate in the same sense that cognition in animals is innate, i.e. the disposition to learn certain things should not in itself be learned. This, though, is dogged by a fundamental weakness, which is that of being able to rule out learning very early after birth, or even prenatally (Samuels 2004). Until we have much more knowledge from neurogenetics and neuroscience, this makes developmental studies aimed at ruling out learning what to learn as the least satisfactory approach to establishing the existence of cognitive constraints in humans deriving from genetic part-causation, and hence natural selection. The developmental empiricists (see Chapter 5) can always say that the constraint is not innate but is itself learned. There are, however, some clues and hopeful observations.

The possible imitation of facial gestures and tongue protrusion in neonates has long been a candidate case for ruling out learning what has to be learned because it occurs immediately after birth (Meltzoff 1996; Meltzoff and Moore 1977, 1983). Early imitation learning, because it is visually guided and hence could not have occurred prenatally, is an obvious candidate for learning based on innate constraints. Another is eye gaze in 2-day-old newborns (Farronni *et al.* 2002) cited a few pages back. Again, explanations in terms of prenatal learning cannot be made in this case.

In the 1980s, the development of habituation–dishabituation methods for detecting infant sensitivity to events displayed, usually visually, to the infants led to a number of reports which showed an understanding of folk physics and causation at ages as young as 12 weeks (Hirschfeld and Gelman 1994; Sperber *et al.* 1995) and a host of other forms of cognition by about 16 weeks. Given the young age even of a 16-week-old infant, and certainly of one of 12 weeks, the tendency of many developmentalists and other psychologists was to assume an increasingly nativist stance, arguing that the infants could not have learned the skills that they were demonstrating. That, however, cannot be taken as evidence of innate constraint. Learning postnatally *could* have been the cause in some, perhaps many of these studies. However, one report using the habituation–dishabituation methodology on sensitivity to faces cannot be thus dismissed.

Johnson and Morton (1991) reported confirmation of an earlier study by Goren *et al.* (1975) of a stunning sensitivity to the human face within an *hour* of birth, using stimuli of normal and scrambled facial displays as well as a blank control. Again, prenatal learning has to be ruled out because attention to faces is a visual response. The infants must enter the world 'with some considerable perceptual "knowledge"' (Johnson and Morton 1991, p. 30), and they concluded that 'the infant is born with some structural information about the general characteristics of faces in a primitive pathway concerned with the control of orienting' (Johnson and Morton 1991, p. 143).

It must be added that Johnson and Morton do not draw only that conclusion. Reviewing their own and others' findings, they conclude that attention to faces and facial recognition is the product of a rich and complex developmental sequence. They also indicate how minimal the innate constraints, their 'perceptual knowledge', need be. Nonetheless, whilst their monograph is a wonderful example of how to marry thinking about cognitive development using both psychological and biological perspectives, they do provide a strong demonstration of constrained learning in humans.

From this most brief of reviews, it would be foolish to conclude that all human cognition is constrained, just as it would be foolish to come to the same view on the basis of the non-human animal findings. If nothing else, the evidence is as yet lacking. Nonetheless, the evidence is strong for some human cognition being constrained. This, in combination with the animal findings, indicates that it is simply not the case that all learning is a general process writing on a *tabula rasa*. Lorenz's assertion that learning is an adaptation is now strongly supported by data on its being focused on specific places in an enormous search space. That said, it remains the case that the notion of adaptation, and its application to cognition, remains in some ways still a troubled one.

CHAPTER 5

Developmental empiricism: old wine in new bottles

The phrase developmental empiricism refers to the school of empiricist thought that denies the existence of innate knowledge, and which provides the conceptual grounding for its general position in the complex cascade of individual development, known universally as epigenesis, for understanding how humans, or indeed other animals, gain knowledge. As indicated in the previous chapter, through the 1980s and into the 1990s the findings of cognitive developmentalists using more sensitive methods than had previously been available, which indicated knowledge in infants at surprisingly young ages, had led an increasing number of psychologists, though by no means the majority, to an acceptance of the rationalist avowal that the notion of the *tabula rasa* belongs in the dustbin of the history of ideas. For this reason, *Rethinking Innateness: A Connectionist Perspective on Development* by Elman *et al.* (1996) is a significant work because of its broad authorship and its explicit and repeated denials of the existence of innate representational knowledge. As a repudiation of the new rationalism, and in its support for general process theory, it was also the natural outcome of a history of constructivist thought that goes back to William James and James Mark Baldwin and which blossomed in the writings of Jean Piaget, though constructivism and a strong empiricist stance are not of necessity linked. The Elman *et al.* book, then, is a modern classic of the developmental empiricist position. In this chapter, we will begin by examining some of the key concepts of the book specifically, as well as its precursors and some recent developments amongst empiricist–constructivist developmental theorists. The constructivist position will then be considered within the wider perspective of the complexity of development and its place within developmental theories of evolution (so-called developmental systems theory and evo–devo). Finally, the relationship between development and learning will be considered within the specific context of the contrasting constructivist and new rationalist positions.

The rethinking of innateness

In many ways, the Elman *et al.* book is an entirely conventional approach to cognitive development. Extreme positions of every kind are repudiated, especially any and every form of cognitive preformism in the specific sense of 'born with knowledge', and so too is the notion of knowledge acquisition as a simple and indiscriminate internalizing of the world. The first page of the preface declares 'that the real answer to the question, *where does knowledge come from*, is that it comes from the *interaction* between nature and nurture, or what has been called "epigenesis". Genetic constraints interact with internal and external environmental influences, and they jointly give rise to the phenotype' (Elman *et al.* 1996, pp. xi–xii—italics in the original). It is impossible to find fault with this statement. No biologist or psychologist would disagree with it. Yet within its obvious correctness it is possible to position oneself in a very large number of conceptual places defined by emphasis and nuance, the division(s) of that conceptual space and any asserted connections or lack of them, to result in major differences in theoretical stance. This potential for small differences of view being geared up to major differences of position is, of course, the penalty paid by most psychologists for the vague manner in which the nature–nurture problem is stated. Elman *et al.* are a good deal less vague than most, but the interactionist stance in general, with its inability, or refusal, to apportion causal power in any explicit way between what is present at conception, and what accrues through development, and what specifically through cognitive functioning, by its nature is going to suffer from a lack of incisive explanatory bite.

Another interesting aspect of the general approach of the book lies in the role that metaphors play in how scientists think. As will be remembered from the previous chapter, for Lorenz a genotype was the blueprint for the phenotype. However, as more and more became known of just how complex is the trail that starts with DNA in a single cell and, via its transformation into proteins, ends with a functioning phenotype comprising many hundreds of billions of cells and, in the case of complex nervous systems such as ours, the orders of magnitude greater number of connections between the billions of cells in our brains, the notion of the genotype as a blueprint receded and then appeared simply as hopelessly incorrect. The blueprint metaphor 'is dreadfully misleading, for it implies a one-to-one mapping between bits of body and bits of genome' noted Dawkins (1982, p. 175). In its place, Dawkins offered another metaphor, much more acceptable to most in the age of molecular biology, of the genotype as a recipe, with the variable conditions of cooking as the equivalent to development. In several ways, including its depiction of development as an irreversible process, it is a far superior metaphor to that of the blueprint. However, many remain wary of the recipe metaphor specifically, and of quite what role, if any, metaphors have to play in science. The price of metaphor, as was once said, is eternal vigilance.

This leads directly to one of the most notable features of the Elman *et al.* book, which is its use of connectionist modelling of nerve net functioning in order to simulate the neurophysiological basis of cognition. There are many different forms of connectionist modelling, but all assume networks of connected units called nodes; models vary in terms of how the weightings or strengths of the connections between nodes are set at the outset of the simulation, how those strengths change with repeated inputs to the network, what that input is, the implementation of learning rules, and the interactions of layers of networks in hierarchical structures (Quinlan 1991). There is no doubt that connectionist modelling has led to simulations that have been remarkably successful in showing patterns of cognitive development and learning, including some features of language learning, that have strong resemblances to known general patterns in cognitive development (such as non-linearities) as well as specific cognitive phenomena (such as grammatical irregularities) that give them a strong claim to being much the most significant form of formal modelling tools that have been developed by cognitive scientists (Quartz and Sejnowski 1997; Elman 2005). It is also the case that even a casual glance at the network diagrams in any connectionist text, with the obvious similarity of functional role as well as general structural features between nodes and their connectivity in the models on the one hand and neurons with dendritic and axonal features in real brains on the other, gives the strong impression by way of its imagery that connectionism really does serve as a model for the brain.

Elman *et al.* (1996) are quite clear that for them connectionist modelling is of value precisely for this reason: 'We do believe that connectionist models resemble biological systems in important ways. We believe that connectionist models will be improved by taking seriously what is known about how computation is carried out in neural systems. We also believe that connectionist models can help clarify and bring insight into why neural systems work as they do' (p. 105). However, the fact is we know little about 'how computation is carried out in neural systems'. We have only speculation. There is a bigger problem. It is that apart from fragmentary knowledge concerning long-term potentiation, the possible role of certain neurotransmitters and their receptors, and a smattering of knowledge about biochemical changes and their relationship to a tiny number of genes, neuroscience as yet can tell us very little indeed about the anatomical, physiological or biochemical bases of learning and cognition of any sort at all (Marcus 2004). At neither the synaptic, subcellular, cellular or network level is anything known as to how learning actually occurs. Everyone expects advances in knowledge soon, where soon covers time periods ranging from a few years to a few decades, but at present our knowledge is so fragmentary that the use of connectionist modelling by cognitive developmentalists, in which the modelling is justified by surface resemblance to neural networks, smacks more of metaphor than of modelling.

The essence of models in science is that they of necessity simplify very complex processes, but are based on a reasonably secure foundation of knowledge. The fourteenth century clockwork by Giovanni de Dondi of Padua was a physical model of the starry heavens based on thousands of years of astronomical observation. It was factually incorrect in many respects, of course, being Earth-centric and deficient in the numbers of planets and stars depicted; nonetheless, it was substantially based on factual observations of the rotations of the heavens that had been documented for thousands of years. It simplified a reasonably well known, if poorly understood, complex system and hence qualified as a model. An entirely different form of successful modelling, mathematical modelling, comes from the unexpected recent conceptual marriage between population genetics and cultural practices known as gene-culture co-evolutionary modelling that Cavalli-Sforza and Feldman (1981) pioneered in the 1970s. Using this methodology, Laland and his colleagues, based on what is known about the genetics of sex determination and the primary sex ratio as well as the cultural practices relating to the sex of children, were able to make predictions about the future demographic trends of countries where sex-biased customs with regard to the support for and raising of children exist. Again the important point is that the modelling was based on a substantial factual basis relating to the primary sex ratio and actual behaviours towards children of different sexes. The modelling simplified the situation, of course, which is one of the points of models: 'substituting a complex model for a complex world does not aid our understanding. When a simple model accurately predicts aspects of a complex world, we have gained some insight into what the important parameters may be' (Laland *et al.* 1995, p. 138).

The success of connectionist model simulations in replicating some interesting features of human cognition gives it a significance that is absent from all other models of cognition. However, it is not clear that connectionism is able to make any forms of prediction, and in this regard it is less a model than a metaphor. If the price of metaphor is eternal vigilance, then perhaps one needs to be vigilant when considering connectionist modelling. It is difficult to overstate the magnitude of our current ignorance about the neuroscience of cognition, apart from neuropsychological and functional imaging information as to where, roughly, in the brain the unknown events relating to cognition are occurring. However, until we have considerably more knowledge than we do have presently about the neurological basis of learning, all forms of cognitive modelling need to be viewed with caution.

One of the attractive features of connectionism is that it has revived one particular aspect of Piaget's theory of cognitive development, namely constructivism. One of its less accurate features is the way it has misled a readership which now seldom studies Piaget's original writings. Like the associationists, Piaget was a general-process theorist; however, he was certainly not an associationist. Also, the references to Hebb (1949) as being the original source that brought together associationism and constructivism is wildly misleading. Hebb and Piaget seldom referred to the work of the other. In his most detailed account of the biology of knowledge (Piaget 1971), there is but a single fleeting reference to Hebb in the context of Piaget's own form of *tabula rasa* theorizing: 'Between a hereditary system and some acquisition imposed on the subject by the environment and its regular sequences, there does, in fact, exist a tertium quid, which is exercise' (p. 188). If there are any links between constructivism and associationism then it is the connectionist modellers themselves who have established them, which is one of the most positive features of connectionism.

Like his predecessor Baldwin, whose work bore such a close resemblance to some of the core ideas of Piaget that it is hard not to conclude that the ideas of the one originated in those of the other, Piaget was a theorist on a grand scale and one of the few truly original thinkers in psychology's history. There were a number of distinctive characteristics in Piaget's ideas. One was the close relationship that he saw between evolution and cognition in terms of both leading to transformation in time by the operation of the same processes (Piaget 1971, 1980). He was also a strong advocate of the notion that behaviour has a causal role to play in evolution (Piaget 1978—see Chapter 6). However, the most striking feature of his writings is how they centre on the notion of change in the world, and the constant flux that he saw in both evolution and cognition which he attempted to formulate in the highly abstract terms of structuralism (Piaget 1973). Change, of course, is what is *wrought* by evolution, by individual development, by cognition and by behaviour; but, equally importantly, all are also *caused* by constant change. He was a theorist for whom causal chains are always two-way streets. For this reason, Piaget conceived of early human cognition being almost entirely action and response orientated—again a view close to that of Baldwin. Interestingly, he defined behaviour itself in terms of goal-directed change: 'By "behaviour" I refer to all action directed by organisms toward the outside world in order to *change* conditions therein or to change their own situation in relation to these surroundings' (Piaget 1978, p. ix—italics added).

Piaget was deeply sceptical of Darwinian evolutionary theory. Just as William James disliked the passivity of the organism that he saw in Spencer's Lamarckianism, Piaget showed a similar antipathy towards the non-dynamic role of organisms he felt he saw in Darwin's ideas. Oddly, he attempted to correct that 'organism inertness' by appealing increasingly to a form of Lamarckian theory, which, of course, was what lay at the heart of William James' intense dislike of Spencer. In this way, James and Piaget held entirely opposite positions to one another with regard to the kind of evolutionary theory they thought appropriate to psychology in general, and cognition in particular, and yet both were at one in demanding that life in general and cognition in particular be understood as generators of change. Piaget also greatly disliked what he described as the role of chance variation in neoDarwinism. In the end, he seemed to embrace a form of neoLamarckianism, which did not endear him to biologists—Lewontin referred to Piaget's idea of adaptation as a form of 'pseudo-Lamarckian response' (Lewontin 1982, p. 167).

Above all, Piaget argued that cognition is an extension of an absolutely fundamental organic autoregulatory process. He conceived of all living organisms as being in a state of constant and dynamic interaction with their environments. This, he argued, comes about through a complex web of information flows between organism and environment by which the organism regulates its activities and functions on the basis of flux within that environment, one of the principal sources of which is the activity of the organism itself. For Piaget, intelligence, i.e. cognition, was conceived as an adaptation: success, i.e. survival, depends in general on achieving a state of equilibrium between any organism and its environment. Cognition specifically he considered to be an extension of this most fundamental of relationships; cognition is a tool that works in order to achieve that equilibrium—that is why it is an adaptation, and the way cognition works as a process is also by way of the maintenance of equilibrium, specifically cognitive equilibrium.

> Intelligence is an adaptation. In order to grasp its relation to life in general it is therefore necessary to state precisely the relations that exist between the organism and the environment. Life is a continuous creation of increasingly complex

forms and a progressive balancing of these forms with the environment. To say that intelligence is a particular instance of biological adaptation is thus to suppose that it is essentially an organization and that its function is to structure the universe just as the organism structures its immediate environment (Piaget 1953, pp. 15–16).

So cognitive processes are at once one of the outcomes of organic autoregulation whilst being at the same time one of the most highly differentiated organs for the attainment of autoregulation. Thus the activities of the organism in its environment, including the operation of its cognitive processes, change and construct both the environment and cognition. He referred to this constant flux between the organism, including a knowing organism such as humans, and its world as a dialectic—a constant give-and-take, a dynamic exchange between organism and environment in which autoregulatory and self-organizing processes result in a construction by the knower of both the world to be known and of its own cognitive processes by which the world comes to be known. Piaget often used the word 'organism' because he believed he was expounding the universal laws of intelligence—be they of humans or of other species of intelligent animal.

It is an extension of Piagetian constructivism that a connectionist such as Quartz (1999) writes thus: 'the development of cortical circuits is a "constructivist" one of progressive elaboration' (p. 50) and of 'activity-dependent mechanisms in the progressive construction of neural circuits' (p. 50). Also 'representational structures are progressively elaborated during development through the interaction of intrinsic developmental programs and activity-dependent growth mechanisms' (p. 50.) In addition, 'constructive neural networks are ones in which the architecture itself can be altered as part of learning' (p. 52). Connectionists may, and often do, play down Piaget's broad picture of cognition or intelligence being embedded within a larger evolutionary picture, especially if that entails processes of selection rather than the instruction of associationism; but what they do give us is a truncated version of Piaget's constructivism in which cognitive development is depicted as a highly complex cascade of developmental processes by which each stage, whether in Piaget's terms or merely successions of time and states, determines what is to develop, and in which the construction can occur by way of sensory input, motor activity or the act of cognition itself being causal in subsequent neural and cognitive states. Here is a pleasing theoretical complexity to complement the complexity of cognition when compared with most general process theories. Contrary to the view that connectionism might save constructivism (Marcus 1998), it may be more appropriate to consider constructivism as one of the positive features of connectionism.

Constructivist developmental models of cognition can be pursued in ways other than through connectionist simulation. Not unlike the comments above about connectionism being as much a metaphor as a model, Cohen and Chaput (2002) suggest that connectionist models 'serve(s) mainly as an existence proof, meant to demonstrate that such a system *can* learn some concept. In that sense it provides a logical counter-argument to postulations of certain types of innate core knowledge. But the field has now advanced to the point where it is important to go beyond existence proofs and attempt to model more closely how these concepts are actually learned by infants and how developmental changes in these concepts actually occur' (p. 173). Like the connectionists, they aspire to a Piagetian constructivist bottom-up process whereby the infant initially processes 'simple perceptual units', which then become integrated into higher order units, and these in turn into yet higher order units forming a hierarchical progression, the whole process being based on six information processing principles (Cohen *et al.* 2002). The first is that infants at birth are endowed with an innate information processing system, but not with a 'preponderance of innate core knowledge' (p. 1325). We shall return to this curious phrase below, though it seems to imply that humans are born without representational knowledge of any kind. The second and third concern the hierarchical structuring of information processing units such that more complex, integrated information is processed at progressively higher levels. The fourth and fifth principles argue that there is a bias in the system such that information is always processed at the highest level possible, with the utilization of units lower in the processing hierarchy only when processing at higher levels fails. The final principle avows that such hierarchical information processing is domain general, and hence that it is not restricted to any modality or any form of information; and that it operates throughout cognitive development and indeed throughout life in the case of expertise that is acquired in adult life. Cohen *et al.* then, using their six principles, offer a constructivist learning architecture, the operation of which is congruent with different aspects of cognitive development such as that relating to causal understanding. If they are correct, this is as good a demonstration of a general process approach as there is. However, whether they are correct or not depends upon their first information processing principle.

Here is their exact wording:

> Infants are born neither with a blank slate nor a preponderance of innate core knowledge. Rather, we would argue that infants are born with a system that enables them to learn

about their environment and develop a repertoire of knowledge. From the outset, the innate system provides architectural constraints in how this learning may be accomplished.
The system is designed to allow the young infant access to
low-level information, such as orientation, sound, colour,
texture, and movement' (Cohen *et al.* 2002, p. 1325).

The *tabula rasa* notion is denied, but what exactly is meant
by 'core knowledge', and just what is meant by 'architectural
constraint' which is accepted as innate? Does architectural
constraint refer to actual computational mechanisms or does
it refer to what information the mechanisms have access to
and which they process?

Elman *et al.* are less confusing and more explicit: 'We have
tried to point out throughout this volume not only that the
tabula rasa approach is doomed to failure, but that in reality, all connectionist models have prior constraints of one
sort or another. What we reject is *representational* nativism'
(Elman *et al.* 1996, p. 365—italics in the original). A few
pages earlier they remarked that 'to explain why mice do not
become men, and vice-versa, we are probably going to have
to work out a scenario involving constraints on architecture
and timing' (Elman *et al.* 1986, p. 361). But where do those
constraints come from? There are two possible answers. The
one is to attribute them to prior *developmentally* caused
constraint and to take it no further back in time. The other
is to attribute them to developmentally caused constraint
whose origins are genetic. However, Elman *et al.* are reluc-
tant to consider the genetics of the case for two reasons.

The first is that they assume implicitely that if the innate
knowledge is representational, then it must be written into
cortical networks. However, tissue transplant and rewiring
studies have tended to demonstrations of considerable plasticity of function for cortical tissue that is re-sited or rewired

(Johnson 1997). That, it is often argued by those disliking notions of the innate, especially the representational innate, reduces the likelihood of specific neural networks coded initially by suites of genes. However, plasticity of function does not absolutely rule out specificity in some other attribute, such as the wiring of cells. As Johnson himself notes, a caveat to the notion of equipotential neocortex is that 'while transplanted or re-wired cortex may look very similar to the original tissue in terms of function and structure, it is rarely absolutely indistinguishable from the original' (Johnson 1997, p. 57). Also 'there is still very little behavioural evidence indicating that the transplanted tissue shows the same functional properties that the host region normally shows' (p. 57). It is perfectly possible, then, that the very small differences that such studies reveal is in fact due to innate factors. There is also another possibility, and that is that whatever, if anything, is innate, it might be located outside of neocortex. There is nothing in the position of anyone who adheres to the notion of innate knowledge that requires that that knowledge be sited in neocortex. In either event, Johnson's statement is reminiscent of that of Marler (see Chapter 4) regarding song development which does indeed point to a core of innate representational knowledge in at least some species of songbird.

The second reason for their reluctance is the suspect interpretation by some psychologists of a linguistic impairment in a single family in which an impaired gene, the FOXP2 gene, has been very strongly implicated subsequent to the publication of Elman *et al.* There certainly is now strong evidence that links the FOXP2 gene to the disorder in question. However, as many have pointed out, this is a gene which is widespread in mammals and which finds expression outside of the brain as well as in it. There is absolutely no reason to conclude that there is 'a gene for language' (Marcus 2004). Elman *et al.* seize on the weaknesses in the FOXP2 case to buttress a general gene-phobic stance. Even the issue of language as species-specific to humans is denied as advancing the case for genetic part-causation of language because it does not follow that 'grammar itself is under strict genetic control' (Elman *et al.* 1996, p. 372). That, however, is a straw-man argument—nothing is under 'strict' genetic control. Nobody has ever made such a claim. However, as argued in the previous chapter, species-specificity is undoubtedly direct evidence for genetic part-causation. It is not an argument for 'a language gene', and it is not an argument against there being other causal elements in the development of language. However, it shows conclusively that some part of the causal chain that results in human beings using language is that of human genes unshared with any other species.

Now, as noted in the previous chapter, cognitive constraint might occur in many different ways, and not just in terms of the computational conjectures that are made when language is under discussion. Lorenz himself, it will be remembered, had considered attentional mechanisms as one possibility. That same possibility was offered by one of the authors of Elman *et al.* in a previous book. 'Nature specifies initial biases or predispositions that channel attention to relevant environmental inputs, which in turn affect subsequent brain development' (Karmiloff-Smith 1992, p. 5). Offering two basic ways in which innate influences on infant cognition might occur, Karmiloff-Smith distinguished between the kind of detailed innate specification that early and middle period Chomsky suggested (Chomsky 1980) for the language organ of mind whose development would be triggered by certain environmental events on the one hand,

and on the other a much more 'skeletal outline' which 'involves attention biases toward particular inputs and a certain number of principled predispositions constraining the computation of those inputs' (Karmiloff-Smith 1992, p. 15). The possibility of innate attention biases is offered at several subsequent points in the 1992 book, attentional biases that fit well with the findings on attention to faces shortly after birth mentioned in the previous chapter. Much the same point was made in a later publication: 'We suggest that in normal development there are distinct, domain-specific, skeletal predispositions for discriminating stimuli relevant to language, face processing, and theory of mind ... with the massive early experience of superimposed inputs (i.e. face, voice and human interaction all take place in a superimposed fashion), these predispositions gradually take over privileged circuits in the brain that become increasingly specialized and progressively interconnected' (Karmiloff-Smith *et al.* 1995, p. 203).

A similar and seminal contribution was made by Clark (1993) in which he advanced the case for a rapprochement between connectionism and what Fodor would later call the new rationalism by way of what Clark termed a form of 'minimal nativism'. For Clark 'the most crucial step in this process is to recognize the important role which innate knowledge and gross initial structure must play in the development of realistic and powerful connectionist models' (Clark 1993, pp. 182–183). Noting that 'it has become increasingly clear that, for certain complex problem domains, connectionist learning algorithms will prove efficient only if they operate on a highly prestructured system' (Clark 1993, p. 183), he argued that the degree of pre-structuring will vary with the complexity of the problem that has to be learned. Following Karmiloff-Smith's 1992 explanation of the Johnson and Morton (1991) findings on attention to faces at birth, he derives a principle of minimal nativism which he stated thus: 'Instead of building in large amounts of innate knowledge and structure, build in whatever minimal set of biases and structures will ensure the emergence, under realistic environmental conditions, of the basic cognitive modules and structures necessary for early success and for subsequent learning' (Clark 1993, p. 185).

This kind of minimal nativism, Clark argued, can be achieved by relatively minor constraints in neural networks, including slight adjustments in weight assignments in neural network connections, in overall structure of inputs to networks of specific characteristics, and how the output of a network might serve as input to another level of network. The point of the principle of minimal nativism is that it is a form of Simon's satisficing. The innate predispositions need only tweak attention or networks to generate a specific 'direction' of cognition; the power of the networks' computation, especially if they are hierarchically structured, will then structure a simple, satisficing, predisposition into a complex form of knowledge.

In the final chapter of Elman *et al.*, the authors insist that they are 'neither behaviourists nor radical empiricists. We have tried to point out throughout this volume not only that the *tabula rasa* approach is doomed to failure, but that in reality, all connectionist models have prior constraints of one sort or another. What we reject is *representational* nativism' (Elman *et al.* 1996, p. 365—italics in the original). In his review of the book, Fodor (1998) notes that this is best interpreted to mean that they accept innate mechanisms but reject innate knowledge content.

There is, however, a contradiction here, a deep and serious contradiction, between the denial of representational nativism, i.e. the denial of innate knowledge in the form of content on the one hand, and between any acceptance of innate bias or predisposition in mechanism, be it an acceptance of innate attentional bias or innate differential weightings within neural networks, on the other. This contradiction lies in the following: how can some feature of a cognitive system which biases attention or differentially weights some aspect of computational mechanism be anything other than a form of representation of that which is to be attended to or computed. If at birth human infants are predisposed to attend to human faces rather than human elbows or the legs of tables, that can only be understood in terms of a predisposition to look at something that has a specific, certain, content. *Such a predisposition can only work if there is content—and that content must be representational.* Otherwise how can an infant know it is the face to which it must attend and not the elbow or shoulder or table leg. It may be, and almost certainly is, only fragmentary and highly reduced content, but if there is no content then the biases in the system will not be able to work. The biases are forms of representational knowledge.

Elman *et al.* consider a specific setting in a neural network that corresponds to a specific linguistic utterance to be representational knowledge (e.g. 'my grandmother was born in the city of Minsk, which is now a part of Belarus'), rather than an innate sensitivity to the linear speech rhythms and recursive structures, amongst other features, of language in general. However, speech rhythms and recursion are as much representations of human language, if less precise, than is a specific utterance. To be sure, they are greatly reduced and fragmentary representational knowledge forms of human language. However, to deny that they are such forms of knowledge is not dissimilar to depicting Plato's rationalism as if we come into the world knowing the names of our parents and the birthplaces of our grandparents, rather than, as Plato thought, the knowledge we have at birth relating to specific qualities of thought such as differences or identities of quantities. The point is, however, more fundamental than a misunderstanding of a philosophical position. If learners, including human neonates, came into the world without innate representational knowledge, no matter how partial and fragmented, they would have to count too heavily on chance to learn what is important to them and hence the things that they must learn. Even in the circumscribed world of the human infant, that world is an unlabelled place, to use Edelman's words again. There is no reason to think that in this regard humans are any different from songbirds. Innate representational knowledge is what makes learning an adaptation because without it learning would not work efficiently—indeed, it would too often not work at all. Without innate representational knowledge, necessary innate knowledge, learning would not be an adaptation. It would instead be an unguided cognitive fumbling.

Development in perspective

How, in each generation, does an intact complex organism arise from a fertilized egg? This is perhaps the most difficult of all problems in biology. Insofar as development, like the genotype of the fertilized egg at conception, stands as the bridge that joins each organism to the evolutionary past, which means to all other organisms that have ever existed and not just to its parents or more immediate ancestors, individual development stands alongside evolution itself as the conceptual heart of theoretical biology. Neural and cognitive development are but a part of this much wider puzzle, and it is instructive to place the issues of what is cognitively innate and what is not within this much broader perspective.

There is a famous diagram by Nicholas Hartsoeker, a seventeenth century biologist and microscopist, of a sperm cell containing a crouching fully formed figure, hands holding drawn up knees, with a very large head filling the greater part of the sperm cell but, oddly, with no visible facial features. The latter lack notwithstanding, the notion of a homunculus, complete in every part, being contained either in a sperm cell or in an ovum, and each had its supporters, was a form of predeterminism that dates back to pre-Socratic times. Hartsoeker's famous diagram was not based on what he saw under his microscope but an imaginative reconstruction of what others had claimed to be so for thousands of years. The notion that one or other of the gametes contained a fully formed individual was a manifestly absurd attempt to answer the question of how development occurs. Insofar as the homunculus had merely to increase in size, it declared development to be a simple matter of growth; and, of course, it implied that each homunculus contains its own homunculus. Even accepting biblical accounts of the limited time human beings have been on the planet and some 50 generations per millennium, the homunculus version of predeterminism presumes a regression of homunculus within homunculus some hundreds deep. Predeterminism of this sort was never going to survive in the age of science, but its crudity reflects the bafflement as to just how development occurs.

The alternative, which began with Aristotle, is that order and organization arise anew from the formless fertilized egg, the gradual transformation from a seemingly unordered cell

into a multicellular, highly differentiated organism characteristic of its species being termed epigenesis. Until the nineteenth century, preformism or predeterminism and epigenesis
were polar opposite explanations, each excluding the other. We
now know that each, in some sense, was correct. Development
is not simple growth in size as Hartsoeker's diagram
suggested. However, nor does the view that development is
a transformation from a homogeneous to a heterogeneous
state now accord with what we know with certainty is a
different form of heterogeneity contained in a fertilized egg
at conception. Development is really a transformation from
one form of heterogeneous state to another.

As has been so often the case in science, earlier, seemingly
opposite, explanations of phenomena, are now seen as both
having a degree of correctness. Oppenheimer (1967) and
Oppenheim (1982) provide excellent accounts of the history
of our understanding of ontogenesis, and what follows is a
necessarily truncated précis of the work of others. In order
to place developmental empiricists such as Elman *et al.* into
a broader perspective, we are concerned here mainly with
the history of ideas about ontogeny, rather than with the
details of individual development itself. Accessible accounts
of the incredible complexity of what is known of the details
of how development actually occurs can be found in Rose
(1997, Chapters 5 and 6) and Carroll *et al.* (2005, Chapters
2, 3 and 4). Marcus (2004) provides a specific application
of what little is understood, and it is only a little, of the
genetics and epigenesis of the mind.

The essential difference between pre-nineteenth century
preformationists and epigenesists is that the former envisaged development as a simple quantitative growth from
some form of organization already present in the fertilized

egg but, to most observers, too tiny to see; whereas the latter conceived of a form of creative process in which the complexity of the organism derives from some kind of qualitative transformation. The notion of a creative process easily attracted vitalist conceptions since, from its inception until the late nineteenth century, epigenetic accounts of development seemed quite at odds with what people could see and understand—epigenesis as a purely material process evoked sheer disbelief and hence it was most often conceived to be driven by vitalist forces such as Aristotle's entelechie. Such vitalism was espoused even by some nineteenth century embryologists, such as Hans Driesch, who were actively pursuing laboratory studies of development.

The first significant scientific breakthroughs in embryological understanding came with the description by Pander of embryonic germ layers which the great Ernst van Baer later developed into the doctrine which held that in vertebrates, specific organs and organ systems develop from specific germ layers—the nervous system derives from ectoderm, for example, and bone and muscle from mesoderm. At this time, in the first few decades of the nineteenth century, embryology was pursued entirely by observation. Out of the mass of data thus accumulated, von Baer developed what became known as Baer's law: 'Most general features that are common to all the members of a group of animals are, in the embryo, developed earlier than the more special features which distinguish the various members of the group (Balinsky 1960, p. 9). This was a generalization that all development proceeds from the general to the specific, which Herbert Spencer modified somewhat and elaborated upon in terms of homogeneity and heterogeneity and which became central to Spencer's interpretation of

Lamarckian evolutionary theory in the widest possible sense (see Chapter 2).

Baer's formulation was made about 1830, when evolution was little accepted and not at all understood. This changed, of course, with the publication of Darwin's book in 1859. With the vastly increased acceptance of the transformation of species in time, the conceptual connection was made by Ernst Haekel, one of Darwin's champions in Germany, between von Baer's embryological generalization and Darwin's evolutionary theory to result in what became known as the biogenetic law. Baer had generalized, but without theoretical context and force, that the common features of a taxonomically related group appear earliest in embryological development whilst the features unique to more restricted groups appear later. However, seen in the light of evolutionary theory, those features common to the larger group are those of the older ancestors, whilst features unique to more restricted groups evolved in more recent times. Haekel took this to mean that the transformations occurring in ontogenetic time are a mirror of the transformations that occurred in evolutionary time. Thus 'ontogeny is a recapitulation of phylogeny', the so-called biogenetic law. Haekel invented the means by which this was done: terminal addition and condensation, all within an implicit Lamarckian framework (Gould 1977) despite Haekel's avowed Darwinian convictions; but, as pointed out before, Darwin himself began to incorporate some features of Lamarck's theory into his own. It is now known that Haekel's biogenetic law is largely incorrect both factually and in terms of the supposed mechanisms driving it. However, Haekel's law seemed to have real theoretical power and dominated embryological thought for a long time. What then ensued for some decades was a phase of intense comparative descriptive embryological study. It was only with the ideas of Weismann in the 1880s and the advent of experimental methods that embryology began to assume a more analytical and proximate causal framework, as well as a perspective that made the way for the acceptance of that most successful of twentieth century sciences, genetics.

Weismann was another German champion of Darwin, but unlike Haekel in a number of different ways. He actually attempted to test experimentally the ages-old belief in the inheritance of acquired characters, and found it to be false, though it must be said the experiment was a poor one in that the acquired character was a product of injury and not an ontogenetic, adaptive, modification. Neither Lamarck nor Spencer would have accepted the evidence against them. Nonetheless, Weismann was a consistent anti-Lamarckian and his most potent weapon was his doctrine of the separation of germ cell lines from somatic cells which expressed his conviction that there is no possible means by which changes in somatic cells could induce corresponding alterations in sex cells, despite over a century of speculation that by some means unknown it had to be so. More than any one else, and that includes Darwin, Weismann purged biology of Lamarck's theory of evolution.

As Oppenheim (1982) points out, an element of preformationism was implicit in the biogenetic law because recapitulation implies the inevitable determination, indeed predetermination, of ancestral structures, albeit appearing in a particular sequence. Weismann recognized this and understood the supreme importance of the demonstration that all cells arise from the division of pre-existing cells that begins with the fertilized egg, and also that gametes themselves arise from primordial germ cells. Thus it was that in the last years of the nineteenth century, Weismann concluded that some form of material substance is contained in both male and female gametes constituting the hereditary factors that link each organism to its parents, and to the evolutionary history of its species. He concluded from cytological work that this material was contained within the nucleus of almost all cells, and he construed from what little was then known that these hereditary factors were, at conception, a complex, hierarchically organized set of structures, some of which migrated from the nucleus into the cytoplasm to 'instruct' the cell on the nature it was to assume, for example a skin cell or a neuron in the case of cell lines deriving from ectoderm. As Oppenheim notes, Weismann's scheme had a striking similarity to what later came to be known about chromosome structure and the general manner by which DNA determines RNA and protein structures, and was a marked contrast from his earlier views on development as wholly unpredetermined epigenesis. In recognizing the existence of hereditary material, as every thinking person had always to do, and giving it a structure which allowed him to grope conceptually towards how cell differentiation might occur, he was uniting the two long-standing different schools of thought: the hereditary material represents a kind of ghost or echo of predeterminism, whilst the complex of envisaged interactions by which that material finds expression in differentiation constituted an attempt to construct some form of understandable epigenesis in strictly non-vitalist form.

Weismann had to consider which of two possibilities is the more likely: does every cell in the body of an organism contain a full complement of genetic material at all stages of development, or, as Weismann thought, do cells contain only a small fraction of the hereditary matter present at conception which has become reduced by successive cell divisions to form the small amount that then directs the fate of each cell? Weismann was eventually shown to be wrong.

Provided that the cell has a nucleus, each and every one of them contains the full complement of genetic material that was present at conception. In that demonstration, experimental embryology was born, in part through the work of a collaborator of Weismann, one Wilhelm Roux. It was eventually shown with absolute certainty that every cell in a blastomere (a very early stage in the development of an embryo) contains the material from which can be constructed an entire organism, and from this it was concluded that Weismann had been too restrictive in his views about hereditary material. Thus arose a new form of epigenesis, or neoepigenesis, which held that, at least early in development, the germplasm did not have anything like the complex structure advocated by Weismann, but instead was initially without pre-organization. An extreme version of this was put forward by Hans Driesch who argued that all cells have an equipotential hereditary basis which is initially acted upon only by its position in the embryo to form a specific hereditary material which then determines cell differentiation. 'In other words, characters are not inherited even in the sense of preorganized genetic material, but rather they are created during development' (Oppenheim 1982, p. 25).

One of Roux's most important contributions was to understand the role of functional adaptations during development, whereby the functioning of an organ or part of an organ during development may itself contribute to further structural and functional development and differentiation. In short, that development is a continuous, interlocking causal process. Importantly, Roux thought this may be of particular significance in the development of the nervous system: 'The sense organs are stimulated by sensory input and this input can participate formatively in the shaping of their perceiving parts' (translation in Oppenheim 1982, p. 30). A century later and this statement would have been part of any constructivist manifesto.

However, the extreme neo-epigenetic position of people such as Driesch, who renounced all forms of predetermined structure or function in whatever form, simply made no sense—it remained a view that evoked sheer disbelief still, and an inability to square possible material mechanisms with anything that was known about the developing embryo. It really was not surprising that Driesch was driven to vitalism. One either had to have recourse to mysticism or to some form of predetermined epigenesis in which some minimal initial structural guidance determines subsequent development, no matter how complex and intricate that subsequent development is. Weismann himself in his Romanes lecture of 1894 pointed the way in a manner central to this book: he noted how a predisposition to respond to certain environmental stimuli *must itself* be determined by germplasm, no matter what developmental events that predisposition subsequently triggers.

As the nineteenth turned into the twentieth century, experimental embryology was rapidly moving into an era in which all the empirical findings pointed to a complex causal cascade of the kind foreseen by Roux: development is contingent on past developmental events entailing interactions within cells between assumed hereditary material, whatever that is, and the cytoplasm, and interactions between cells, between differing developing organ systems and between all parts of the developing organism and the environment. Then came the discovery of Mendel's work carried out and obscurely published decades before, and the new science of genetics was born. In some 10–20 years Mendel's plant breeding ratios had been understood within the context of reducing divisions, dominant and recessive genes, and the ways in which gene expression can be changed by mutation, gene linkage and gene–gene interactions. Yet the great irony of the Mendelian revolution is wonderfully well expressed by Oppenheim: 'the only field that Mendelian genetics failed to shed any light on at all, however, was that of development' (Oppenheim 1982, p. 42). It was only with the discovery of the structure of genes some 30–40 years later, and the astonishing understanding that came with regard to the linkage between DNA, RNA and proteins, that molecular genetics began to shed light on just how intricate and complex the relationship is between genomics, proteomics and individual development. Even now, a few years on from the first unravelling of the human genome, no general 'laws' of development relating genetic structure to phenotypic structure exist beyond the way in which the nucleotide sequence determines amino acids and that genes control the production of enzymes which in turn control intracellular biochemical reactions. Hence Oppenheim's comment still largely holds true in 2006.

By 1920, however, no scientist or informed member of the public doubted the existence of genes. The details of genetic knowledge kept changing for the next 30 years, and then accelerated dramatically in the 1950s. It is likely the case that the thinking of no scientists working in any area of biology for the last 80 years and more was unaffected by that knowledge, with one exception. This was the small group of radical behaviourists working in psychology in the first decades of the twentieth century, of which Watson, Kuo and E.B. Holt were amongst the most prominent members. Almost everyone understood that whatever the general principles of ontogeny are, they apply as much to the nervous system as to any other organ system. That the nervous system's function is to mediate between the interactions of the organism and its environment in a manner more direct than any other organ system does not in itself alter the basic principles of development. Yet somehow a small group of psychologists believed that it did. Lashley partly explained why. Some of the early instinct theorists in psychology, notably McDougall, appeared to invoke non-material forces. 'The psychology of instincts was a dynamics of imaginary forces and the anti-instinct movement was primarily a crusade against such conceptual dynamism. Somehow the argument got twisted. Heredity was made the scapegoat and the hypostatization of psychic energies goes merrily on' (Lashley 1938, p. 447).

It is not clear how the argument 'got twisted', but what is clear is that heredity somehow was scapegoated as a causal force that had to be kept out of psychology, notably through advancing a particular set of ideas about development. An absolute *tabula rasa* view ruled amongst the extreme behaviourists. Kuo denied the causal relevance of heredity even to the earliest motor patterns of neonates (see the previous chapter for his claims about beak movements, heart beats and post-hatching pecking movements in chicks) which he attributed to 'gross bodily architecture' (Kuo 1922, p. 344). He was silent on the sources of the gross morphological architecture, that final silence as to what links the earliest stages of development to the genetic structures contained in the fertilized ovum, which marks all *tabula rasa* theorists, but he was repeatedly explicit in rejecting the possibility of 'pre-established nervous arrangements' (Kuo 1922, 1924). As Oppenheim notes,

> … if species-specific neuroanatomical patterns (including reflex arcs) are found to exist in the newborn, then they must have been acquired (molded) by prenatal learning or conditioning mechanisms. Although this argument may have been

entirely consistent with their extreme environmentalism, it
was so patently implausible (why, for instance should natural
selection act on general bodily structure but not on the structure of the nervous system?) that one can only attribute its
popularity to an overenthusiastic desire to rid psychology of
all vestiges of instinct theory no matter how illfounded the
substitute (Oppenheim 1982 p. 64–65).

It should be noted that Oppenheim himself is no expo-
nent of an extreme hereditarianism. He is merely pointing
to the inconsistency and implausibility of the *tabula rasa*
position which refuses to trace development back to its
beginnings which is, alas for the enemies of all forms of
predeterminism, a heterogeneous structure in the form of a
genotype that exists in every fertilized egg.

There are two postscripts to be appended to this sorry tale
of biological illiteracy amongst the extreme behaviourists.
In the 1970 volume dedicated to the memory of T.C. Schneirla
and his work, Lehrman, who in his anti-Lorenz paper of 1953
(see Chapter 4) had leaned quite heavily on Kuo's ideas and
observations, noted that 'I would not now use Kuo's work as
an example of the study of behavioural development'
(Lehrman 1970, p. 37). In a later chapter of the same volume,
perhaps the last paper he wrote before he died in 1970, Kuo
himself wrote: 'Ontogenesis of behaviour is a process of
modification, transformation, or reorganization of the existing patterns of behaviour gradients in response to the impact
of new environmental stimulation; and in consequence a
new spatial and/or serial pattern of behaviour gradients is
formed, permanently or temporarily ('learning'?) which
sometimes adds to the inventory of the existing patterns of
behaviour previously accumulated during the animal's
developmental history' (Kuo 1970, p. 189—parentheses in the
original). Attempting to explain the behaviour of hatchlings

to certain specific stimuli he invoked '(a) sensory factors, (b) developmental antecedents or previous experiences, (c) the environmental complex, and (d) the position of the hatchlings at the moment of tests' (Kuo 1970, p. 183). True to the last, genetic part-causation is wholly omitted.

At least Kuo was consistent and clear. The last chapter of the otherwise excellent book by Elman *et al.* (1996) is not. They deny that they are empiricists (p. 357) and avow that the *tabula rasa* approach is 'doomed to failure' (p. 365) with 'all connectionist models have(ing) prior constraints of one sort or another' (p. 365). However, in denying the existence of representational knowledge, 'representational nativism' (p. 365), they leave that same inexplicable gap in the causal chain: where do the constraints originate? Also, if the constraints ensure that the learner learns what it is imperative that it learn, then the only possible reason is because the constraints constitute a form of representational knowledge. As noted above, this, as Clark (1993) demonstrates, is not beyond connectionist models. Why, then, the denial of innate representational knowledge when that is exactly what cognitive constraints are, if in minimal and fractionated form? Unlike Kuo, Elman *et al.* are not zealously against causal genetic explanations. 'At some level, of course, we all concur in the existence of some degree of innate specification' (Karmiloff-Smith 1998, p. 389). A more recent publication is explicitly directed at 'cognitive genetics' (Scerif and Karmiloff-Smith 2005) though largely in terms of cognitive disorders. Well, if some forms of cognitive impairments can be understood as part-genetically caused, it follows absolutely that so too can normal cognitive functions be explained within the same causal structure.

One final point needs to be made in the context of connectionist modelling and other forms of general process theory based on associationism. In Chapter 1 it was noted that some psychologists and cognitive developmentalists show a reluctance to consider human cognition to be a product of recent human evolutionary history, especially of the Pleistocene, a period that extends from the first appearance of *Homo habilis* to around 10 000 years before the present, this same period being the one consistently targeted by a particular school of evolutionary psychology with regard to the origins of human cognition (Barkow *et al.* 1992; Pinker 1997). On the other hand, they cannot deny the necessary evolutionary origins of cognition without appearing to be against evolutionary theory of any sort, and thus appearing to be scientifically illiterate. One solution is to accept implicitly that learning evolved a very long time ago, and has altered relatively little since. As indicated in Chapter 1, placing the evolution of learning in remote geological time from human evolution may be thought somehow to reduce the causal strength of the genes that were selected and which still provide the neural network structures by which associative learning occurs. It does not, of course. The causal strength of evolution is not attenuated however old associative learning is, but it is possible that cognitivists who dislike notions of the innate are deluded into feeling that remoteness of past somehow equates with remoteness of causation. In any event, associationism fits that bill very well indeed. A centralized nervous system very probably evolved not long after the evolution of multicellularity. The advantages of being able to predict causal relationships, which is what associative learning does (Dickinson and Shanks 1995), is likely to have been strongly selected for. It is thus perfectly possible, and likely, that simple associative learning evolved in the region of 500–400 million years ago. If that associative learning is the same associative learning that we now see across

a number of phyla, and probably universally amongst chor-
dates, then that might be the 'level' of innateness mentioned in
the previous paragraph that connectionists are prepared to
accept. However, even if that is all that human cognition is,
and it seems extremely doubtful, it would not alter the essential arguments presented in this book for necessary innate
representational knowledge. The world remains a complex
place and, if learning is to supply the adaptive need that
drove its original selection, then it still has to be pointed to
specific places in that complex world about which learning
has to occur.

The main issue of this chapter is the adequacy of developmental empiricism as an account of how humans, and other
learners, acquire knowledge of the world. As adjuncts to this
principal theme, there are two questions to be touched upon
briefly. In the context of cognition they may appear to be
mere footnotes. In the world of science at large, at least one
of them, how development may relate to evolution, is one of
the central questions of biology. The other concerns the
tidying up of conceptual relations: how should development
and learning be understood in relationship to one another?

Development and evolution

Although natural selection alters the frequencies of genes
within a breeding population, selection does not act on
genes. It acts on the phenotype, and that includes all stages in
the development of the phenotype. Since development itself
is never the automatic and inevitable embodiment of the
information contained in arrays of genes linearly arranged
along the chromosomes but instead is contingent upon the
conditions of development, development in its broadest sense
becomes one of the sets of causal factors that determine

evolution. West-Eberhard (2003) phrased this position thus: 'if recurrent phenotypes are as much a product of recurrent circumstances as they are of replicated genes, how can we accept a theory of organic evolution that deals primarily with genes?' (p. 4). Her answer was that we should not: an evolutionary theory that fails to take development into its causal account is incomplete and unsatisfactory. As noted in Chapter 1, this is not a book on evolutionary theory as such, and hence no account of conventional neoDarwinian or alternative theories of evolution is a part of its remit. However, since the relationship between individual learning and evolution is the theme of this book, and since learning may be, and often is, construed as a part of ontogenesis, it is necessary to provide a brief overview of this issue.

Gottlieb (1992) provides an extensive and authoritative review of the history of ideas relating individual development to the transformation of species. St George Mivart, born just a decade before Darwin discovered the idea of natural selection as the major force in evolution, was an evolutionist who believed natural selection to have much lesser causal force in speciation than did Darwin. Mivart differed from Darwin in two significant ways. The one was his belief that changes in development, brought about by severe environmental events, are what induce significant phenotypic changes. This is in contrast to the Darwinian notion of slow and gradual transformation resulting from selection acting primarily on the adult phenotype. Secondly, and in even greater contrast to Darwin, Mivart also believed that the possibilities of transformation are not infinite but strictly limited by internal organizational forces, malleability itself being a species-specific character. Gottlieb points out that Mivart's ideas were the start of a lineage of evolutionary thought that remains very much alive in the present, perhaps the best known example being the controversial work of Stephen Jay Gould. Gould, however, like all scientists, was standing on the shoulders of others. If developmental theories of evolution were to advance beyond Mivart, then the dead hand of Haekel and his biogenetic law had to be removed. The repudiations of recapitulation doctrine by Walter Garstang and Gavin de Beer were essential to this process. In addition to the empirical demonstrations that recapitulation was factually incorrect, Garstang's statement that 'the real phylogeny of Metazoa has never been a direct succession of adult forms, but a succession of ontogenies or life-cycles' (Garstang 1922, p. 82) spelled out the theoretical death of Haekel's law. As Gottlieb put it: 'Phylogeny is thus not the cause but the product of a succession of different ontogenies' (Gottlieb 1992, p. 90).

The modern evolutionary synthesis of Theodosius Dobzhansky, Julian Huxley and Ernst Mayr, amongst others, building on the theoretical structures of R.A. Fisher, J.B.S. Haldane and Sewall Wright, failed to incorporate individual development into a larger evolutionary theory. It did not take account of the ideas of Baldwin, Waddington and Schmalhausen (see Chapter 3). Some judge the synthesis especially remiss in ignoring the ideas of Waddington because of his explicit attempts to marry his ideas of buffered developmental trajectories, which he pictured as epigenetic landscapes, within an otherwise entirely conventional view of genetics and evolution; and remiss also because while he consistently expounded the idea that evolution must be seen as entirely Darwinian and never Lamarckian, Waddington nonetheless considered that a truly complete theory of evolution could only be arrived at by way of a four-system conception through adding what he called the exploitive and the epigenetic systems to the natural selection and genetic systems (see below as well as in the following chapter).

Gottlieb's own theory, which can be found in journal sources as well as in his book (Gottlieb 1976, 1987, 1998), envisages evolution as occurring in three stages. The first is a change in ontogeny that leads to a novel behavioural shift (he called this the behavioural neophenotype) which in turn results in new organism–environment relationships; the second is the consequent morphological and physiological changes which may include changes in genetic regulation; the final stage is genetic change due to isolation of the relevant breeding population by behavioural or geographical factors, this last being an entirely conventional modern synthesis view. It might be noted that while the first stage is characteristic of virtually every account of developmentally led evolutionary change, for the rest Gottlieb's theory is close to Baldwin's 'new factor in evolution' (see Chapter 3), which Gottlieb freely acknowledged.

Related calls for the reformulation of evolutionary theory by the incorporation of causal developmental factors can be found in Ho and Saunders (1979, 1982) and Oyama (1982, 1985, 2000b). More recent accounts of what has come to be known as developmental systems theory (Griffiths and Gray 2005) and, unfortunately, evo–devo, can be found in Oyama et al. (2001). West-Eberhard (2003) herself provides a magisterial review. The common theme from Waddington in the 1950s onwards has been to broaden the account of the causal forces operating to result in species transformation. In the language of replicator theory, the notion of replicators (genes) in some sense being causally superior to the vehicles or interactors (phenotypes) is increasingly rejected. Vehicles or interactors are increasingly being seen as causally significant in evolution, and by some as being at least as causally potent as replicators, if not more so.

It is probably futile to assign quantifiable causal influence
to replicators and interactors. The arguments advanced in the
1960s and 1970s by Williams (1966) and, later, Dawkins
(1976a) as to the significance of replicators were cast in terms
of the copying fidelity of genes and hence their longevity as
causal agents dictating the spread and retention of adaptive
phenotypic features over long periods of time. It was
another way of saying what has been stated repeatedly in
this book: genes are one of the principal means by which
any one individual retains causal contact with the evolutionary past of its species. However, whether that warranted
replicators (genes) being cast as the most important unit of
evolution is another matter. What the gradual encroach-
ment of developmental systems theory and niche construction (see Chapter 6) has done is the re-establishment of the
more traditional view that the phenotype, that upon which
selection acts (though niche construction invests the phenotype with a more active causal role), is just as important as
the propagation of genes. Also, if both replicators and vehi-
cles/interactors are invested with causal power in the explanation of how species are transformed in time, as they must
be, then both have equal potency of cause. If learning, which
some see as a special form of individual development, is a
product of evolution then, as a part of development, learning also has a causal role in evolution. That is yet another
aspect of the relationship between evolution and learning,
and one which will be returned to in the next chapter.

Learning as a causal force in evolution is also, of course,
part of Baldwin's 'new factor'. Conventional new synthesis
theorists such as Mayr were critical of Baldwin's new factor
precisely because learning itself is a product of evolution,
and hence, they asserted, there is nothing 'new' in the

Baldwin effect. As noted in Chapter 3, this, however, was never a criticism of any potency. The only point it makes is that evolution has given rise to evolved features which facilitate the process of evolution itself, and there is nothing new in that. A complete theory of evolution needs to take into account these facilitating factors, evolved or not. No one has ever thought of sexual reproduction as anything other than as a product of evolution, and no one denies the power of sexual reproduction in leading to more rapid species transformation. Phenotypic plasticity, including learning, is also a product of evolution and yet also a cause of further evolution. It is precisely because they enrich evolutionary causation, providing a causal pluralism for evolutionary theory, that notions such as the Baldwin effect, genetic assimilation and developmental systems theory in general have value.

Is learning different from development?

As noted earlier in this and other chapters, interactionism of some kind is an inevitable stance for anyone seeking to explain any aspect of development, especially behavioural and cognitive development. As also noted, however, interactionism can also be a relatively non-specific and hence empty explanation when defenders of the *tabula rasa* on one side and some form of nativism, extreme or otherwise, on the other, cannot be conceptually separated by way of their common adherence to an interactionist stance. To paraphrase Karmiloff-Smith from an earlier part of this chapter: 'At some level, of course, we all concur in the existence of some degree of interaction'. Thus it is only in terms of their interpretation of the small amount of behavioural data, usually developmental or comparative (Gomez 2005), that might bear on the issue, and the extent to which their formal models, or less formal metaphors, are compatible with their views, that support or denial rests as to whether we, and other creatures of cognition, are or are not born or hatched with knowledge which is *a priori.*

There is another way of putting this matter. Interactionism in this context simply means more than one causal force determining a behavioural or cognitive outcome. However, interactionism does not address the precise nature of those causal forces. The massive complexity both of the genome and of brain development seems to exclude precision, at least in terms of current knowledge. It is simply not known how genes do or do not determine specific aspects of neural network structures, even though there are known to be certain cognitive disorders that can be firmly tied to specific genes. It is also likely that the causal arrows do not point in a single direction starting with genes and leading in a straight causal line to functioning neural networks underlying cognitive skills. Developmental events, including experience in the case of cognition, will turn those causal arrows around such that phases of development will feed back to further gene–intracellular–extracellular interactions. It is also the case that at present it is not known how developed neural networks determine cognition. Parenthetically, bringing individual development into evolution presents the same problem in terms of a kind of causal chaos which is uncomfortably close to an undiscerning holism.

It must also be said again that what *is* known with certainty regarding brain–cognitive relationships impinges not at all on these matters. An increasing flood of reports using functional brain imaging during specific cognitive activities, supported by more conventional neuropsychological studies on cognitive impairments resulting from brain injury, continue to build the evidence that goes back a century and more. All of it points to a localization of cognitive function extending from imitation and the attribution of intentional mental states to facial recognition and the making of economic decisions, amongst many other forms of cognition. The great majority of such studies report data from children far removed in time from birth or, most commonly, from adult subjects. Thus not even the contentious issue of whether such localized cognitive function is evidence for innate modularity (Pinker 2002, for example) or for a developmentally determined modularization (Elman *et al.* 1996) is addressed, much less how to sort out the causal networks that are invoked by any form of interactionism. Localization of function, whatever that function might be, is simply irrelevant to the main issue of this book.

Quite apart from the 'how' of development, it is also as yet not known with any certainty which genes are involved in brain development generally, and learning specifically. Studies of *Aplysia*, a marine gastropod whose common ancestry with vertebrates is to be traced back to the proterozoic, have begun to show something of the complex relationship between specific genes and different forms of learning (Hobert 2003; Cohen-Armon *et al.* 2004). Studies with rodents also implicate early activity-dependent genes (Izquierdo and Cammarota 2004), though the likelihood of such widely unrelated species of learner having molecular mechanisms in common must be remote indeed. Once again, Marcus (2004) provides a balanced review of what is known. Another recent development implicates neuronal network oscillations in cognitive function (Buzsaki and Draguhn 2004), which adds another level of complexity. None of these advances, however, shows the way to an empirical separating of different forms of interactionism.

That is the point of the preceding few paragraphs. On the one hand, what is known with increasing certainty, localization of function, and the constantly improving specification of just what those functions are, speaks not at all as to whether the developmental empiricists or the new rationalists are correct. On the other hand, the fragmentary knowledge of both the genetics and the epigenesis of cognition is insufficient for making any judgement as to whether any form of knowledge might be innate.

In the light of such difficulties, is there any reason to draw further theoretical distinctions which cannot be empirically supported? Specifically, is there any need to draw a distinction between individual learning and ontogenesis, or should all forms of learning be seen as an extension of development? There surely is such a need, because while all forms of learning might be depicted as special forms of ontogenesis, not all forms of ontogenesis have the characteristics of learning. This fundamental asymmetry alone justifies the distinction. It does not, however, exclude the necessary view that cognition, like every other feature of the phenotype, itself is a product of epigenesis.

Considered in the broadest context, the distinction between development and learning is easy to maintain. Development is a necessary process in all multicellular organisms. Epigenesis is an intrinsically flexible process whose responsiveness to environmental circumstances results in phenotypes adopting a range of forms that are adaptations to the conditions of development. The most extreme examples supporting the distinction are plants, which develop epigenetically as do animals, but which have neither nervous systems nor cognition. Animals with complex nervous systems also provide many examples which support the distinction. For instance, whether locusts develop as solitaries or whether they swarm is determined by a number of conditions during the development of each individual. It has nothing to do with learning; whether locusts can learn at all is as yet unknown. In the same way, the alteration of receptive fields in the visual cortex in kittens as a result of specific restricted visual experience after birth (Hirsch and Spinelli 1970; Blakemore and van Sluyters 1975) is not a consequence of learning but of visual experience. The maternal behaviours of rats are determined by hormonal levels during development and proximate external stimuli such as the presence of rat pups, not by learning (Rosenblatt 1967, 1970). There are many other such examples. All can be contained within the distinction that Schneirla (1956) drew between 'experience' and learning.

Baldwin and Waddington were explicit in assuming that individual learning and cognition were narrower processes, in some way different from the larger notion of epigenesis. Waddington, though he wrote very little about his notion of an exploitive system and raised it as part of his wider vision of evolution in order to encourage others to do so, seemed to locate learning within the exploitive system, which he separated from the epigenetic system. Lorenz (1969) had also drawn the distinction in terms of flexible behaviour to which no memory attaches, and flexible behaviour which is based on some form of changed internal representation— memory, in short. Campbell (1974) too distinguished various forms of learning and cognition from more fundamental processes within his hierarchy of knowledge-gaining processes (see Chapter 6). Most psychologists, be they learning theorists or developmentalists, have implicitely assumed that the gaining and storing of information by the individual in some kind of memory system is something that is separate from the epigenesis that they equally implicitely held to account for development at large, including that of the brain and cognition.

One way of drawing the distinction with some empirical support arose in the 1970s with the much noted, and replicated, findings of the effects of enriched environments on both the learning and brain structures of rats (Greenough *et al.* 1987). Animals exposed to environmental complexity were shown to have 20–25 per cent more synapses per neuron in visual cortex, and somewhat lesser, but still significant, increases in synapses per neuron in auditory and somaesthetic cortex, as well as for hippocampal neurons. From their survey of the literature, Greenough *et al.* concluded, on the basis of data deriving from long-term potentiation studies as well as the presence of polyribosomal aggregates, so-called protein synthesizing 'factories' which are characteristic of new synapse formation, that 'there is a fundamental difference between the processes governing the formation of synapses in early, age-locked sensory system development and those governing synapse formation during later development and adulthood.' (Greenough *et al.* 1987, p. 550). The age-locked early changes Greenough *et al.* referred to as 'experience-expectant information storage', whereas the later changes they called 'experience-dependent information storage'.

The 'experience-expectant' and 'experience-dependent' distinction is in effect the cognitive development and learning/cognition distinction. Greenough *et al.* proposed that there are two different kinds of plasticity involving storage of information about the environment. The first, which they suggested underlies sensitive-period phenomena, 'we term experience expectant, is designed to utilize the sort of environmental information that is ubiquitous and has been so throughout much of the evolutionary history of the species' (Greenough *et al.* 1987, p. 540). Light itself and with it visual contrast borders, for example, would be a form of environmental information that for a species with an evolved visual system would be 'expected' by every member of that species, and utilized in the development of functioning sensory, motor and, presumably though they are silent on the issue, cognitive systems. In Greenough's view, the advantage of experience-expectant systems is that genes need supply only a 'rough' outline of the pattern of neural connections, the details of which are established by expected experience. What sets such processes apart from 'many later developmental processes, as well as from adult learning and memory, is the degree to which they are age dependent and subsequently irreversible' (Greenough *et al.* 1987, p. 545). It is not clear what 'later developmental processes are', but there is no mistaking 'learning and memory'.

It is the 'subsequently irreversible' that is key, and links Greenough's scheme with those presented by others. Waddington (1957, 1959*a*) had earlier presented a schematic image of heavily buffered developmental pathways which he called chreods, whose underlying control processes were considered to be 'homeorhetic' in character, not homeostatic. For Waddington, that meant that while such developmental pathways could vary somewhat and hence be capable of compensating to a degree for fluctuations in the environment, they were incapable of undergoing drastic change in response to environmental conditions that shifted radically, or even reversed themselves, in a single lifetime. In short, for Waddington, development had severe limitations for establishing adaptive structures across a whole lifetime, which squares reasonably well with Greenough's conception of experience-expected and experience-dependent development. It was because of the limitations of individual development that Waddington appeared to place learning within his exploitive system rather than in the epigenetic system—though again it must be stressed that Waddington wrote little on either the exploitive system or learning. What is clear from his writings is a preoccupation with a dynamic and constantly changing world. This emphasis is so important as to warrant several quotations, though in a context somewhat different from Chapter 4: 'The fitness of a population is the degree to which its gene pool gives it the ability to find some way or other of leaving offspring in the temporarily and spatially heterogeneous range of environments which its dispersion mechanisms offer to it' (Waddington 1969b, p. 121). However, he continued, 'how to know what the "temporarily heterogeneous range of environments" may bring?' (Waddington 1969b, p. 121).

This is not just a matter of how learning and development are related to one another. For Waddington, this was a matter at the heart of all theoretical biology: 'The systematic exploration of the evolutionary strategies in facing an unknown, but usually not wholly unforecastable, future would take us into the realm of thought which is the most challenging and very characteristic of the basic problems of biology. The main issue in evolution is how populations deal with unknown futures' (Waddington 1969b, p. 122).

This general conception, that development of all kinds, including the development of cognition, has time-limited utility as a device for establishing adaptive relationships of fit with the environment was subsequently used by Plotkin and Odling-Smee (1979, 1981) to distinguish between flexible epigenesis and learning. 'Epigenesis cannot respond adaptively to any environmental changes that recur and reverse, possibly rapidly and possibly frequently, within the lifetime of an individual because epigenetic development, like every other form of development, is firmly linked to one-way developmental trajectories' (Plotkin and Odling-Smee 1979, p. 25). Learning, as an organ-specific device for adapting to rapid and repeated change in the world, it was suggested, evolved precisely because it could respond throughout a learner's lifetime to what Plotkin (1994) later referred to as short-term stabilities, such as the shifting position of vital resources, and the identities of individuals forming alliances in social groups. What developmental flexibility cannot achieve, because of the very nature of irreversible epigenetic pathways, learning can achieve. Whether the molecular/physiological mechanisms of learning are an extension of epigenetic neural network processes and mechanisms is as yet unknown. Certainly work of the kind cited by Greenough does not answer this question. However, whether it is or is not, within the larger question posed by Waddington, learning is an extension of development in the evolution of the means by which some organisms deal with 'uncertain futures' that can be characterized by the rates at which different aspects of the world change.

The idea of change, and of different rates of change, and of adjustment and adaptation to change, is very close to Piaget's constructivism. It is no coincidence that Waddington was so influential in Piaget's writings. As will be seen in the next chapter, culture too can be captured within the same general framework of a differential sensitivity to rates of change.

In conclusion, any argument against developmental empiricism should not be construed as an argument against the absolutely central role of epigenesis to both cognition specifically, and evolution as a whole more generally. However, the centrality of epigenesis does not in any way exclude nativism, unless one is going to repeat the errors of the neoepigeneticists and the radical behaviourists. There is no contradicting the argument of connectionists that the plasticity of neocortical tissue, and the prolonged postnatal development of neocortex in apes, especially humans, is more compatible with a general learning process stance than an extreme innatist position. It is the very flexibility of neural networks, and their stunning connectivity, that developmental empiricists look to support their argument. The new rationalists with their notions of innate knowledge have no well-defined neuroscience to support them. However, neural net plasticity is not in any way denied by rationalists of any cast. The notions of minimal nativism, and the conceptual contradiction of a clumsy and slow cognition that must be a consequence of unguided learning in a very complex world when the reason why learning evolved at all was to deal with rapid environmental change, argues for compatibility between the notion of innate representational knowledge, necessary knowledge, and the constructivism of cognitive development.

CHAPTER 6

Complex causal architectures

If humans are born with some of their cognitive slates already partially written on, one of the implications is that the products of those forms of cognition are multiply caused. Assuming that present at birth is innate representational knowledge, an informationally small and fragmentary feature of the human face, subcortically sited, if the findings and reasoning of Johnson and Morton (see Chapter 4) are correct, then when an infant later learns to discriminate between the faces of its care-givers and those of others, the cognitive mechanisms then being sited in cortical networks, suits of genes as well as visual developmental experience and individual learning are causally implicated. Genes, developmental experience involving shifting neural networks from subcortex to cortex, and individual learning are all necessary, *and none are sufficient causal forces*, for facial recognition.

In and of itself, multiple causation does not necessarily imply causal linkage between causes. This is the case in many physical systems, where multiple causal conditions may be necessary for some state to occur, but in which such multiple causes are not linked other than as necessary conditions for that occurrence. For example, the internal combustion engine converts chemical into kinetic energy and will propel a vehicle through space provided that the appropriate mechanical connections are established between the kinetic energy of the moving engine parts and the means by which the vehicle as a whole moves across a surface, provided that the vehicle itself does not exceed a weight the initiation of movement of which is not greater in energy requirement than that contained in the fuel source of the engine, and provided that there is an appropriate spatial configuration of the vehicle and surrounding objects, amongst many other necessary conditions. However, engine size is not causally linked to the position of the vehicle in space and neither is linked to the mechanical connections between the movement of pistons and the turning of wheels or tracks. Necessary multiple causation of physical systems does not impose a condition of causal linkage beyond some combination that results in an overall effect. Such is not the case for biological systems. Polanyi's notion of 'life's irreducible structure' (Polanyi 1968) was not just an argument for complex structures and complex causation in biological systems, but for necessary linkage, causal linkage, between multiple causes. The genes which somehow direct an infant's visual attention to faces via an as yet unknown chain of events involving enzymes and other protein products resulting in the development of neurons, their migration to specific parts of the brain, and their synaptic contacts with other neurons, are causally linked with necessary appropriate developmental experience to result in neural networks sensitized to the acquisition of specific forms of knowledge. The capacity to learn facial patterns is thus the product of multiple genetic and developmental events, each causing the other to be expressed and acted upon in certain ways; the products of such a cognitive mechanism will then feed back and become causal in initiating behaviours that in turn will have causal consequences for subsequent individual development, other cognitive events, and may also be causal in evolution itself. Causation in living systems is not a one-way street.

No biologist would dispute the notion of multiple linked causes for any aspect of living forms where the effect of one cause may be causal in some other effect, including an effect on the initial cause. Many, however, whilst cognizant of such causal complexity, have been content with 'flat' causal explanations. Others have considered what Simon (1962) called the 'architecture of complexity' to be integral to complete explanations of living systems. Beginning with the appearance of general systems theory in the late 1940s, whose appearance was initially owed to an increasing awareness that technological and social phenomena have to be understood in terms of the inter-relationships of the parts of complex wholes, of the need to 'confront ... *problems of organized complexity at all levels*' (von Bertalanffy 1969, p. 59—italics in the original), in the words of one of general systems theory's founding fathers, the extension of such ideas to biology was inevitable. The series of symposia organized by Waddington in the late 1960s and early 1970s, and whose published proceedings he edited (Waddington 1968, 1969a, 1970, 1972), were awash with attempts to construct adequate theoretical approaches to complex biological systems. Indeed, the consensus view at those meetings was that an architecture of complexity is at the heart of theoretical biology—if life is indeed irreducible, then the architecture of complexity is essential for complete causal accounts of any living phenomenon, including, of course, cognition. It was unsurprising that these ideas began to be applied to evolutionary theory itself, some using behaviour and cognitive mechanisms as part of such complex structures. Any attempt to understand the relationship between evolution and learning has to consider such possible theoretical developments.

Complexity in evolutionary theory

von Bertalanffy's conclusion that an adequate theory of evolution has to include 'exploration of organismic systems beyond the molecular level; regularities in evolutionary processes; the "grammar" of the genetic code; thermodynamic and information-theoretical considerations; a theory of dynamic hierarchic order; generally speaking, the consideration of evolution as not completely "outer directed" but co-determined by laws at the organismal level' (von Bertalanffy 1969, p. 75) is a theoretical world away from Darwin's original conception. Any direct comparison between Darwin and a systems theorist of the mid-twentieth century is not just unfair, but absurd. Nonetheless, the kind of perspective someone like von Bertalanffy brings is revealing. Darwin's genius was to build upon some previous insights such as that of Malthus, as well as evidence such as that present in the fossil record and his own data, together with what was widely known about artificial selection, to arrive at an explanation for the transformation of species by way of natural selection driving heritable changes in organisms such that under appropriate conditions of divergence of form and function, new species would arise from those previously existing. Darwin knew nothing of the physical basis of heredity or ontogeny; what he observed were the distributions of organismic forms in both space and time, and the ways in which some features, adaptations, seemed to increase the likelihood of a living creature surviving and producing offspring. If he had even begun to think in terms of causal structures, Darwin would doubtless have gladly declared himself satisfied with a relatively 'flat' causal framework: selection acts upon variations in form to result in differential propagation across generations.

The establishment of genetics as the science of heredity, and its expansion to take in understanding the basis of genetic change, gene linkage and gene–gene interactions, as well as its application at population levels, when married to natural selection led to the synthetic theory of evolution of Fisher, Haldane and Sewall Wright. Dobzhansky, Julian Huxley, Mayr and others then completed the synthesis by constructing plausible theoretical scenarios for speciation itself. However, in one sense, the addition of genetics to the explanation of speciation did not much change the explanatory landscape. Darwin had known that there must be a material basis for heredity; he just did not know what it was, and its relevance to the central idea of differential survival and reproduction transmitted to offspring, no matter how that transmission occurred, was of little importance. Dobzhansky and others would have agreed with him that there were no structural considerations to be taken into account when considering the causes of evolution.

von Bertalanffy, however, was looking at the world through rather different eyes. He needed no convincing about the common descent of all living forms and the transformation of species. However, his 'conceptual ontology' of evolution was very different from that of the founding fathers of Darwinism and the new synthesis: 'Organizing forces and 'laws of organization'—in whatever way defined—are evident at the various levels, from protein and nucleic acid helices to fibrils and fibrillar structures, to organelles like mitochondria reconstituting themselves after severe disturbances, to tissues like hydra or embryonic organs re-organizing themselves after dissociation' (von Bertalanffy 1969, p. 68). He admitted that such organizing forces were 'insufficiently known' but considered that such forces will differ at each 'level' and that they are 'non-summative', by which he invoked the notion of emergent properties that 'cannot be obtained from the isolated parts'.

von Bertalanffy was not expressing a wholly isolated view. The embryologist Paul Weiss had for decades been writing along similar lines. Waddington's notions of developmental and exploitive systems functioning in tandem with genetic and natural selective systems was another expansion of evolutionary thinking beyond the neoDarwinian conception of selection acting on phenotypes to change gene frequencies in breeding populations. Waddington's writings had been appearing in prominent publications (Waddington 1952; 1959b, for example) since the 1950s, and in Waddington's case the general framework had always been a strict adherence to Darwinism, though with an expanded conception of what exactly was necessary for a complete theory of evolution. Waddington's ideas should have received wider recognition. For more traditional evolutionists, however, notions such as organizational complexity and exploitive systems simply had no place in evolutionary theory—even though there may have been the acceptance that they had some role to play in understanding other areas of biology, such as ecology. It is significant that neither von Bertalanffy, Weiss nor Waddington receive a single mention in Mayr's magisterial account of 'biological thought' (Mayr 1982). It should be noted in fairness to Mayr, however, that he did make brief reference to hierarchical structure.

If complexity of any kind were acknowledged by the new synthesis, it was contained within a two-tier structuring of the genotype and phenotype. What Waddington attempted was an expansion of the phenotype into three components, though his diagrams were so ambiguous that any ordering of those components into levels, or any other kind of structure, is not possible. He presented a simple time line extending from one generation to the next. The first 'system' in that time line, though why it should be first is unclear, is the exploitive system; the second the epigenetic system; the third, and seeming to overlap, and presumably strongly interact with the first two, is the natural selective system; and finally a genetic system. It is not possible to understand the ordering of these systems. What is clear is that he envisaged a necessary extension of conventional neoDarwinism to incorporate development on the one hand, and the complex of factors that fall within the scope of what he called the exploitive system. As noted in earlier chapters, Waddington's attention to the causal force of development in evolution, his explication of developmental landscapes, buffered developmental pathways (chreods), and the effects of stress in exposing previously unexpressed genes to the forces of selection, make of him one of the earliest of the developmental systems theorists. However, at least of equal importance was his inclusion of causal force residing in the exploitive system.

Waddington wrote sparingly of his fourth (or first, diagramatically) system, and only in a small number of places. In the paper he gave marking the centennial celebrations of the publication of *Origins*, he described the exploitive system as 'the set of processes by which animals choose and often modify one particular habitat out of the range of environmental possibilities open to them' (Waddington 1959a, p. 400). He never expanded his discussion beyond such vague phrases in any of his other writings, save when discussing humans in which he explicitely considers culture and its effects on human evolution (Waddington 1961, reprinted in Waddington 1975) which he probably (though even *this* is also unclear) would have included within an extended exploitive system. In any event, what is clear from his very few words, is that what he envisaged as the exploitive system are processes that drive behaviour, processes that involve 'choice' and the consequent modification of the environment as a result of such choice. Environmental modification by organisms is an issue that will be considered later in this chapter in terms of John Odling-Smee's notion of niche construction. However, as to what underlies and drives an animal to 'choose', it is reasonable to assume that this would include aspects of learning and cognition.

The point of Waddington's adding epigenetic and exploitive systems to his conception of evolution was his belief that the theory of evolution cast only in terms of genetics and natural selection is an oversimplification of a set of interacting and complex factors.

> These four component systems are not isolated entities, each sufficient in its own right and merely colliding with one another when impinging on the evolving creature. It is inadequate to think of natural selection and variation as being no more essentially connected with one another than would be a heap of pebbles and the gravel-sorter onto which it is thrown. On the contrary, *we have to think in terms of circular and not merely unidirectional causal sequences.* At any particular moment in the evolutionary history of an organism, the states of each of the four main subsystems have been partially determined by the action of each of the other subsystems. The intensity of natural selective forces is dependent on the condition of the exploitive system, on the flexibilities and stabilities which have been built into the epigenetic system, and so on (Waddington 1959a, p. 401—italics added).

Thus, a bird 'choosing' a nesting site as a result of developmental experience such as exposure to song with a specific regional dialect, behaving in such a way as to bring it to that site and constructing a nest there, and possibly employing cognitive mechanisms such as acquiring and then singing its own song, is having the selection pressures that act on it partially determined by its own epigenetic and exploitive systems. A nest site in one position may result in significantly different predatory pressures from that of a nest site differently positioned; it also may be closer or further from food sources, and so on. Behaviour and choice may modify selection forces. Waddington not only anticipated later calls for widening of evolutionary theory, but he also foresaw the need to understand what he termed the 'organization' of interacting and mutually dependent subsystems of processes.

It will be remembered from Chapter 2 that both Lamarck and Darwin in their different ways considered behaviour to have significant bearings upon evolution. For Lamarck, behaviour mediated between the effects of need and his law of use/disuse; and he had hinted that behaviour, autogenously generated, may play a similar role—a notion not far off Waddington's exploitive system. For Darwin, behaviour, at least in *Origins*, was mostly conceived within an instinct framework, but one which was, like all phenotypic characters, variable, and hence provided a source of variation— especially when guided by a 'little dose of judgement or reason'. For Baldwin, adaptive behaviours, whether acquired through flexible development or learning, might provide a 'holding' role until the evolution of similar but directly inherited behaviours relieved and replaced them—his 'new factor' in evolution. Yet while Waddington was not alone from around the mid-twentieth century onwards in subscribing to a causal role in evolution for something approximating to an 'exploitive system'—a set of processes that drive behaviour, including learned behaviour—it has not until recently been prominent in evolutionary theorizing. There was, nonetheless, a trickle of such ideas.

Thus wrote Mayr in 1963: 'A shift into a new niche or adaptive zone is, almost without exception, initiated by a change in behaviour. The other adaptations to the new niche, particularly the structural ones, are acquired secondarily. With habitat and food selection—behavioural phenomena—playing a major role in the shift into new adaptive zones, the importance of behaviour in initiating new evolutionary events is self-evident' (Mayr 1963, p. 604). This is explicit reference to an exploitive system, yet it appears towards the end of the book and the implications are never spelled out beyond that stark statement. A similar incongruity appears in the monumental 1982 survey: 'Since many ecological factors are ultimately behavioural characteristics, such as predator thwarting, feeding strategies, niche selection, niche recognition, all evaluations of aspects of the environment, and many others, one can perhaps even go so far as saying that, at least in animals, the greater part of ecological research is now concerned with behavioural problems. Furthermore, all work in plant as well as animal ecology ultimately deals with natural selection' (Mayr 1982, p. 122). Put in other terms, Mayr is assigning a central role to behaviour in how evolution occurs, yet there is no discussion, beyond that most general assertion, as to how this might happen.

Waddington was not alone in his view that behaviour, including learned behaviour, should be recognized within a more inclusive evolutionary theory. Bateson (1979), Hardy (1965), Piaget (1979) and de Wolsky and Wolsky (1976), amongst others, all made similar cases, if within different contexts. Some were, to say the least, unorthodox, and verging on the heretical. Piaget, for example, invoked notions of 'disequilibria' partly resulting from behaviour and partly resolved and compensated by behavioural change, acting in some wholly unstated and improbable way to alter the genome. In effect a Lamarckian stance, it was not surprising that ideas like that gained no recognition. If anything, they harmed the case for an expansion of evolutionary theory. Others were much more credible, and built on the then expanding understanding of behavioural ecology, and specific issues such as mate choice. More recent reviews can be found in Bateson (1988) and Plotkin (1988*a,b*).

The specific case of learned behaviour, and cognition generally, will be returned to shortly. The story as regards evolution itself must be completed with a brief account of the attempts to introduce hierarchy theory into mainstream evolutionary theory.

Evolutionary theory and hierarchy theory

In 1643, the poet John Milton wrote 'there is a certain scale of duties, there is a certain hierarchy of upper and lower command' which the complete *Oxford English Dictionary* cites as one of the earliest English usages of the word hierarchy. The relevant section of the dictionary was compiled in 1898 and defines hierarchy either as some division of angels, or a system of ecclesiastical rule, or an organized body of priests, or 'a body of persons or things ranked in grades, orders or classes, one above another'. Whilst the earliest usage was religious, the concept of hierarchy was incorporated into systems theory, and introduced to a much wider readership by Simon (1962) in his 'architecture of complexity' paper (see also Simon 1973) in which he argued that hierarchy 'is one of the central structural schemes that the architect of complexity uses' (p. 468). Pattee was even more emphatic in arguing for the place of hierarchy theory in biology at large:

> *If there is to be any theory of general biology, it must explain the origin and operation (including the reliability and persistence)*

of the hierarchical constraints which harness matter to perform coherent functions. This is not just the problem of why certain amino acids are strung together to catalyze a specific reaction. The problem is universal and characteristic of all living matter. It occurs at every level of biological organization from the molecule to the brain. It is the central problem of the origin of life, when aggregations of matter obeying only elementary physical laws first began to constrain individual molecules to a functional, collective behaviour. It is the central problem of development where collections of cells control the growth or genetic expression of individual cells. It is the central problem of biological evolution in which groups of cells form larger and larger organizations by generating hierarchical constraints on subgroups. It is the central problem of the brain where there appears to be an unlimited possibility for new hierarchical descriptions. These are all problems of hierarchical organization. Theoretical biology must face this problem as fundamental, since hierarchical control is the essential and distinguishing characteristic of life' (Pattee 1970, pp. 119–120—italics in the original)

The generally accepted view is that hierarchical order, which is a partial ordering of entities based on dimensions such as size, energy levels, connectivity and strength of inter-action, is so pervasive in living things as to be one of the defining features of life. It is the means by which it is possible to attain 'efficiency in a large collection of interacting elements' (Pattee 1973*b*, p. 73). Simon's well known parable of the watchmakers, Hora and Tempus, made the point wonderfully well. Both men made fine and complex devices comprising some 1000 separate parts, but when the partially completed product had to be laid down, as when the phone rang with customers submitting orders, it would fall apart and return to its original unordered form. Hora discovered that he could construct subassemblies, each of some 10 component parts, a hundred times more rapid to build than a watch in its entirety. Though when laid down the subassembly would also fall apart, it did so only to those original 10 parts. In all, each subassembly grouped with 10 others, and 10 of these formed the clock in its entirety. Given some stated time for construction of the entire watch, piece by piece by Tempus, versus the time to build one of Hora's subassemblies and then to put the subassemblies together to form larger assemblies and ultimately an entire watch, and the frequency with which customers called in their orders, it is a simple arithmetical exercise to work out why Hora completed most of his watches, whereas Tempus was able to construct only very few. Hora thrived whilst Tempus did not. Simon's story illustrates the stability of hierarchies, even when some parts of a complex system are changing. As Pattee noted, a characteristic of any hierarchy is both to limit and yet increase freedom of activity and function within a system. It is a simple extension to see how such compartmentalization, or layering, is at once a means of simplifying interactions within component parts whilst making more complex the whole. It is a framework which demands attention both to the fine detail and to the larger whole. In hierarchies, the devil is in both the detail and the overall structure: or as Simon put it in that classic 1962 paper 'in the face of complexity, an in-principle reductionist may be at the same time a pragmatic holist' (p. 468).

All-inclusive definitions of hierarchy are necessarily diffuse and unhelpful given the widespread understanding that hierarchies are of at least two kinds, structural and control hierarchies, and that other forms of hierarchical organization, such as those of classificatory hierarchies, are outcomes of the operation of both (see Dawkins 1976b; Salthe 1985; Grene 1987; and the other essays in Pattee 1973a).

Structural hierarchies are characterized by literal containment, as in a Chinese (or Russian) doll, where each doll contains another doll, which in turn contains yet another, until a level is reached, the fundamental level, where the final doll does not contain another. Mayr (1982) calls this a constitutive hierarchy, and the obvious example is a hierarchy whose fundamental level are molecular components, which are contained within subcellular organelles, which are contained within cells, then organs, organ systems, whole organisms, demes, species and ecosystems.

Literal physical containment is absent in control hierarchies where the principal causal dependency can be envisaged in the term 'is boss of' (Dawkins 1976b). Military organizations are control hierarchies. A general exerts control over all other members of that army, including her senior officers, who in turn control more junior officers, who exert control over the soldiers without rank. There is no physical containment. The general is not made up of the rest of the army, nor do the senior officers contain junior officers. Modern armies have a relatively complex layering of command but smaller organizations may comprise flat hierarchies with just a small number of levels. One of the characteristics of control hierarchies is that despite a differential degree of control being exerted across levels—generals have greater power to cause things to happen than do junior officers—the system as a whole is characterized by a greater degree of dynamism than occurs in structural hierarchies. Dependency, be it control or flows of information or both, moves fluidly in all directions. Within-level interactions may be more frequent than between-level interactions, but between-level interactions are essential if the system is to maintain coherence and effectiveness—lower ranks report events, problems and possible solutions to higher officers, who in turn report to the general whose orders may, and often will be, altered in accordance with the information that feeds into the higher levels of control. Campbell (1974b) referred to this as 'downward causation'. (Those working within the framework of hierarchies come in two types. There are those who refer to the more fundamental levels of either structural or control hierarchies as 'lower', and there are those who refer to them as 'higher'. The latter would, in Campbell's sense, use the phrase 'upward' causation.) Thus, causal powers are not rigidly fixed in complex control hierarchies, and within-level interactions may be exceeded in importance by those occurring between levels, such shifts responding to changing circumstances.

Most social systems are control hierarchies. Control hierarchies may also operate in complex organ systems such as the immune or central nervous systems. Information flows from sensory surfaces into neural networks in the central nervous system which process the input and then pass it on for further processing and integration within existing networks; feedforward and feedback loops (upward and downward causation) operate to adjust the functioning of the whole system, including control exerted on or close to sensory surfaces by 'higher' control centres which act to modulate further sensory input. Just as Pattee noted, the brain must operate as a control hierarchy on a massive scale.

Complex control hierarchies also operate within cells, with intracellular events turning the expression of genes on and off, which in turn control the production of specific enzymes and protein concentrations, which in turn alter gene expression. The development of a single fertilized egg into the complex structures and functions of complete organisms with billions of cells, that ancient mystery of epigenesis (see Chapter 5), is a cascade of control hierarchies.

Genealogical hierarchies (Grene 1987), or what Mayr (1982) refers to as aggregational hierarchies, are the product of structural and control hierarchies operating over long periods of time, and a specific outcome of human cognition—our understanding that life has a single origin and a branching history resulting from species transformation. Thus biologists classify species as 'contained' within genera, which cluster to form families, orders, classes and phyla. However, strictly speaking, they are neither structural nor control hierarchies. They are hierarchies that we 'make in our minds' (Plotkin 2002a). Mayr refers to genealogical hierarchies as 'strictly an arrangement of convenience' (p. 65) and dismisses them as 'essentially only classificatory devices' (p. 66).

Hierarchical ideas were introduced into evolutionary theory by biologists attempting 'to rethink the problem of causality in their discipline' (Grene 1987, p. 504). Eldredge and Gould's (1972) theory of punctuated equilibrium, the most radical of competing 'reformulations' of evolutionary theory of the 1970s and 1980s, was partly the result of an extension of evolutionary theory by conceiving the process within a hierarchical structure; ecologists also embraced the notion of hierarchy as a means of understanding the complexity of ecosystems (Patten and Odum 1981; O'Neill et al. 1986). A sample of such work can be found in Arnold and Fristrup (1982), Gould (1982a), Vrba and Eldredge (1984) and Vrba and Gould (1986); Wicken and Ulanowicz (1988) provide a more abstract formulation. As Gould himself put it, the issue was not just the possible independence of macroevolution from microevolution—much the most revolutionary notion of punctuated equilibrium theory—'but the question of whether evolutionary theory itself must be reformulated as a hierarchical structure with several levels—of which macroevolution is but one—bound together by extensive feedback to be sure, but each with a legitimate independence. Genes, bodies, demes, species, and clades are all legitimate individuals in some situations, and our linguistic habit of equating individuals with bodies is a convention only' (Gould 1982b, p. 98).

An attempt to sort through the fundamental assumptions that a hierarchical theory of evolution must be based on can be found in Eldredge and Salthe (1984). These include how to define different levels in any hierarchical system by non-transitivity of effects across levels; the confinement of forces to specific levels; the constraints that act on contiguous levels (initiating conditions acting 'upwards', and boundary conditions 'downwards' which, they claim, maps onto the division of Aristotle's four causes, more of which in the final chapter); the necessity of understanding levels as individuals and not classes (Ghiselin 1974; Hull 1976) and thus envisaging biological hierarchies as a nesting of individuals not of classes (which is how they save genealogical hierarchies from the kind of dismissal meted out by Mayr); and the connected-ness of what they conceive as the two fundamental hierarchies of living systems, genealogical and ecological hierarchies, and how the former is the seat of replication and the latter that of interaction. The distinctions that have been drawn between replicators, vehicles and interactors are summarized in Hull (1988a), and hierarchies of replicators and interactors can be found in Brandon (1988).

As stated in earlier chapters, this is not a monograph on evolution specifically, but on the relationship that holds between evolution and learning. Whether the introduction of hierarchy theory into evolutionary theory has been successful is debateable. Certainly there is not yet a consen-sus as to which hierarchies are the important ones (note again the contrast between Eldredge and Salthe's views as to the importance of genealogical hierarchies, and the dismissive approach of Mayr who, like many of the older school of the synthetic theory, was never impressed by, or absorbed in, notions of complexity), and that lack of consensus may be fundamental or may merely indicate the extent to which we all concentrate on, and perhaps exaggerate, the importance of our own interests. There continues, however, to be a more general acceptance that hierarchies are central to any area of biology, and the likely equally general acceptance that a single grand theory of biology grounded within a complex structural architecture is not yet with us, and may never be so. Growth in the popularity of developmental systems theory and niche construction, however, suggests an increasing acceptance that evolutionary theory itself needs to be expanded. It might be noted in ending this section that in his last major testament on evolutionary theory, Gould, who was so important in generating interest in hierarchical thinking amongst biologists, devoted the longest chapter of a very long book to hierarchies (Gould 2002). In any event, the broader acceptance that thinking in terms of complex structures is a legitimate and important aspect to an understanding and depiction of every part of living things, grants us licence to consider the relationship between learning and evolution in this light.

Cognition and evolution within a hierarchical framework

Late in his life, Piaget (1979) wrote a monograph in which the central idea was that behaviour is the 'motor' of evolution. As noted before in this and earlier chapters, Piaget's was not a novel point of view. Lamarck and Spencer had offered roughly the same notion, and Lorenz had also accorded special evolutionary significance to behaviour. Mayr too had judged behaviour to have major importance in initiating evolutionary change. In each case, the claim arose from the intuitively obvious connection between a set of phenotypic attributes, behaviours of many different kinds, that present a highly active form of interaction with the environment. The very basic act of movement in space provides for the strong probability that the act contributes to changing environmental circumstances. Yet the conception of a highly reactive and interactive set of traits, very recent developments regarding niche construction apart, did not change the conceptual framework of evolution as a two-step process in which selection acting on phenotypes results in the differential propagation of genes. Behaviour may be an especially dynamic characteristic, but it seemed not to present any need for novel ideas as to how evolution might be occurring. Some behaviours, however, in some species of animals are subject to change in the future as a consequence of events in the past. That is, some behaviours are under cognitive control in the broadest sense that changes in central nervous structure are wrought by experience which subsequently alter those behaviours. If the arguments and evidence of Chapter 4 are correct, this decoupling of such behaviours from the conventional processes of evolution as a two-step process is only ever partial, cognition being subject to evolved constraints, but a decoupling it nonetheless is. Cognition of any kind introduces an additional locus of causation sited in neural networks. Evolution becomes, at a minimum, a three-step process with an increased causal complexity.

Just how complex is the required architecture depends on how encompassing is the scheme being put forward, and one of the most ambitious of all was that offered by Donald Campbell. In a long series of papers beginning in the 1950s

(Campbell 1956, 1959), Campbell had developed a form of evolutionary epistemology which advanced the notion that all forms of knowledge are based on the same set of selection processes embodied in different mechanisms. There are three essentials to such processes: mechanisms for introducing variation; selection of a small subset of the variants generated; and the means of preserving and propagating the selected variants. He referred to it as a 'blind-variation-and-selective-retention process', which was essentially the Darwinian conception of change driven by selection which from T.H. Huxley onwards, including the luminary likes of James Mark Baldwin, William James, Poincaré and Popper amongst many others, all had offered a similar set of processes to account for adaptive transformations in time, ranging broadly from simple trial-and-error learning to the fundamental means by which the immune system and science work. Campbell's universal variation–selective-retention scheme was very similar to that described in the influential paper of Lewontin (1970) which analysed all evolutionary processes in terms of three principles: variation; differential fitness; and heritability.

In his 1974 review of evolutionary epistemology, offered in honour of Karl Popper, Campbell presented the most ambitious and complex 'nested hierarchy of selective-retention processes' (Campbell 1974a, p. 416) that had ever been developed. The scheme was intended to include all forms of knowledge and knowledge-gain, beginning with 'nonmnemonic problem solving' in protists such as paramecium, through 'vicarious locomotor devices', 'habit', 'instinct', 'visually supported thought', 'mnemonically supported thought', 'socially vicarious exploration' (which includes imitation), 'language', 'cultural cumulation' and 'science'. It was, and probably remains, the most ambitious and far-reaching epistemological scheme based on a single set of processes that has ever been proposed, far greater in scope than that offered by Lewontin in his 1970 paper, or by any of the proponents of replicator theory as applied to culture (see later in this chapter), such as Dennett (1995) or Blackmore (1999).

Campbell's scheme was entirely conceptual. The 'hierarchy' comprised each knowledge form as a 'more or less discrete level(s)' (p. 417) without formally relating them to any specific type of hierarchy. What connects them is an identity of process, and an unspoken and informal evolutionary 'progression' in time. Campbell was also not concerned with any kind of empirical underpinning for his scheme.

A far simpler approach, though with less explicit reference to causal structure, has resulted from a cluster of questions concerning brain size, the reasons for systematic changes in brain size across species, and whether brain size does or does not relate to cognition and intelligence (Jerison 1973, 1985; Armstrong and Falk 1982; Martin 1983) on the one hand; and these being run together with, on the other, a related set of issues concerning the nature of environments driving the evolution of cognition, specifically the notion that social environments in particular are potent sources of selection for specific forms of cognition (Humphrey 1976; Whiten and Byrne 1988; Aiello and Dunbar 1993). It is clear that absolute brain size is indicative of little, given the extent to which learning in the honey bee (Bitterman 1988, 2000) shows remarkable similarities to associative learning described in many vertebrate species whose brain sizes are orders of magnitude larger. Relative brain sizes within restricted taxonomic groups, however, may speak with greater precision to the issue of how cognition, brain size and evolution are related.

A series of papers by A.C. Wilson and his colleagues (Wyles *et al.* 1983; Larson *et al.* 1984; Sage *et al.* 1984; Wilson 1985) were based on a 'behavioural drive' hypothesis that related rates of evolution to relative brain size. The argument was that behaviours which expose animals to changes in selection forces increase the rate at which mutations become fixed in populations—with the unstated further assumptions that involve individuals that are reproductively highly successful and that such individuals will occur in reproductively isolated populations. Whilst the evidence to support the notion was necessarily indirect, it nonetheless was startlingly vivid. For example, using several hundred species of birds belonging to 26 different orders, they were able to show significant differences in rates of evolution, contrary to older views that birds are anatomically more uniform than other classes of vertebrates. In some cases, as in songbirds, the rates of evolution exceeded those of most placental mammals. Taking into account the putative 'ages' of living genera of amphibia, reptiles, birds and mammals, the age differences being based on both fossil and molecular difference data, they concluded that 'anatomical divergence among birds had been unusually fast in relation to both point-mutational divergence and to time' (Wyles *et al.* 1983, p. 4396). Similar findings among fish, especially cichlid fish in lake Victoria which display 'explosive rates' of evolution comparable with those of some orders of birds and mammals, provide some confirmation for their view that evolutionary rates vary widely. What, however, is driving the variation? Wilson and his colleagues did not give measures of learning ability, but they did provide tables showing apparent correlations between rates of anatomical evolution and relative brain sizes. Songbirds and hominids showed both relative brain size and anatomical evolution rates some two to three times greater than in other mammals; the equivalent brain sizes and evolution rates in *Homo* were found to be some four or five times greater than those of songbirds and other hominids. These are startling findings. Wyles *et al.* concluded that

> ... during the history of land vertebrates, the relative size of the brain has increased in a manner that is reminiscent of an autocatalytic process in the lineages leading from amphibians through reptiles to birds and several mammalian groups, especially in the lineage leading to humans. In light of the strong correlation between relative brain size and rate of anatomical evolution, we propose that this rate has also been accelerating along these lineages. Our view of anatomical evolution as an autocatalytic process, mediated by social learning, contrasts with the old view that the pressure to evolve has been rather steady through geological time' (Wyles *et al.* 1983, p. 4397).

Wilson had no direct evidence regarding social learning, or indeed learning of any kind, as the process driving accelerating rates of evolution. The reasoning was based on the, perhaps careless, assumption that brain size correlates with increases in intelligence, though, as noted earlier, this has in the past been an issue of some contention. A recent study by Reader and Laland (2002) does, however, provide additional evidence of the relevant correlations between cognition and brain size. An unconventional form of 'meta-analysis' of some 1000 journal articles on primate behaviour showed significant correlations between a basket of measures of cognitive capacity and the volume of neocortex and striatum, those areas of the brain thought to be most closely tied to executive function and hence linked to complex cognitive processes. The cognitive forms that Reader and Laland were using underpinned specific behaviours recorded in the primatology literature, these being behavioural innovation (behaviours not observed before in a species according to the claim of the original investigator), instances of behaviours that appeared to be the result of social learning, and tool use. As Reader and Laland note, most of the observations from which their data were drawn had lacked the empirical authority of experimental studies; only tool use carries a degree of certainty in terms of any kind of cognitive classification, innovation and especially social learning being vague behavioural and cognitive catch-alls with little consensus amongst those studying them as to what these are and what form they may take. Nonetheless, whatever caution attaches to the work, the correlations with brain size are impressive.

It may be reckless to bind together a series of correlational studies, one grouping of which, the A.C. Wilson studies, measures brain size and evolutionary rates in different classes of vertebrates, and a quite separate analysis, that of Reader and Laland, of brain size and cognitive ability amongst species in a single order, to conclude that some general measure of intelligence is correlated with evolutionary change. This is especially the case when correlations speak little to the causes involved, and especially to the direction of that causation. If Wilson was correct, there is no way of establishing whether evolution rates were being driven by cognitive abilities, social or otherwise, or whether it has been the other way around. Nonetheless, these are a cluster of studies and ideas that collectively point to some kind of causal linkage between intelligence and evolution which goes beyond the simple formulation of cognition as a product of evolution. What might be the architecture of such complexity?

If, as suggested in an earlier chapter, cognition or intelligence in a generic sense evolved in response to what Waddington referred to as 'the uncertain futures problem', cognition in every form is a response to the information sampling limitations inherent in the process of evolution (Plotkin and Odling-Smee 1979, 1981; Plotkin 1994). This abstract and strongly adaptationist argument was based on that same general notion of Campbell that biological transformations of every kind, including evolution as generally understood, are forms of knowledge gain that occur by way of a general information-gaining algorithm of variation and selective retention. The selectionist nature of cognition, however, is contentious and besides the main point of the claim. This is that one of the limiting conditions in the evolution of sexually reproducing organisms conforming to such a generate–test–regenerate algorithm of evolution, the Darwinian processes that most evolutionists accept, is the delay inherent in the process: the conjunction of genetic information from separate organisms that occurs at conception has then to be translated through epigenesis into a novel phenotype before that phenotype can contribute to its own gene pool. In other words, there is a time lag between an organism receiving the genetic information from which its own development constructs its phenotype, and the time at which it is reproductively capable: '... the frequency of environmental change relative to the rate of generational turnover' (Plotkin and Odling-Smee 1979, p. 30) determines the uncertain utility of genetic information in the face of possible environmental change. Flexible development, especially important in plants, and flexible behaviours moulded by learning in animals, are devices by which organisms can track changing features of the environment by incorporating into the phenotype adaptive structures. Flexibility of development is limited by the point at which epigenesis is complete. In the case of learning, the memory that guides behaviour in the event of repeated and life-long environmental change, which epigenesis alone cannot deal with, can accommodate behaviour to such rapid environmental flux, to change which is occurring too fast for the main evolutionary programme to track, by incorporating such change into neural network structures with great rapidity.

If this very general argument is correct, then learning has a specific hierarchical relationship to the main evolutionary programme, and to the developmental processes by which the phenotype is constructed, including the neural networks whose structures and functioning will cause them to become the substrates of memory. The main evolutionary programme, epigenesis and individual learning and cognition form a control hierarchy, each level of which is responsive to different rates and durations of environmental change. Individual learning is nested within the main evolutionary programme and serves as a proxy information-gaining system sensitive to the more rapid rates of change in the environment to which the slower acting main evolutionary programme is insensitive because of the temporal limitations of selection acting on phenotypes; and nested also within individual development whose responsivity to environmental events is limited and unable to track environmental events which may change repeatedly across the lifetime of the phenotype.

Such a nested control hierarchy has specific consequences. The most important is that learning, if it is to serve its evolved function, must occur rapidly. The second is that information can be transmitted across levels; both evolution, working over repeated trials of selection in geological time, and epigenesis working within the restricted period of individual development, are able to feed information to the learning processes and mechanisms such that cognition is primed and focused towards specific features of the world that have to be learned. This does not ensure absolute accuracy of learning, but it certainly does make it more rapid, and increases the likelihood of the relevance of cognition to the overall life history strategies of different species of learner. What appears to be *a priori* knowledge in the learner, the necessary knowledge of the title of this book, is transformed, by this relatively simple architecture of complexity, into the *a posteriori* knowledge accumulated over long periods of selection by the main evolutionary programme and its transformation and fine-tuning by epigenesis into specific organs of cognition. The scheme presented by Odling-Smee and Plotkin was explicitly developed to place learning within the context of evolution. It does not, of course, preclude the possibility of further hierarchical structure within cognition itself, as presented in Campbell's grand scheme or more specific applications to particular kinds of cognition (for example, Greenfield 1991; Byrne and Russon 1998).

The nesting of learning within evolution and development provides the explanation for the well-documented constraints on learning described in Chapter 4, and also explains why learning constraints vary in line with life history strategies—why, for example, aversive conditioning involving the ingestion of food is associated so readily with one set of conditional stimuli in one species or group of species on the one hand, and a quite different set of conditional stimuli in another group of species. It also accounts for how developmental experience is crucial in the way in which birdsong is acquired in songbirds, as well as in the acquisition of language by human infants.

The structure of causal complexity also provides insight into a further issue. Unless one further condition evolves, within the framework of a control hierarchy linking evolution, epigenesis and individual cognition, the products of cognition, individual knowledge, remain trapped within the neural networks of individual learners. The utility of such cognition is tested like any other phenotypic character in that it either adds to individual fitness or it does not, and the consequences are then the increase or reduction in the gene pool of those genes, or combination of genes, that part-cause the specific form of cognition. In either case, the knowledge or information gained by learning/cognition remains trapped within the neural networks of the individual learner. Genetic transmission is the sole means of transmitting information between learners, and it takes the form not of highly specific information but of the capacity to so gain such information by way of the fragments of what is here referred to as necessary knowledge, the latter itself gained through the hard discipline of standard Darwinian selection processes. That further condition referred to above is when evolution results in learners able to transmit information directly between themselves—'short-circuiting', as it were, the genetic channel of information transmission. This alters evolution in a dramatic and significant manner; it forms a major transition in the evolution of life on earth (Szathmary and Maynard Smith 1995), and it adds further complexity to the causal structures of behaviour in those species able to learn from one another.

Cultural complexity

Even as Szathmary and Maynard Smith were writing in terms of the major evolutionary transitions, and listing the last of these as the evolution of protolanguage in *Homo erectus* and then the emergence of 'human language with a universal grammar and unlimited semantic representation' (Szathmary and Maynard Smith 1995, p. 231), questions were being raised as to whether the consequence of such a transition, from a non-cultural to a cultural state, was unique to humans. Language undoubtedly is an aspect of culture, but language *per se* is not the issue—what is, are the presumed consequences of language, human culture as a product of language; also what psychological processes and mechanisms apart from language are necessary for culture; and whether culture is present in other species of animal and, if so, what psychological mechanisms support such non-human culture. These are largely unresolved questions and, since they are not central to the main concern of this chapter, which is the architecture of causal complexity, they will be touched upon only briefly.

The acquisition of species-specific song in some species of songbird, as is clear from Chapter 4, requires the learning of that song during a relatively restricted period after hatching. This is a form of social learning in which the behaviour of one animal is learned by another. Social learning, however, is a generic phrase and certainly encompasses a number of specific and different forms of learning (Heyes and Galef 1996; Fragaszy and Perry 2003). Nonetheless, it is not absurd to assert that since songbirds do share behaviours through learning, they should be considered to be species that do have culture of a kind, even if only of a very limited kind. Certain species of cetaceans, notably bottlenosed dolphins and killer whales, share complex behavioural, especially vocal, traditions, which again qualifies them as cultural animals (Rendell and Whitehead 2001). Orangutan cultures (van Schaik *et al.* 2003) have also been described, as have those of chimpanzees (Boesch 1996; Whiten *et al.* 1999; McGrew 2004). The principal forms of evidence in the case of the great apes takes the form of regional variations in behaviour which cannot be explained by genetic or ecological differences. In the case of chimpanzees, Whiten *et al.* reported 39 different behavioural patterns, including courtship behaviours, grooming, gestures and tool usage, which are habitual and widespread in some communities and different, or entirely absent, in others. In the Tanzanian communities, for example, fishing for ants is common, but distinctively different in the individual animals of each community. The west African communities show equally striking differences. Nuts and stones are universally present for all, but whereas west of the Sassandra-N'Zo river nuts are cracked open using the blows from hand-held stones, east of that river such nutcracking does not occur. Recent experimental evidence from the laboratory (Whiten *et al.* 2005) confirms that specific forms of tool use are learned by observing others and, quite strikingly, recorded the presence amongst captive chimpanzees of a conformity bias never reported before outside of our own species, and accorded considerable importance amongst the psychological processes and mechanisms that support enculturation in humans (Boyd and Richerson 1985; Plotkin 2002*a*; Richerson and Boyd 2005).

There is no reason, then, to think that culture is an exclusively human attribute. There is also no reason to doubt that whatever constitutes the culture of chimpanzees and orangutans, seemingly in large part the sharing of gestures, manual skills and, perhaps, vocalizations, is also present in modern humans and probably was also present in other species of *Homo*. However, what it is certainly also reasonable to assert is that culture in humans takes a significantly different form from that of any species, and it is this difference that marks out humans as a species with a special feature—the ability to construct social reality (Searle 1995; Plotkin 2002*a*). Literally hundreds of definitions of culture have been offered (Kroeber and Kluckhohn 1952), and different anthropological schools have emphasized the importance of different aspects of culture. Within the context of this book, what is emphasized here is the ideational definition of culture, because that is the means by which direct links can be made between the social science conceptions of culture on the one hand, and on the other hand the psychological world in general, and cognition specifically. 'A society's culture consists of whatever it is one has to know or believe in order to operate in a manner acceptable to its members' (Goodenough 1957, p. 167) encapsulates wonderfully well two key elements of human culture: the first is that what is learned from the learning of others is knowledge, values, beliefs, customs and rituals, all of which are part of a different conceptual realm from the gestures and tool use of chimpanzees; the second is that Goodenough's 'acceptable to its members' points to the important issue of social acceptance and social force. The findings of Whiten *et al.* clearly demonstrating a conformity bias in at least one non-human ape species indicate that the role of social force as the 'glue' binding cultures together is not exclusive to our species. However, what makes human culture special is the variety of shared ideational forms, and the enormous quantity of knowledge contained within each of those. Two of these forms are of particular significance: social constructions (Searle 1995) and higher order knowledge structures (Plotkin 2002a, 2007).

Social constructions are forms of social reality that exist by virtue of the agreement of the individuals out of which the social group is composed. Social constructions cover an enormous range precisely because they are formed by agreement between the members of a culture. Money, justice, patriotism, capitalism, socialism, ethnicity and specific religions are all social constructions. Many social constructions give rise to physical structures: justice gives rise to court houses and prisons; money is embodied in pieces of paper, coins, banks and entries on computers. Nonetheless, agreement is central to the existence of money. The pieces of paper or the memory in a bank's computer system of themselves have no value; it is the agreement between the individual offering money for a commodity or service and the person who accepts the money in return for a product of some kind wherein the value lies. Social constructions cease to exist when the agreement between members of a culture ceases to exist; that is exactly what happened in a number of cultures at different times in the previous century when money became worthless.

The absolute necessity for agreement makes social constructions especially strange entities, but, of course, their oddness does not mean they are without material structure. Social constructions are interlocking neural network states inside the brains of the individuals making up a culture. That one is married, a member of a specific religious institution, a citizen of a particular country, all of these are 'social facts'. If humans had not evolved to the point of having consciousness and its accompanying intentionality, these psychological states being also biological and hence physical states, social facts would not exist. Britain is a social fact. It is also a 'brute fact', an island of some 250 000 km^2 off the northwest coast of a much larger land mass in the northern hemisphere of the planet. The differences, the origins and the consequences of the differences between brute facts and social facts are analysed by Searle (1995). A resumé of his analysis can be found in Plotkin (2002a).

Social constructions, and the social reality that results, form the basis for the specific forms of higher order knowledge structures that characterize cultures. Attendance at a religious ceremony is an act embedded within a set of social constructions deriving from agreed metaphysical beliefs and moral values, and it occurs within, and is guided by, complex knowledge structures such as what a religious temple is, as opposed to, say, a school or a bank, and how one must behave in that specific context. As Sperber (2000) points out, the cultural world is freighted with such complex knowledge forms that go far beyond simple motor acts such as donning the appropriate headwear. One of the corner-stones of such higher order knowledge structures is Bartlett's conception of the schema (Bartlett 1932), a cognitive structure wholly at odds with the atomism of associationism. For Bartlett, memory was not a passive recollection of stored associations but a form of creative reconstruction that is guided by schemas, deep-lying generic knowledge structures that are products of features specific to different cultures, and which fashion and mould that reconstructive process. Minsky (1975) revived Bartlett's idea of scripts when he understood that artificial intelligence needed generic knowledge structures of the kind Bartlett had conceived of; scripts (Schank and Abelson 1982; Rumelhart and Norman, 1985), actions appropriate to specific complex settings, were a further enlargement of this general conception of a knowledge structure that acts as a kind of memory attractor that structures remembering and action. There is much evidence that non-human primates (Tomasello and Call 1997) and at least some other mammalian and avian species (Pearce 1987) are able to acquire limited forms of generic knowledge. There is also some evidence that young children and great apes may share common cognitive features in both social learning and forms of cognitive abstraction, so-called secondary representations (Suddendorf and Whiten 2001; Horner and Whiten 2005). However, whether the psychological processes and mechanisms that result in human culture are the same as those generating culture in non-humans remains, for the present, speculative.

There can be no doubting the crucial role of language in the evolution of culture, cultural evolution and the enculturation of every human child as a part of essential cognitive development. However, whether language alone could have engineered that eighth evolutionary transition without the necessary presence of other psychological processes and mechanisms is increasingly considered to be doubtful (Donald 1991; Tomasello 1999; Plotkin 2002a, 2003; Tomasello et al. 2005). At a minimum, in addition to the ability to form higher order knowledge structures, intentional mental states, perhaps including the capacity for collective intentionality or 'we-intentionality' (Tuomela and Miller 1988; Bratman 1992) are necessary. There is an increasing awareness that understanding the intentions and goals of others relates to specific brain region activity, what is known as the mirror neuron system (Rizzolatti and Craighero 2004), which appears to be separate from the object-recognition systems of the brain (Frith and Wolpert 2004). Mirror neurons have been observed in primates other than humans, and may be widespread in monkeys and apes, thus providing a possible mechanism out of which initially very simple cultures might have evolved. There is also a likely role for the mechanisms that control social force, as mentioned above, in the process of enculturation. Conformity and obedience are social phenomena about which nothing is presently known in terms of neuroscience when compared with language and theory of mind, but there are increasing signs of recognition of the importance of understanding the brain as a 'social' device (Dunbar 2003).

Whatever the essential psychological mechanisms are that have given rise to culture, it has unquestionably given our species a power and dominance unprecedented in the history of life on earth. That does not mean that culture should be placed within the conventional notion of an adaptation. If indeed a number of mechanisms are necessary for culture to become possible in a social species, it is likely that each evolved as a consequence of whatever separate advantage each bestowed on the individual. Their coalescing into a unitary process with properties that increase both individual and group fitness can only be understood within a framework of multiple exaptations—mechanisms as exaptations of exaptations leading to an unparalleled complexity of process. A natural science account of culture may yet be a long way in the future. However, there are two questions that can be raised with reasonable clarity. The first concerns the causal force of culture; the second is how to conceive of culture in terms of a complex causal architecture.

Galton was utterly mistaken in his dichotomizing of nature and nurture; and was even more in error, if that were possible, in assigning very much greater power to the former, to biological inheritance and evolution, than to culture. Evidence for the causal power of culture (Plotkin 2007) is to be found in two stark figures. The one is the growth of the human world population in the last 5000 years, and especially the last century. Increased population numbers are owed entirely to the spread of agriculture and, in recent years, advances in medical science increasingly available worldwide. Both are products and/or forms of culture. The second figure, in a strange contradiction of the first, is the number of people killed in the twentieth century by armed conflicts. The members of the International Committee for the Red Cross estimate this to be a number somewhat exceeding 100 million; the causes of warfare, they avow (personal communication), have overwhelmingly been social constructions such as ideologies, religion, ethnicity, national identity and attempts to control financial and other resources.

One need only also consider climate change and the effect we are having on other species, all consequences of human culture, to understand its power. Furthermore, religious and other moral injunctions on how to live one's life determine the daily behaviour of billions of people across the planet. Galton could not have been more wrong. Aspects of culture, notably social constructions, are curiously fragile owing to that need for social agreement; but once that agreement is present, human culture is awesomely powerful, sufficiently so to have determined human evolution and, in the present, the evolution of other species. Reviews and specific instances of the effects of human culture on human evolution can be found in Durham (1991), Aiello and Wheeler (1995) and Wrangham *et al.* (1999). Whether such causal power is unique to our species is now debateable (Whiten *et al.* 2003; Byrne *et al.* 2004). There is even tentative evidence for genetic effects of culture in four species of matrilineal whales (Whitehead 1998).

The causal power of culture is also seen in the way in which specific enculturation experiences determine psychological phenomena, as touched upon briefly in Chapter 1. Quite apart from the long appreciated and pervasive effects that early experience has on fundamental aspects of behaviour and personality, such as a propensity to violent behaviour when exposed to cultures in which firearm crime is common (Bingenheimer *et al.* 2005), culture is a force moulding cognition itself. Lillard (1998), for example, argues for the effects of different cultures on theory of mind variations. The European–American (EA) theory of mind results in an understanding of intentional mental states within a specific cultural setting in which the individual mind, focused on individual needs and desires, is central. This contrasts with many different forms of intentional causal attributions in which the individual mind has little or no role to play. The individual has little relevance amongst the Illongot of the Philippines, Tibetan Budhists or the Tallensi of Africa, where the group is the dominant unit, and the individual mind is subsumed within complex concepts that include notions such as heart, ancestry and the spirit world. '… although the mind is still behind the action, it is a different sort of mind than EAs think of' (Lillard 1998, p. 15). Even the primacy of senses and our principal means of sensory identification vary across cultures. The EA theory of mind is dominated by vision and hearing, but amongst the Ongee of the south Pacific, the nose and odour is central. Such ethnographic differences are undeniable, even though a form of social causation is at the heart of all theory of mind—it is what constitutes the realm of the social that differs.

More fundamental cultural effects on cognition have been reported by Richard Nisbett and his colleagues (Nisbett *et al.* 2001; Nisbett and Masuda 2003; Nisbett and Miyamoto 2005). East Asians are reported to be significantly more 'holistic' and context-dependent, attending to larger fields of causation and making little or no use of categories and reasoning that approximates to formal logic. Westerners, in contrast, are more analytical, guided in their thinking to the object, the category to which it belongs, and using general rules, including aspects of formal logic, to understanding the behaviour of that object. Nisbett argues that cultural and social organization directs attention to certain features of 'the field' whilst detracting from the relevance of others causing specific kinds of dominant metaphysics to emerge, metaphysics that guides tacit epistemology, which in turn 'dictates the development and application of some cognitive processes at the expense of others' (Nisbett *et al.* 2001, p. 292). Their conclusions were that 'the cognitive processes triggered by a given situation may not be so universal as generally supposed, or so divorced from content, or so independent of the particular character of thought that distinguishes one human group from another' (Nisbett *et al.* 2001, p. 307).

An even more focused account of culturally induced psychological *and neurological* difference is to be found in a recent functional imaging study of dyslexic children whose native language is Chinese. Impaired reading of alphabetic script is associated with dysfunction of left temperoparietal regions of the brain where grapheme-to-phoneme conversion occurs. The Chinese language, however, is logographic and reading requires conversion from a graphic to a syllabic representation. The Chinese dyslexic children showed dysfunction of the left middle frontal gyrus. This demonstrated that 'rather than having a universal origin, the biological abnormality of impaired reading is dependent on culture' (Siok *et al.* 2004, p. 71). It may not be that surprising that writing systems of such fundamentally different designs as Chinese and English should impose different psychological and neurological requirements for reading; but what is absolutely clear is how this study demonstrates culturally driven causes of altered psychological mechanisms to achieve the same end of decoding written language.

Yet another example is to be found in the work of Atran and his colleagues (Atran 1998; Medin and Atran 2004) who have shown how urban and rural children in north America categorize and generalize biological forms, with the children raised in cities using similarities to humans as their criteria whereas rural children employ more expert-based taxonomies which do not focus on humans. Other cases and studies can be found in reviews by Greenfield *et al.* (2003) and Cole (2006).

Culture, then, exerts causal force on basic developmental experience in humans, on possibly quite fundamental aspects of human cognition, and it almost certainly has played a role in the evolution of *Homo sapiens*, if not of other species of human. How can culture be meshed into the complexity of living forms? The anthropologist George Murdock had speculated on the possibility of analysing cultural change as being evolutionary in form, a notion akin to William James' conception of creativity as being a parallel form of evolutionary process. The application of this form of evolutionary epistemology to how science works by Ernst Mach and Jules Henri Poincaré in the early twentieth century was a variation on this idea, and found expression in the writings of Campbell (see earlier in this chapter), and subsequently of David Hull (1988*b*) amongst others. Dawkins (1976*a*) mused on the possibility of analysing culture in terms of replicator theory in which cultural entities called memes are to be seen as replicators, the cultural equivalents of genes in biological evolution. Dawkins envisaged memes as 'leaping from brain to brain via a process which, in the broad sense, can be called imitation' (Dawkins 1976*a*, p. 206). The conception of cultural change as a form of evolution to be understood in terms of replicator theory has been recently revived (Dennett 1995; Blackmore 1999; Aunger 2003), and criticized (Bloch 2000; Boyd and Richerson 2000; Plotkin 2000, 2002*a*; Sperber 2000). The criticisms take a number of forms, not least being that an evolutionary conception adds nothing to ideas of cultural change, that it is an extreme form of oversimplification of just the destructive nature that has occurred in the past when biologists have stepped into the territory of the social scientist, and that in its essential features it is plain wrong. Children do not learn what money is, or that their family, and hence themselves, are adherents to a specific religion, by any process or set of processes remotely resembling imitation. In the terms of this chapter, there is a further weakness to the whole conception of memetics as an adequate science of culture. This is that it provides a flat causal structure that belies its complex nature.

Gene–culture co-evolutionary theorists (Cavalli-Sforza and Feldman 1981; Boyd and Richerson 1985; Laland 1993) have long built into their models a form of causal inter-action between biological and cultural evolution; what occurs in the one realm may, and often does, have causal implications for what happens in the other. The implicit conception is of a complex causal architecture. A complex control hierarchy of multiple levels (Plotkin and Odling-Smee 1981), of which culture is either one or part of one, is an explicit account of just such an architecture. Human culture cannot be understood in terms of imitation. However, it certainly is a product of complex cognitive processes. One causal structure would have biological evolution, devel-opment and individual cognition as separate hierarchical levels, with a further set of sublevels within cognition, of which culture would be one. The advantage of this is that, like Campbell's 10 epistemological levels, the forms of cognition that result in cultural phenomena such as social constructions can be seen against the rather lesser motor forms of learning that are indeed acquired by imitation, both in humans and in other apes. It might also allow a better understanding of how different forms of cognition interact to form human culture in all its astonishing forms. In many ways, this would be an appropriate architecture within a psychological context.

An alternative architecture would have culture as a level in a control hierarchy in its own right. The advantage of this conception is that it signals culture as a phenomenon and as a source of potent causal force whose effects on the other levels of the hierarchy are no less significant than the effects of the other levels of the hierarchy on culture itself. Given that science is at once an outcome of culture, as well as one of its forms, and given the extent to which science is beginning to change nature itself—whether it be genetic engineering, drug therapies or the interconnecting of brain activity with that of computers, to mention just some—the conception of human culture as a distinctive level within a control hierarchy in which causal force and information transmission between levels are almost as significant as those occurring within levels, may be the more appropriate. Certainly it is this latter conception that has been chosen by those broadening evolutionary theory with the notion of niche construction.

Extending the theory of evolution: niche construction

In his 'paradigm for an evolutionary process', Waddington (1969*b*) had reasoned that there are two absolutely essential elements for evolution to occur: one is some form of stable memory, and the other is the need for something 'reactive enough to be an effective operator' (p. 115). This combination of retaining aspects of the order of the past together with a reactivity to test and hence ascertain the order of the present as defining the conditions for evolution, anticipated by decades what complexity theory would later term the conditions of evolvability (Kauffman 1995) which are 'poised between order and chaos'. DNA, argued Waddington, is just too unreactive to carry the conditions of evolvability on its own; a probing, testing, reactive component is necessary, the operator, or what later Hull (1988*a*) would term the interactor in contrast to Dawkins' vehicle (Dawkins 1982b). For Dawkins, the replicator dominated its vehicle (until memes, another form of replicator, evolved). This was not so for Waddington's operator or Hull's interactor. The operator/interactor, the phenotype in less abstract terms, is an active, causal, agent in the evolutionary process.

Lewontin's criticism of neoDarwinism that the organism is envisaged as too passive in the process of evolution, and his conviction that what is needed for an adequate theory of evolution is a more constructivist approach in which the activities and autogenous states of the organism are at least as important as changes in gene frequencies and forms (see Chapter 4), led to his presentation (Lewontin 1983) at one of the events commemorating the centenary of Darwin's death, of a paper centred around two differential equations which conveyed for him the quintessence of neoDarwinist theory: the one represents the change of the organism in time as a function of the current state of that organism and its environment, whilst the other states that environmental change is a function of environmental events. Lewontin's main point was that contemporary evolutionary theory holds these two equations as separate, with adapted organisms not being causal in environmental change—the very point of Lewontin's criticism.

John Odling-Smee (personal communication) was influenced by both Waddington's paradigm for the evolutionary process in which the operator is an essential component, and Lewontin's argument that those two differential equations should be coupled such that they depict the necessary linkage between environment and organism—the history of change in both organism and environment is a function of both organism and environment. The result was a series of chapters and papers, beginning with Odling-Smee (1988), and later including his collaborators Kevin Laland and Marcus Feldman (Laland *et al.* 1996, 1999, 2000, 2005— which is not an exhaustive listing), culminating in a monograph (Odling-Smee *et al.* 2003), the overall effect of which some (for example, Griffiths 2005; Okasha 2005; Sterelny 2005; and various commentaries in the 2000 *Behavioural and Brain Sciences* paper) consider to be one of the most significant additions to the theory of evolution since the work on inclusive fitness and the units of selection writings of Hamilton and Williams in the 1960s.

The epigram at the start of the monograph comes from George Orwell: 'to see what is in front of one's nose requires a constant struggle'. What Odling-Smee saw in front of his nose, which everyone aside from Waddington and Lewontin simply did not see in terms of its explanatory power, was what Odling-Smee called 'niche construction'—organisms alter their environments, either passively (leaves shed by deciduous trees, for example) or actively (the building of burrow systems by rabbits or dams by beavers) which have two consequences: one is that the constructed niches form an ecological inheritance which may be stable across many generations and so constitutes an additional inheritance system to that of genetics; and the other is that in both changing the world and passing these changes on to their offspring, many organisms have a causal role in altering the selection pressures that act on them and their offspring.

A frequent response to niche construction (Dawkins 2004, for instance, as well as in many of the reviews of the monograph) is that this is nothing new. Darwin himself wrote a book on earthworms and how they alter their environment, an example frequently invoked in the writings of Odling-Smee *et al.* It has also long been understood that the evolution of cyanobacteria, whose metabolism released oxygen into the atmosphere, altered the conditions for the evolution of life on earth in a profound manner. Additionally, Dawkins' own conception of the extended phenotype (Dawkins 1982a) had touched on many aspects of niche construction and ecological inheritance. There are, however, two differences between Odling-Smee *et al*'s treatment of the notion when compared with that of everyone else, from Darwin to Dawkins.

The first is that Odling-Smee and his collaborators incorporated niche construction into formal mathematical modelling of evolution, using population genetic models, and have demonstrated that the 'effects of niche construction can override external sources of selection to create new evolutionary trajectories, which leads to the fixation of otherwise deleterious alleles, the support of stable equilibria where none are expected, and the elimination of what would otherwise be stable polymorphisms. Even small amounts of niche construction that only weakly affects resource dynamics can significantly alter both ecological and evolutionary patterns' (Laland 2004, p. 317). Niche construction, in other words, can be demonstrated as having real causal force, and this is presented within a context that has predictive power. These are significant advances in how to understand the role of organisms in their own evolution. Niche construction is not without its critics (Dawkins 2004), one of Dawkin's main points being a distrust of circular causation. Complex causation, however, is to be distinguished from circular causation, and one of Odling-Smee's most significant contributions has been to provide the conceptual framework from which to understand such complex causation.

This relates to the second way in which Odling-Smee's conceptions are different from everyone else who has understood the need to incorporate the organism's own activities into evolutionary theory, though, as outlined previously in this chapter, Waddington's four-component theory of evolution was a move in this direction. What Odling-Smee did was incorporate the notions of niche construction and ecological inheritance into an architecture of complexity which included ontogeny, learning and intelligence, and culture as parts of a complex hierarchy, at each level of which niche construction occurs and leaves a legacy of ecological inheritance.

Niche construction, in a burrowing species such as the mole rat, or insects that provision their eggs with a food supply and a specific environment within which development occurs, are examples of the innumerable cases in which the activities of individual animals have consequences for the development of their offspring, and in which the activities of individuals affect the conditions of their own development. Not all forms of learning are instances of niche construction, but some certainly are. All forms of learned tool use would entail altering the environment, i.e. what tools are for, and hence qualify as niche construction. A particularly interesting instance of tool use is cited by Odling-Smee *et al.* (2003). This is the work of Grant (1986) and Tebbich *et al.* (2001), both describing how, by learning to grub with a tool, selection pressure in woodpecker finches alleviates selection for the form of the birds' bill. What is fascinating about these observations is that they reveal the Baldwin effect in action. As noted in Chapter 3, the Baldwin effect can be understood as a form of niche construction (Laland 2003), which places Baldwin's 'new factor' in a broader and hence more meaningful context. All forms of learned behaviours which alter the selection forces acting on the learner are an instance of niche construction. Another category of learning which will often constitute a form of niche construction is social learning where the activities of one animal become the source of learning for another, as in diet choice.

Finally, culture is another form of niche construction, and cultural inheritance another instance of ecological inheritance. It is certainly conceivable that the controlled use of fire for cooking altered the selection pressures acting on *Homo erectus* and resulted in the alleviation of selection for gut size which then allowed for further increases in brain size (Aiello and Wheeler 1995). It is clearly the case that the invention of agriculture created conditions that changed human history. It is equally clearly the case that the invention of social constructions such as religious beliefs and values provides a niche and an inheritance that powerfully affects how people think.

Niche construction and ecological inheritance are significant additions to the theory of evolution. They expand the causal structure of the theory. In placing these concepts within a hierarchical framework, Odling-Smee has expanded that very causal structure itself such that individual learning and culture can be incorporated into the central theorem of biology, the theory of evolution.

The complex structure of interdependent multiple causation is what makes living systems different from non-living systems. The addition of other sources of causation sited in neural networks, be it individual learning or shared learning and hence culture, makes the causal structures even more complex. The nature of these structures is central to the concern of this book. If constrained cognition is the product of evolution, with all constraints comprising small amounts of representational knowledge that prime learning to particular features of the environment that have to be learned, then it is only within a framework of interdependent causal structure that the seeming *a prioris* that constrained cognition implies can be understood as the products of *a posteriori* evolutionary selection within which is nested all forms of cognition. Simon's architecture of complexity is absolutely essential to understanding the relationship between learning and evolution.

CHAPTER 7

Cognitive science, philosophy and the problem of unbounded culture

The principal aim of this book is to examine exactly what is the relationship between evolution and learning. An integral part of that relationship, it has been argued, is the notion of *'necessary knowledge'*, necessary knowledge referring to some probably very small, perhaps fragmentary, innate representational knowledge. Such necessary knowledge is the embodiment of the relationship between evolution on the one hand, and the surrogate knowledge-gaining process, i.e. learning, to which it has given rise, on the other. What this minimal innate representational knowledge does is constrain, and hence aim or guide, learning towards specific features of the world that must be learned. Such necessary knowledge converts a potentially slow and wholly inefficient process to one that is appropriately 'fast and frugal' in Gigerenzer's words (see Chapter 4).

For reasons of clarity and simplicity of argument, previous chapters have presented a single, and probably overly strong, form of the notion of innate representational knowledge. This strong form of the hypothesis of *'necessary knowledge'* is that it is present in all instances of learning in all animals that have evolved the capacity for learning. This is, however, unlikely to be the case. Habituation, for example, is a necessarily undefined form of learning, the effective operation of which does not require that the learning mechanisms be pointed at specific features of the world. There is also evidence for learning in some species of invertebrates (Corning *et al.* 1973) whose limited sensory sensitivity makes necessary knowledge redundant. The evidence for constraints on learning is most strong in vertebrates, and so a weaker form of the hypothesis is appropriate. This states that necessary knowledge is essential for learning that is limited to a specific form of information, such information constituting a very small part of the patterns of sensory input to which the learner is receptive, for instance facial pattern learning in humans, language in humans and specific forms of auditory input in songbirds, in each case the learning being restricted to a tiny subset of input from the relevant sensory surfaces; or in the computation of behavioural strategies under specific circumstances appropriate to the life-history strategies of the learner of the kind described by Gigerenzer and his colleagues in the case of humans, and in studies of learning strategies in some species of birds. The key to the weaker form of the hypothesis is specificity of learning requirement within a context of exceedingly large quantities of potential information, and patterning of that information, flowing into the cognitive mechanisms of the brain from the sensory surfaces.

Determining exactly what kinds of learning, and in which species of learners, innate representational knowledge is necessary is an empirical matter in which formal modelling could act as a guide. In any event, the weaker form of the hypothesis of such necessary knowledge is a specific and empirically testable, or at least potentially testable, outcome of the relationship between evolution and learning. In general, the evidence currently available supports the existence of constraints on learning, and hence of that necessary knowledge, in a range of different species and in different cognitive forms.

Previous chapters have been concerned with the evolutionary, cognitive and comparative science that informs us of how one should understand the relationship between learning and evolution. However, the issues raised, and the answer given in the form of the thesis of necessary representational knowledge, also derive some support from aspects of philosophy of science, and may also be seen as having specific implications for at least one central problem of classical epistemology. In addition, it raises questions concerning the powers of culture, and how in humans that relationship between evolution and learning may be altered with profound consequences for our species. These, then, are the subjects of this final chapter.

It must be stated that this is not a philosophical text and the author is not a philosopher. Philosophy, however, has always stood at the centre of all scholarship, comprising systematic analysis of the most fundamental questions of human existence and experience. For this reason, it is no surprise to find that philosophy of science, especially that dealing with issues of explanation and causation, may shed light on some of the issues raised in this book. The reversal of this influence, the possibility that contemporary science may be reaching the position where it begins to inform classical philosophy about one of the central questions of epistemology, is an especially pleasurable outcome.

Explanation and causation

One of Aristotle's many great contributions to thought was his insistence that scientific understanding entails causal accounts of the world (Kenny 2004 provides a recent and relatively detailed account). For Aristotle, however, causation was not of a single kind. He argued instead for the doctrine of four causes. Examples illustrating the distinctions Aristotle drew between the four causes abound in the philosophical literature. Wedin (1995) in his entry on Aristotle in the *Cambridge Dictionary of Philosophy* used that of a house and the causes of that house; the material cause of a house is the substance from which it is built; the efficient cause is the builder; the formal cause is its plan or form; and its final cause is the purpose of a house or what a house is for, which is to provide shelter. It is the last of these, final cause, that in recent centuries has given rise to a great deal of thought and unease, especially when applied to living forms. Amongst philosophers of science, Aristotle's notion of final cause is directly linked to the issues of the nature of biological explanation and that of teleology.

The difficulties of one of the most common forms of causal explanation in biology were nicely summarized by Hull (1974):

> Both physicists and biologists use ordinary causal language in describing and explaining natural phenomena. Just as a physicist might say that heating a gas causes it to expand, a biologist might say that heating a mammal causes it to sweat. But a biologist might also say that a mammal sweats when heated *in order* to keep its temperature constant, while no physicist would say that a gas expands when heated in order to keep its temperature constant—even though that is exactly what happens …' (p. 102—italics added).

Goal-directedness, or function, is the heart of the problem, especially the implied intentional goal-directedness.

As a part of Aristotle's cosmic philosophy, the four causes applied to all objects, whether animate or not, and in the case of natural objects, though not when considering human artefacts, the efficient and formal causes became one with the material cause, whilst final cause was considered applicable in the case of every object in the world. The universality of material and final causes meant that for Aristotle and his followers it would not have been outrageous to consider a gas as acting in accordance with a goal or final state—behaving in a manner in order to achieve a particular end state—any more than it would be wrong-headed to accord end states to living creatures: sunflowers partially rotate their flower heads across the day 'in order' to maximize exposure to the sun, or carnivores have enlarged incisor teeth 'in order' the better to disable prey. The problem with the notion of final cause, of course, is that it implies prescience of future events. The predator 'knows' that it will need slashing teeth to disable and dismember prey, just as the sunflower must 'know' that it will need to maximize its access to sunlight. This is the problem of teleological thought, which refers 'to all statements couched in terms of goals, purposes, and functions' (Hull 1974, p. 103). However, prescience apart, who exactly has that knowledge? Some animals may have purposes and knowledge, of course, but what about plants? Unsurprisingly, Aristotelian finalism was naturally acceptable to Christian thinking, because it is entirely commensurate with the idea of an omniscient Creator who does indeed know about future events and who thus created all the creatures of the world in the light of that prescient knowledge. Well, whether Aristotelian or Christian in form, finalism implies *a priori* cause and effect, where the effects appear before their causes. Renaissance science, however, rejected such causal notions (Grene 1972) and insisted that all causation be understood as *a posteriori*. Teleological thought thus commits three errors: it implies knowledge of the future, places the effects temporally in front of their causes, and attributes appropriate end-directed actions and forms to all living things. For these reasons, teleology is a thoroughly discredited way for a scientist to think (Beckner 1957; Goudge 1961; Nagel 1979)— or is it?

One of the difficulties in making a judgement either way is that at least for one species of animal, namely ourselves, end-directed action cannot be denied. With this in mind, philosophers such as Beckner (1969) have offered classifications of different kinds of teleology: intention-ascription (John intends to learn philosophy by reading many appropriate texts); goal-ascription (the goal of the honey bee is to find and harvest food sources to take back to the hive); and functional ascription (the function of the heart is to pump blood). Regarding Beckner's intention-ascription, except for the likes of eliminative materialists, teleology in the form of human intentions is denied by nobody. As to goal-ascription, the issue of goal states in non-human animals has been an area of discussion and contention for well over a century, receiving considerable support with the timely death of behaviourism and the rise of animal cognitivism. It is now, for example, commonplace to ascribe goals, such as attacking members of a neighbouring troop, to individual chimpanzees. Well, if chimpanzees have goals, why not squirrels or crocodiles? What of invertebrates, plants or single-celled organisms? These are not trivial questions, because they confront again the problems raised by the original critics of teleological thought who considered it unacceptable and unprovable to ascribe such properties to all living creatures. To many observers and commentators, it seems plausible to ascribe goal, and even other intentional states, to some great apes. Where, then, lies the line between creatures who do have such states and those that do not?

This question aside, most philosophy of biology textbook treatments of teleology (Hull 1974; Ruse 1973, 1988; Sober 1993) consider what Beckner called functional ascription to be the real centre of the problem of teleology. Asserting that the function of the heart is to pump blood may now seem obvious and uncontroversial. However, the heart has many properties, including its special muscular structure, its overall form, its position within the body and the noises that it makes. It is easy enough to argue, or even demonstrate, that these are properties secondary to its function, but the suspicion remains that if physics can do without functional explanations, then so too should biology.

Several lines of argument, however, converge to save the idea that structures in living forms should indeed have functions ascribed to them. One of these is that function is what makes biology different from physics, and hence is no trivial matter, much less an error of thought: 'To surrender functional individuation is to surrender biology altogether in favour of organic chemistry' (Rosenberg 2001, p. 742). A related argument is that Darwin turned functions into science. The notion of function becomes intelligible, as Sober (1993) argues, when teleology was naturalized by the theory of evolution through natural selection. Darwin bound together the ideas of function and adaptation and, despite the misgivings noted in Chapter 4 of this book about the adequacy of both the concept and empirical measurement of adaptations within conventional evolutionary biology, provided an explanation for adaptations. The concept of adaptation linked to fitness by way of natural selection is not an optional extra for biologists of any sort: 'The study of adaptation is not an optional preoccupation with fascinating fragments of natural history; it is the core of biological study. The organism is not just a system some features of which may or may not be adaptive; the living system is all adaptation insofar as it is organized' (Pittendrigh 1958, p. 395). Whatever may be the logical and practical difficulties attaching to functions (Wright 1973), their incorporation into evolutionary theory by Darwin simply banished the problem of teleology as a form of finalism. What appears to be *a priori* causation was turned into wholly acceptable *a posteriori* causation in the form of a cumulative history of selection events in the past being the cause of adaptive features in the present.

This is the key to the argument that turns teleological language into acceptable scientific explanation. Gould (1986) stated it forcefully thus: 'Darwin was, above all, a *historical methodologist*. His theory taught us the importance of history, expressed in doing as the triumph of homology over other causes of order. History is science of a different kind— pursued when done well, with all the power and rigour ascribed to more traditional styles of science. Darwin taught us that history matters and established the methodology for an entire second style of science' (p. 60—italics in the original). Gould was largely, but not wholly, correct. Part of Darwin's genius was to understand that change in time is what characterizes most of the universe. His theory of evolution provided the process by which such change in living forms can be understood, and it served as a pioneer to twentieth century scientific explanation which, with the exception of the deepest laws of quantum mechanics and relativity theory, came to understand that even entities such as the chemical elements or the galaxies have not always had the form that they do now.

Historical narrative couched within the concept of homology (similarity of structure in different species caused by descent from a common ancestor) was powerfully assisted as an explanation of adaptation and function by the developments during the 1930s and 1940s of goal-directed mechanical devices such as rockets and torpedoes whose ability to guide themselves towards a specific end-state or goal were seen as non-living and wholly un-Aristotelian teleological systems whose effectiveness formed the basis for non-finalistic models of biological adaptation and function (Rosenblueth *et al.* 1943; Sommerhoff 1950; Nagel 1979). Indeed, so effective was this form of analysis that Sommerhoff's classic analysis of adaptations received scant observance from biologists, yet a great deal of attention from the cybernetics and artificial intelligence communities. As Nagel noted: 'Goal-directed processes in living systems are patently programmed, containing "instructions" for the development (among other things) of "feed-back" subsystems; and the origins of the programs are left to be explained by evolutionary theory' (Nagel 1979, p. 288).

How, though, can history have general laws? And if biology is so saturated with historical explanation, can biology ever be said to have general laws in the way that the physical sciences have general laws? These questions have been much pursued in the philosophy of biology literature (see Goudge 1961; Smart 1968; Ruse 1973; Sober 1993 for contrasting views). It is not the purpose of this chapter exhaustively to summarize the arguments and counter-arguments. Suffice it to say that no scientist, whatever discipline within biology they are a part of, would accept that general laws lie outside of their particular science. To do that would be to relegate their role in scholarship to that of mere describers, not explainers. The specific line of argument that will be followed here relates to the ascription of teleological function within an evolutionary framework as a form of explanation, and not just a description.

The covering law model of explanation in science is a deductive argument amongst whose premises is a universal law (Dray 1957). Description alone does not constitute a science. Thus describing, no matter how exhaustively and accurately, the temperatures at which different metals melt, does not constitute a scientific explanation of why what is being described occurs. 'Scientific explanation, prediction, and postdiction all have the same logical character: they show that the fact under consideration can be inferred from certain other facts by means of specified general laws' (Hempel 1965, p. 174). Such a deductive–nomological explanation can, and must, be applicable to biology as history, but not history merely as narrative (what Hempel described as the 'story of evolution'), but as narrative bound to the process of evolution by natural selection (what Hempel labelled 'the underlying mechanisms'). 'All we need to do is recognize that the only laws biology—in all its compartments from the molecular onward—has or needs are the laws of natural selection (Rosenberg 2001, p. 735). Furthermore, '... the principles of the theory of natural selection are nomological generalizations of the sort we are familiar with in physical science' (Rosenberg 2001, p. 752). Of this Rosenberg is rightly convinced: 'Thus evolutionary theory describes a mechanism—blind variation and natural selection—that can operate everywhere and always throughout the universe. Evolution obtains whenever tokens of matter have become complex enough to foster their own replication and variation so that selection for effects can take hold' (Rosenberg 2001, p. 755).

Thus the reason that Gould was only partly correct in his avowal that Darwin's significance lay in his realization that biology is history, is that it appears to play down the importance of the nomological status of Darwin's principles of variation, selection and heritability. That is what makes biological explanation scientific in the same sense that explanation in chemistry and physics is scientific. There is, however, a complicating factor. However law-like Darwin's principles might be, the process of natural selection acting under differing circumstances, even only slightly different circumstances, results in differing structures subserving the same functions. As Rosenberg so nicely puts it, in biology 'conditions are never constant and *ceteris* are never *paribus*' (Rosenberg 2001, p. 739). For this reason, the stories of evolution equal the number of different species and, while many will share adaptations whose functions are determined by identical or closely similar mechanisms, the complexity of the history of life is such that frequently adaptations with similar functions have evolved which are based on different structures and mechanisms. Flight, vision and the transport of oxygen are examples of functions subserved by different structures. There is no reason why the ability to gain and act on knowledge of the world should be any different from other adaptive functions. Cognition, across different species, and even in the same species, is likely to be subserved by different mechanisms, and different forms of innate representational knowledge.

The notion of necessary knowledge is inherent within a teleological analysis of learning and cognition. In whatever manner neural networks that could track changes in the environment and conserve cause–effect relationships first arose in multicellular animals, probably several hundred million years ago, their properties must have been selected for because of that function of tracking environmental change which occurs faster than can be detected by the main evolutionary programme and hence which adds to the fitness of each individual learner. However, it is extremely unlikely that the identical neural network architectures that allowed the conservation of information in the first non-chordate learners have been preserved unchanged over the hundreds of millions of years that have since elapsed. The shifts in the kinds of environmental events to be tracked will have been unceasing as the world changed and as did the life history strategies of organisms in response to those changes. The general properties that an organism has, including any possible cognitive properties, and the nature of the world in which it lives, determines the evolutionary fitness of that organism. However, fitness is not determined by precisely what properties the organism has. The fitness of a hare and a tortoise might be the same, whereas the properties possessed by each are different from those of the other. This asymmetry in the relationship between the properties of the organism in its specific environment and the fitness of an organism in that environment is called supervenience (Rosenberg 1978). 'Natural selection makes for the supervenience of the functional on the physical' (Rosenberg 2001). Put simply, identical functions and fitness can be attained by different physical mechanisms. In the light of the long history of the evolution of cognition and the different circumstances within which it has evolved, the likelihood that cognition has not evolved functional embodiment in different physical mechanisms is vanishingly small.

In short, any general process approach to learning and cognition, such as some single form of associationism that can explain all forms of learning in all organisms that do learn, is biologically unlikely. The complexity of evolution occurring over deep geological time implies, if not demands, the expectation that supervenience will result in different mechanisms of learning, and different forms of necessary knowledge to make that learning effective.

There is another general aspect of explanation of causation, especially in the social sciences, that a teleological approach to learning and cognition addresses. This is the matter of reductionism and reductionist explanation, an aspect of causal understanding that has for long been a source of anxiety, if not resentment, amongst social scientists when biology has intruded into their domain. There are a number of different approaches to reductionism—approaches in the sense of a view as to when reductionist explanation is desirable, if not essential; and there are a number of different forms of reductionism, i.e. what procedures are to be followed in the event that reduction is deemed desirable (Schaffner 1967; Ruse 1973; Hull 1974). There is also a great deal of difference amongst philosophers of biology as to the importance of reductionism in scientific explanation. Cohen *et al.* (1974) provides striking examples of such differences within a single symposium proceedings; Schaffner (1974) referred to the 'peripherality' of reductionism with regard specifically to molecular biology; whilst Sober's (1993) provision of less than a page to the issues suggests that the traumas of the molecular biology revolution of the 1950s and 1960s, when much weight was given to the matter of whether Mendelian genetics could be reduced to molecular structures and mechanisms, and the controversy raised by the sociobiology writings of the 1970s, had been significant forces behind arguments that are now seem much less pressing.

In general, 'reductionism is pursued because of a belief that some other realm is more fundamental—that is, it can provide deeper understanding, can correlate disparate insights, and so forth—than the one that has been studied. It is necessarily a fundamentalist enterprise at least in this mild sense' (Sarkar 1998, p. 46). It is precisely for this reason that questions were raised about the relationship between

Mendelian and molecular genetics, and around which arguments raged regarding the selfish gene notions of the likes of G.C. Williams and Hamilton, and their application to human social behaviour by E.O. Wilson, amongst others. However, it was the emerging sciences of renaissance Europe and the subsequent age of enlightenment that drove from science a different form of fundamentalism. Ontological reductionism, sometimes referred to as materialism or physicalism, is now the universal view of all sciences, which consider matter and its associated phenomena, including that which lives and thinks, as entirely physical and subject to the laws of chemistry and physics. There is no *elan vital*, no life force other than that which is bound up in chemistry and physics. The same arguments later were applied to the human mind which is to be explained in terms of the functioning, by way of explicable chemical and physical forces, of billions of neurons and their connectivity.

Some forms of reductionism are simply inappropriate to certain, if not all, areas of science. What Hull (1974) calls epistemological reductionism, which is the elimination from scientific theory of any reference to theoretical entities, and which derives from the empiricist assertion that all knowledge originates in sensory experience, is rightly dismissed by Hull as not having much to do with biology, and clearly has no application to psychology and cognitive science unless we were to return to the explanatory emptiness of behaviourism.

Much more cogent forms of reductive explanation are theory reduction and explanatory reduction. Theory reduction has occurred as both casual and informal ways of thinking in the past, as well as in more deliberate and formal exercises. The former would encompass examples such as

Lavoisier's theory of oxidation replacing the notion of phlogiston; rather more formal was the subsuming of Keppler's laws of planetary motion as a special case of Newtonian mechanics and the laws of gravitation; and even more formal yet was the relating of thermodynamics to statistical mechanics as explanations of, for example, how gases behave at different temperatures. Philosophers argue for the importance of specific procedures by which formal theory reduction must occur but, since they involve formal theory structure, which is barely present in psychology, including cognition in almost any of its aspects, theory reduction is not at present part of the explanatory forms, and arguments, available to cognitive science.

Explanatory reduction is another matter. One of the contributors to the 1974 symposium asked:

> ... what is the point of defending the formal model of reduction if it doesn't actually happen, or if the defence has the consequence that if reductions occur, they are trivial and uninformative, or merely incidental consequences of the purposeful activity of the scientist *qua* scientist in devising explanations? ... At least in biology, most scientists see their work as explaining types of phenomena by discovering mechanisms, rather than explaining theories by deriving them from or reducing them to other theories, and *this* is seen by them as reduction, or as integrally tied to it (Wimsatt 1974, p. 477).

What Wimsatt was arguing was that in their search for mechanisms whose functioning embody fundamental processes such as evolution itself, epigenesis, or cognition, reductionism is the natural province of all biologists—it is what they do as an entirely normal part of their task. The formalities of theory reduction by philosophers are an irrelevance, and explanatory reduction in terms of mechanism is all that matters. This is not, however, always the case, even when it is a biologist who is doing the explaining. G.C. Williams, for example, noting that 'reductionism is the seeking of explanations for complex systems entirely in what is known of their component parts and processes' went on to assert 'that reductionism is more likely to provide valid answers to questions about evolution, especially about adaptation, than recently suggested alternatives that evoke emergent properties at various levels of complexity. The currently most important reductionist device is to regard gene frequency change as the essence of evolution' (Williams 1985, p. 1).

If there is any potency to this claim, this can only, however, be an argument for the adequacy of genetic explanations of some limited forms of adaptation, albeit very fundamental ones such as limb form and basic metabolic properties. It does not apply to adaptations that potentially, and in most cases actually do, alter during the lifespan of an animal, often continuously as in the case of cognition, and always in response to change in the world. Flexible development and learning enveloped within the complexity of niche construction result in adaptations in which gene frequency is so remote and devoid of immediate explanatory mechanism as to make them trivial.

In that same 1974 paper, Wimsatt noted the importance of regarding levels of organization as a primary determinant of the kind of causal explanation required in biology: '... the majority of readily definable entities will be found in the ... neighbourhood of levels of organization, and (that) the simplest and most powerful theories will be about entities at these levels (Wimsatt 1974, p. 484). In short, in complex systems, including hierarchical ones, that are defined by structural and/or control levels, explanation has to be at a level congruent with that structuring and control. Referring all explanation to the most fundamental level, whatever that is, will not have adequate, or even plausible, explanatory force in the way that Williams asserts. This is especially the case with learning, which, if the arguments presented earlier in this book and in other places are correct, has evolved precisely because the main (or fundamental level) evolutionary process cannot provide behavioural adaptations to rapid forms of environmental change. In the case of learning, that fundamental level, evolution itself together with its changes in gene frequencies, concedes a great deal of functional autonomy to cognitive processes, and causal explanations have to be aimed primarily at the neural/cognitive level—not completely, however. The capacity for learning together with the constraints, including the necessary knowledge of this book, that guide it to learn efficiently about specific forms of change, must have causes within genetic structures. However, of course, the specific outcome of learning will have causes concentrated in neural network mechanisms.

If causal explanation of cognition cannot adequately be reduced to genetics and changes in gene frequencies alone, the argument against the possibility of reductionist accounts applies even more strongly to culture and the products of culture. Culture in all its forms is defined by shared knowledge. Proper causal understanding of culture needs not just the neural network mechanism of the individual learner, but the interaction of the neural networks of more than a single learner. There is no question but that culture is the outcome of a number of evolved cognitive mechanisms, whose evolution probably was independently driven by separate selection forces (Plotkin 2002a). However, as argued in the previous chapter, culture and its products requires the minimal participation of the cognitive forces of at least two individuals. That makes a genetic, and perhaps even a neuroscience, causal explanation so remote as to be wholly unrealistic if not unrealisable. Culture is a natural phenomenon that absolutely defies reductionist explanation.

Rationalist and empiricist epistemology

Rationalism is the epistemological stance that reason takes precedence over all other forms of acquiring knowledge (Garber 1995). In its strongest form it is an argument for reason being the only and unique way of acquiring knowledge. This stands in sharp contrast to empiricism, which asserts that knowledge begins at the sensory surfaces. This is a fundamental division and debate within classical philosophy, and modern evolutionary and cognitive science can make a positive contribution to its solution. First the bare essentials of each school of thought need to be presented.

Some of the earliest known Greek philosophy, that of the Milesians of around 600–500 BC, sought to pass beyond the flux and change of sensory experience to some postulated unchanging permanence. However, the last of the important early Ionian philosophers, Heraclitus, believed that everything is in a state of constant change. Plato described Heraclitus thus in the *Theaetetus* (one of the most important of Plato's dialogues regarding his views on knowledge): 'You cannot step twice into the same river; for fresh waters are ever flowing in upon you' (cited in Russell 1946, p. 63). The implication is that under conditions where every thing is constantly changing, if knowledge is possible at all it is but fleeting and tenuous. However, it was only with the Sophists in the fifth century BC that something like a specific theory of knowledge was developed. The most famous member of this school of thought was Protagoras, almost entirely owing to his view that 'man is the measure of all things'. This was taken to mean that what any person could know is the outcome of each individual's nature and needs; this is a relativistic epistemology that pre-dates the relativism of postmodernism by some two and a half millennia. On this account then, at best, knowledge is partial and entirely personal to each knower. For the Sophists, knowledge in the sense that Descartes meant some one and a half thousand years later and which chimes well with what is now commonly held to be knowledge, namely an experience or understanding that accords to some degree with what is in the world outside of the knower, is unattainable. Gorgias, another of the significant Sophists, said 'nothing exists, and if it did, no one could know it, and if they knew it, they could not communicate it'—as extreme a form of intellectual anarchism and scepticism as can be found anywhere in the history of thought.

Many argue that Plato was the greatest of all the Greek philosophers. However, the history of thought has no beginnings and all ideas have their precedents (Plotkin 2004). More pertinent in this regard was the view of Democritus, expressed some decades before Plato, that there are two kinds of knowledge: one comes through the senses and the other through thought and reasoning, only the latter being legitimate knowledge, since the senses are unreliable. Democritus expressed a judgement that was to echo through virtually all of two and a half thousand years of epistemology. Between Democritus and Plato there was Plato's mentor, Socrates. It is unclear as to the extent to which Plato's own writings reflect the views of his teacher. As Kenny (2004) notes, Socrates left behind him not a single written word. However, we do know from Plato's own writings that the 'invented' Socrates of the dialogues held the Sophists in contempt.

Whether echoing the ideas of his mentor or developing them further, it is clear that Plato himself differed profoundly from the archetypal relativism of the Sophists and developed a theory of knowledge closely similar to that sketched by Democritus. Real philosophers such as Kenny and Russell cannot disentangle the views of Plato from those of Socrates. For the purposes of this brief review, all of Plato's writings will be assumed to reflect his own philosophy, whatever debt he owed to his master.

Plato (427–347 BC), like so many great philosophers, wrote a very broad-based philosophy in which his theory of knowledge was not the most central feature of his thinking. Plato laid a much greater stress in his writing on metaphysics and his strongly held views about how people should live their lives, govern themselves, and the beliefs they should hold; in short, morals and politics. Nonetheless, his epistemology was consistent with these other issues. What follows is owed largely to Russell (1946), Hare (1991), Kraut (1995) and Kenny (2004).

For Plato, knowledge is the apprehension of certain specific features of the world that are unchanging, which he called ideas or forms. Exactly what the ideas or forms are is not easy to understand, Hare arguing that one needs to comprehend certain features of 'Greek idiom' contemporary to Plato in order fully to grasp just what Plato thought are the objects of knowledge—what it is we humans can know. In Plato's *Republic*, Socrates asks 'does the man who knows know something or nothing'. Socrates declares that the obvious answer is that she or he knows something, and reasons further that that 'something' has to be an entity, a thing that exists. Ideas or forms, then, are not propositions (such as the assertion that three is a prime number or that all dogs bark), but *things* existing in an eternal realm. As Hare puts it, 'it must be understood that he meant by these (i.e. ideas or forms) a kind of object independent of the mind, with which the mind could become acquainted, and not anything merely mental (i.e. existing only in the mind)' (Hare 1991, p. 37).

What is difficult to reconcile in Plato's epistemology is just what it is that can be known, on the one hand, and what is the nature of knowing, on the other. In the context of Plato's epistemology, the latter is less problematic than the former: knowledge is a kind of 'mental looking—a vision of the Eternal' (Hare 1991, p. 41). In short, it is a state of mind that is achieved by a specific route. What it is a state of mind *about* are the ideas or forms, which must be understood as entities, *things*, that exist independently of the individual moral or physical qualities or things for which they are the absolute models. Whether it is holiness or goodness, a mathematical relationship, or the difference between dogs and cats, that which is known is an eternal entity.

However, our senses do not reveal to us the ideas or forms. What our sensory experiences provide are mere examples of these eternal truths, and in forms that are not to be trusted. Plato makes clear in many of his dialogues that the senses are limited at best, corrupt at worst. Kenny points to the *Theaetetus* as one of the dialogues (the other is the *Republic* with its famous allegory of the cave) where the point is made most strongly by Socrates that knowledge cannot come to us by way of perception. After all, argues Socrates, the senses are different channels; we see with our eyes and hear with our ears, and the resulting percepts, sights and sounds, are different. We cannot hear colours or see sounds, and we *know* that sights and sounds are different. However, how, asks Socrates, do we know this? The answer is that we know this by thought. Knowledge is not perception, which is a product of the body, but of true thought (because, of course, we can have false thoughts), which is a product of the soul.

Plato's dualism, his distinction between body and soul, fits precisely with his epistemology. Knowledge, he argued, is a form of thought; specifically, it is a form of recollection of the ideas and forms that exist within us at birth. Within the context of this book, all knowledge is innate. Perhaps his most famous example is in the *Meno* where Socrates questions a young slave about problems in geometry. The slave has had no prior formal tuition in mathematics, and at the start of the dialogue claims to have no knowledge of such matters. Yet, by asking the right questions, Socrates reveals that the young slave does indeed have knowledge of matters mathematical. Socrates' questions simply provoke a remembrance of knowledge that the slave had at birth; for Plato, knowledge of all of the forms and ideas is *a priori* and hence present at birth.

Plato's was an extreme form of rationalism, and he even prescribed a specific form of training by which the knowledge of the eternal forms and ideas, knowledge that has always been within them, might be recollected by the would-be philosopher kings who would best run society: it began with showing how unreliable and corrupt sensory information is, and then continued through arithmetic, geometry, astronomy, harmonics and finally a form of reasoning he termed 'the dialectic'. The way to knowledge for Plato was thus to give up any reliance on the senses and, via training in reasoning, to discover the knowledge that has always been within us.

For some 20 years, the young Aristotle was pupil, then colleague, to Plato and it was inevitable that much of early Aristotle was suffused with Plato's influence. Kenny or Russell should be read to understand Aristotle in relation to

Plato's ideas. Aristotle worked in areas widely different from Plato, adding a great deal to Plato's work, especially in terms of formal logic and the notion of causes (see earlier in this chapter), as well as his scientific observations, particularly in biology. Epistemological issues were not central to his thinking, but in one respect he remained faithful to his mentor's teaching. He believed in 'eternal universal axioms' as the essence of knowledge, or what he would have thought of as knowledge in a scientific sense. Such universal axioms, similar to Plato's ideas and forms, could not be revealed by the senses alone but were arrived at by thought. Aristotle did, though, admit that knowledge of particulars did come through the senses and that reasoning on particulars might lead to universal axioms. In this sense, Aristotle really was the first scientist, both as observer and theorist, and he departed from the extreme rationalist position of his teacher.

Philosophy did not cease, of course, with the deaths of Plato and Aristotle. Indeed, as will be seen shortly, later Greek philosophical schools taught some very un-Platonic epistemological views. Subsequent developments by neoPlatonists of Plato's account of the innate knowledge of ideas and forms centred on the origins of such innate knowledge, an issue on which Plato was unclear. Plato had invoked what now would be called reincarnation, with knowledge coming to us from souls with previous lives but, aside from an unsatisfying infinite regress, this does not account for the very beginnings of innate knowledge. As Kenny (2004) notes, Plotinus, a Roman philosopher of the third century AD, was an important figure in the revival of Platonism and Aristotelianism, and he did not shirk from attempting to account for the origins of knowledge. These, he believed, derive from 'the One', thus invoking a divine source for knowledge. A century later, Augustine invoked the 'intelligible realities', which Kenny (2005) notes are very close to Plato's ideas, and married Plotinus with Plato within the framework of his own religion and thus Christianized Plato—we come into this world with knowledge already in our minds, knowledge that is placed there by God.

The next significant rationalist was Descartes, over a millennium later. The brief sketch that follows is drawn mainly from Russell (1946) and Kenny (2006), as well as from Descartes' own *Discourse on Methods* (1637) and *Meditations* (1641), both reprinted in a translation by Wollaston (1960). Kenny notes that scepticism enjoyed a considerable revival in sixteenth century European thought, typified in the writings of Montaigne, which were an echo of the extreme scepticism of Gorgias of some 2000 years previously. Montaigne had argued that our senses are limited, unreliable, and conflicting in the information they bring us. Reason is no more trustworthy. In combination, our senses and reason can lead only to falsehood. It was against this backdrop that Descartes set out to argue just what it is that we can know, and in doing so revived a form of rationalism not greatly different from a Christianized neoPlatonism—Descartes himself being a devout Christian.

Descartes argued that in one form the sceptics were correct. Much of conscious experience deriving from the senses might be wholly wrong. Not only are our senses unreliable and conflicting, but we might be experiencing events that do not relate to what is actually in the world outside of ourselves— we might be dreaming, or possessed by evil demons, or even deceived by a devious God. However, of one thing we can be certain: even if all his doubts are correct, he, Descartes, must exist in order to have them and in having them he is thinking. Hence the famous *Cogito*: 'Suppose, however, there were some extremely powerful and cunning deceiver filled with zeal to trick me. But there is no doubt that I exist in being deceived, and so, let him deceive me as much as he likes, he can never turn me into nothing so long as I think that I am something. Whence, after due thought and scrupulous reflection, I must conclude that the proposition, *I am, I exist* is true of necessity every time I state it or conceive it in my mind' (from the 1960 translation—italics in the original).

Descartes went on, then, to question his own doubts about a deceiving God. He concluded that God, of course, exists; and that since God is the ultimate and eternal good, God would not be a deceiver; more, God would impart certain universal truths captured within the mathematical reasoning of arithmetic and geometry. Whatever additional forms of knowledge humans can have, and remember from Chapter 1 that for Descartes it is only humans that can think and hence have knowledge, 'the *Cogito* is the rock on which Descartes' epistemology is built' (Kenny 2006, p. 120). Thus it is that Descartes revived rationalism as a theory of knowledge. What every human knows comes to her or him through thought, and never through sensory experience. God Himself is the source of such knowledge, which is implanted within every person at birth, and it is on the principle that God is good and never a deceiver that we are saved from scepticism.

As Kenny and Russell note, modern philosophers raise many serious doubts about the arguments from which Descartes reasoned for a rationalist epistemology. Why, for instance, is 'I am thinking and therefore exist' significantly different from 'I am walking and therefore exist'?—the answer to which must surely lie in Descartes' view that only humans have rationality, whereas many other animals can walk. The *cogito* only applies to humans because, Descartes believed, only humans can think. More problematic to twentieth and twenty-first century philosophers is the existence of God, though, as will be argued below, one might substitute certain laws of nature for God or other metaphysical agencies and still arrive at some form of 'new rationalism'. In any event, Descartes' was not a lone voice.

Not long after his death, Spinoza and Leibniz both published philosophical works in which rationalism figures large. In his early work, Spinoza described four 'levels' of knowledge, the first two of which are rooted in sensation and perception, and the third and fourth of which derive from different forms of reasoning—in later writings he confined himself to three levels. Spinoza's third level of knowledge is apprehension of the 'essence' of one thing achieved by knowledge of the essence of another. For example, we come to know that the sun is very large by knowing something about the size of a football. The fourth level of knowledge concerns knowledge of things by their own essences, and derives largely from Euclidean geometry. Thus, while Spinoza recognized that knowledge from the senses might be 'auxiliary aids to genuine knowledge' (Garber 1995, p. 674), like others before him he held that the senses are imperfect and that knowledge through them alone is impossible. Leibniz's epistemology was an explicit criticism of Locke's empiricist theory of knowledge. He expounded the theory that no features of the thinking mind derive from the senses and that all are innate in the strictest sense of that word: they are all present at birth—a view that to a degree chimes well with what has passed in the previous chapters of this book. It is therefore unsurprising that in his account of Leibniz, Kenny comes to a view of Leibniz's theory of knowledge that is remarkably close to that adopted in this book:

> These ideas, then, are innate in the fullest sense. This does not mean that a newborn child already thinks of them; but it has

more than a mere ability to learn them: it has a predisposition to grasp them. If we want to think of the mind as being initially like an unpainted canvas, we can do so; but it is a canvas already pencil-marked for painting by numbers (Kenny 2006, p. 143).

Subsequent developments in epistemology, until modern times, were dominated by the empiricists and by Kant, more of whom shortly. It should, however, be added though that philosophers of the last 100 years have tended towards issues that are only indirectly related to the classical rationalist–empiricist distinction, a glance at contemporary philosophical anthologies, such as those in Greco and Sosa (1999), will show many familiar features of the old divisions. A sample of modern texts devoted solely to epistemology shows wide variation in the extent to which the classical rationalists are presented: Plato and Descartes are barely mentioned in Chisholm (1989), whereas they are liberally represented in Williams (2001) and Norris (2005), with Dancy (1985) somewhere in between. These are some of the texts readers may want to sample to see what philosophers are writing about the theory of knowledge in the last 20 years. It is hardly surprising that the subject has moved on, with much less emphasis being now given to the sources of knowledge, and much more to the issues surrounding notions such as coherence, truth conditions, pragmatics and knowledge as justified belief, though everyone acknowledges that the latter is an issue first raised by Plato in the *Theaetetus.* What is clear is that modern epistemology, be it that of Russell or Ayer, Rorty or Putnam, gives much more credence (and space) to knowledge deriving from the senses (e.g. Feyerabend 1968) and it is of these that a brief account must be made.

Rationalism did not rule unchallenged in ancient Greek philosophy. Within a century of the death of Plato, epistemology had become much more central to philosophers than it had been for the master, and with a view quite the opposite to that of Plato. Epicurus, and the Stoics who followed him, considered the senses to be entirely reliable and the foundations of all knowledge; whatever concepts and memories contribute to our knowledge of the world, they all begin with sensory knowledge. Medieval philosophers such as Bonaventure and Duns Scotus inclined towards an empiricist stance (Kenny 2005), with the exception of the understanding of God's existence, which was argued to be innate. God and medieval philosophers aside, an epistemology very similar to that of the Stoics was the view advanced over one and a half thousand years later by Hobbes, whom Kenny (2006) considers to be the founder of British empiricism. In his *Leviathan*, published 1 year after the death of Descartes, Hobbes wrote that 'there is no conception in a man's mind, which hath not, at first, totally, or by parts, been begotten upon the organs of sense'. Hobbes had been a very early critic of Descartes—indeed Kenny notes that Descartes' *Discourse* was the first refereed text in the history of scholarship, and Hobbes was one of those referees—and the differences between them marked the beginnings of the enduring differences between English-speaking empiricists with their focus upon the senses, and continental philosophers who argued for reason as the basis of knowledge.

Hobbes' successor, like Plato, was born into and lived through turbulent times—in the case of John Locke, of the English civil war. Locke was a contemporary of Spinoza and Leibniz, but unlike them was no metaphysician with a monumental scheme of thought that purported to explain the universe. Newton and Boyle, both scientists for whom knowledge begins with observation, were his friends; a materialist and pragmatist, 'Locke wanted to get away from the imagination, from the vague glamour of medieval things, from unthinking adherence to tradition, from enthusiasm, mysticism, and *gloire*; away from all private, visionary insights and down to the publicly verifiable, measurable, plain, demonstrable facts' (Cranston 1961, pp. 21–22). His epistemology was entirely in line with this general approach.

Locke rejected any scepticism about the reliability of our senses on two grounds according to Dunn (1984). The one, ironically since they were epistemologically polar opposites, is a partial echo of Descartes that God would not have endowed humans with senses that systematically deceive them. The other was an argument that the knowledge that comes to us through our senses retains it veracity through time, and the knowledge we get from different senses support one another. Thus we can trust our senses, a trust that is essential to practical living. Locke rejected utterly any notion of innate ideas. He believed that we are misled into the idea of innate knowledge by simple lack of memory of the early sensory experiences that lead to conceptions such as sameness or difference. He famously expressed this in his *Essay on Human Understanding* thus:

> Let us then suppose the mind to be, as we say, white paper, void of all characters, without any ideas: how comes it to be furnished? Whence comes it by that vast store, which the busy and boundless fancy of man has painted on it with an almost endless variety? Whence has it all the materials of reason and knowledge? To this I answer in one word, from experience: in that all our knowledge is founded, and from that it ultimately derives itself (from Nidditch 1975, p. 48).

It should be noted that despite Locke's assertion that we come into the world as blank slates, Kenny (2006) argues that the differences between him and Descartes are not as great as they may first seem. Both had considered the possibility of thought in the unborn infant, and both had believed it possible. Kenny also asks whether both philosophers had believed in an inborn (i.e. innate) general capacity for understanding which is specific to humans? We know from Chapter 1 of this book that Descartes' response to the question was a clear affirmative. So too was it for Locke who at the very opening of the *Essay* asserts that it is understanding that sets man apart from other animals. In modern parlance, if human cognition is in part species-specific, then that portion of human cognition must be innate in the sense of being part-genetically determined, and probably a product of evolutionary forces (see Chapter 1). Locke was an empiricist in denying the existence of specific innate knowledge in the individual but, if he had understood then what cognitive scientists and evolutionists understand now, his arguments for the supremacy of the senses over reason may not have been so strongly stated, being tempered by the apprehension of knowledge at the level of the species.

Locke's most important successor was David Hume, whose empiricist credentials were established in his first book, the *Treatise on Human Nature*, the essence of which was revised and shortened into his *Inquiry into Human Understanding* because, as Hume himself remarked, the first work 'fell dead-born from the press'. The second work certainly did not, and was the stimulus that Kant claimed had aroused him from his 'dogmatic slumbers', and so the *Inquiry* is of 2-fold importance. Hume was as explicit an empiricist as there ever was, entirely rejecting the notion of innate knowledge and asserting that there is 'no idea without an antecedent impression'. For Hume, there 'is nothing in our intellect which has not entered it through our senses.' He proposed a kind of layered classification of knowledge, which begins with impressions, the strongest and most vivid form of knowledge that stem directly from the sensory surfaces. The second layer of knowledge is 'ideas', mental images that derive from impressions but are less forceful, simple ideas being mere copies of impressions, with complex ideas being combinations of impressions or simple ideas. The third layer, based on ideas and memory, are ideas of imagination. The latter are the least intense or vivid but, unlike either impressions or ideas, are freed from the time and space of the original impressions.

Both Russell (1946) and Kenny (2006) are somewhat dismissive of what they see as a rather simplistic structuring of knowledge: 'Hume's treatment of memory and imagination tries to pack a great variety of mental events, capacities, activities, and errors into a single empiricist straitjacket' (Kenny 2006, p. 152), and Kenny is also unduly critical of another of Hume's achievements, which was his advocacy of a form of Newtonian mental mechanics as a new form of a science of knowledge. Hume laid great emphasis on the association of ideas as the means to provide a scientific understanding of reasoning specifically, and thought more widely. Kenny considers this aspect of Hume's thought a 'pitiable ... delusion' (p. 154), but one whose origins lie in the 'impoverished philosophy of mind' that he inherited from his forebears with 'gaps and incoherences in the empiricist tradition' (p. 154). However, Kenny makes no reference to the modern science of mind. The founding of psychology as a science led rapidly to the notion of some form of associationism based entirely on input from the senses as the key to understanding learning and memory, including most distressingly the sad attempts to understand the learning of language within that impoverished framework—leading one again to the conclusion that the learning theorists in psychology of the twentieth century did not include the most gifted minds in science. Nonetheless, associationism does have an important place in the history of psychology, and however naïve and incomplete Hume's ideas on the association of ideas may seem to some, given the time and context within which he formulated the notion, it was a significant and important achievement anticipating psychology by almost 200 years.

Whilst not directly relevant to this brief survey, Hume's notion of the association of ideas led him to consider our understanding of cause–effect relationships within this same framework, and hence to generate a new form of scepticism. In a nutshell, Hume considered the notion of cause and effect as being merely a habit of thought and denied that there is any reason to assume that it corresponds to the structuring of the real world. This, in turn, connected to what has since come to be known as the problem of induction and whether it is reasonable to proceed upon the principle that 'instances of which we have had no experience must resemble those of which we have had experience, and that the course of nature continues always uniformly the same'. Hume thought not. This was the startling idea that awoke Kant. As Ayer put it, 'the propositions that "every event has a cause" and that "the course of nature continues always uniformly the same" were regarded by Hume in the light of natural beliefs. They cannot be proved, but nature is so constituted that we cannot avoid accepting them' (Ayer 1980). Thus did Hume move from an empiricist–scientific approach to knowledge to a scepticism that questioned whether we could ever have certain knowledge.

One final point needs to be made about Hume. He clearly held, at least at a certain stage in his unfolding work, that a real understanding of knowledge rests upon a science of mind, and that how the mind works is set by 'human nature' which is already present at birth. In other words, what now would be termed the processes and mechanisms of cognition are innate. So too are the sensory surfaces. He went even further than that in the *Enquiry*: 'if by innate be meant, contemporary to our birth, the dispute seems to be frivolous; nor is it worth while to enquire at what time thinking begins.' As Fodor (1998) emphasizes, Hume's objection was not to the conception of the mechanisms of association as being innate, but to the impressions and ideas that become associated.

Russell argued that in order to understand Kant, one needs to see the failure of the empiricism of Hume. Because he had cast doubt on the notion of cause, Hume could not really argue for how simple ideas relate to their antecedent impressions and hence could provide no workable definition of what an idea is.

> Obviously, on his view, an 'impression' would have to be defined by some intrinsic character distinguishing it from an 'idea', since it could not be defined causally. He could not therefore argue that impressions give knowledge of things external to ourselves, as had been done by Locke, and, in a modified form, by Berkeley. He should, therefore, have believed himself shut up in a solipsistic world, and ignorant of everything except his own mental states (Russell 1946, p. 676).

Russell's argument is correct and shows the empiricist epistemology of Hume as a failure. Forty years later, Kant's *Critique of Pure Reason* presented a different position. Whilst early in his philosophical life Kant was a follower of

Leibniz, in his later writings he was neither an empiricist in the British tradition nor a rationalist—at least not in the manner of Descartes. No one was more galvanized than Immanuel Kant by Hume's scepticism and the extent to which his analysis of causation and the problem of induction left epistemology at large in something of a hiatus. The *Critique of Pure Reason* provided a wholly different approach to a theory of knowledge, based upon two fundamental distinctions which Kant drew. One of these could not be more pertinent to the necessary knowledge of this book and, whilst the other is much less relevant, Kant's argument cannot be presented unless both are sketched out.

One distinction is indeed epistemological and concerns knowledge that derives from experience, what he termed *a posteriori* knowledge, and knowledge independent of experience, *a priori* knowledge. The other distinction is between analytic and synthetic propositions. The former are *a priori*. They are propositions that are self-contained and non-contradictory. In contrast, a synthetic proposition cannot be arrived at by reasoning alone, some degree of experience being necessary. However, and this is what is at the heart of Kant's epistemology, whilst all analytical propositions are *a priori*, not all *a priori* propositions are analytic. For Kant there is no contradiction in the idea of a synthetic *a priori* proposition. Mathematical knowledge is part *a priori*, involving truths that are necessary and universal. Yet many mathematical propositions are synthetic as well, with an absolute experiential link to the analytical propositions. The example Kant gave was of the quality of 'straightness' of a line, experience showing that a straight line is the shortest distance between two points, but 'my concept of straightness contains no notion of size'. The latter is a synthetic proposition based on experience.

'How such synthetic *a priori* judgements are possible is the principal problem for philosophy' (Kenny 2006, p. 158). The answer Kant delivered was that human knowledge is an inextricable mix of sensory information and an understanding of those sensations. As Kenny puts it, 'our senses determine the content of our experience; our understanding determines its structure' (p. 158) In Kant's words, 'the understanding is aware of nothing, the senses can think nothing. Only through their union can knowledge arise'.

For knowledge to emerge from sensation requires a marriage of the sensory input to understanding by way of certain *a priori* intuitions and categories. Thus the world impinges upon the senses, the effects of which are ordered by our mental apparatus in terms of space and time (the intuitions) as well as 12 categories of *a priori* structuring with regard to quantity, quality, modality and relationships, the last of these including the apprehension of cause–effect relationships, the existence of which understanding Hume had caused so much doubt.

Kant had no doubts as to the existence of entities in the world, the noumena or things-in-themselves, that excite the senses. However, his analysis of the kinds of knowledge we have of those entities made of him the 'progenitor of the view, later expressed in many different ways, that the methodological concepts and principles of enquiry are not reflections of a "logos", resident in the nature of things, but rather procedural ideas and rules that are adopted "pragmatically" for the purpose of controlling the world in which we live' (Aiken 1958, p. 34). Kenny (2006) phrases the same issue thus: 'If so much of what we perceive is the creation of our own mind, can we have any genuine knowledge at all of the real, extra-mental world?' (p. 160) There are two extensions to these criticisms. The first concerns the relationships between the things-in-themselves and our immediate knowledge of them. For Kant, the *a prioris* by which we make sense of our senses are categories and intuitions that do not necessarily represent the ordering of the world as it actually is. They constitute an ideal representation, not necessarily a real one. Indeed, as Russell points out, they are even more limited than Kant makes out: 'Kant holds that the mind orders the raw material of sensation, but never thinks it necessary to say why it orders it as it does and not otherwise' (Russell 1946, p. 687). Thus the categories and intuitions act as filters or processes that bring us to a form of knowledge; but in standing between our mental apparatus by which we come to have knowledge and the noumena, they prevent us from ever having true knowledge of what is really out there in the world.

The second response concerns not the entities of which we have immediate experience, but of the wider world beyond this. If we attempt to extend the application of the *a prioris* such as cause or substance to the phenomenal universe as a whole, whatever these may be and including the universe itself, we are led into imponderable paradoxes the resolution of which are beyond the powers of human understanding. 'Better, thinks Kant, to give up the whole wretched game of speculative metaphysics, lest the very categories themselves fall into disrepute and the human understanding become frozen in the grip of scepticism' (Aiken 1956, p. 36).

A gentle judgement of Kant's epistemology is simply that the inner world of the mind is better known than the outer world of the noumena; that the outer world is something that we can only infer from inner experience. Kenny suggests a harsher judgement: Berkeley, Locke's successor to the empiricist tradition, had preached a physical immaterialism; 'Kant, however, can distinguish his position from that of Berkeley only by claiming that there exists a noumenon, a thing-in-itself underlying the appearances, to which we have no access either by sense or by intellect, and which cannot be described under pain of uttering nonsense. He is emphatic that it is false to say that there is nothing other than appearance, but to many of his readers it has seemed that a nothing would do just as well as a something about which nothing can be said' (Kenny 2006, pp. 162–163). Kant's epistemology, and the criticisms of it, show just how difficult it is to develop a theory of knowledge on purely analytical grounds without recourse to science. However, it was only in the nineteenth century that a science of knowledge became possible.

How, then, do the views of constrained cognition given us by modern cognitive science, and the specific notion of this book of necessary knowledge albeit in the weaker form expressed at the start of this chapter, fit with the empiricist/rationalist divide. Clearly, any conception of, and evidence for, constrained cognition, the sources of which are innate in the sense of Chapter 1, is entirely contrary to the empiricist stance. Whether attentional or due to constrained computational mechanisms, any innate biases in cognition mean that humans, and probably many other species as well, especially those where the evidence is most strong, as in songbirds, do not come into this world as 'white paper, void of all characters, without any ideas'. Kenny's comments cited earlier with regard to Leibniz's notion that some ideas are 'innate in the fullest sense', that every child has a 'predisposition to grasp them' and that the mind of a child at birth is like 'a canvas already pencil-marked for painting' (Kenny 2006, p. 143) are entirely congruent with what is now known about cognitive development. Furthermore, if the argument presented at several points throughout this book that for cognition to be effective it *must* be constrained if it is to serve the purpose for which it evolved, then the *tabula rasa* position of the empiricists is not just factually wrong but makes no biological sense at all.

On the other hand, whilst the stance taken on necessary knowledge is akin to some generalized form of rationalism, it does not accord with the specific forms that Plato or Descartes wrote of, in large part because of their metaphysical assumptions about what is in the world to be known in the case of Plato and the role of God for Descartes. Furthermore, the innate representational knowledge reviewed in Chapter 4 takes many and diverse forms when compared with classical rationalist epistemology. Some of it, such as the sensitivity to and facility for number and an intuitive knowledge of physics, would indeed be familiar not only to Plato and Descartes, but to all rationalists of all times. Others, such as the extraordinary facility displayed by all infants apart from those suffering pathology of some sort, to acquire their native language in all its stunning complexity, would not have discomfited some rationalists like Descartes. However, innate knowledge of the structure of the human face or the attribution of intentional mental states would have been foreign to almost all classical rationalists.

In one curious respect, the notion of innate representational knowledge presented in this book is not wholly at odds with one of the, to modern minds, more outrageous aspects of Plato's rationalism. It will be recalled that for Plato the immediate source of inborn knowledge was in lives previously lived and reinstated in the mind of a newborn through some form of reincarnation. No scientist in the twenty-first century would accept this as an explanation of anything. Yet, the transmission of information in genetic form that predisposes the functioning of the brain of the newborn in specific ways, information in genetic form that has been accumulated by the processes of evolution operating on previous generations and passed down to succeeding generations, constitutes a scientifically respectable substitute for Plato's conception of knowledge as remembrance from previous lives. In the same way, Descartes' notion of the innate coming from God can be substituted by evolution as a law of nature.

The major philosopher who comes closest to the evolutionary notion of innate knowledge, of course, is Kant. It is not surprising that Lorenz was happy to be described as an evolutionary Kantian, and that Shepard was pleased to see his ideas placed within the context of Kant's epistemology. Yet whilst Kant's *a priori* intuitions and categories come closer to the conception of necessary knowledge of this book than any of the other conventional rationalist philosophers, in one respect an evolutionary account of cognition must utterly reject part of Kant's formulation. This is that the *a prioris* stand between the observer and the things-in-themselves; that the intuitions and categories are not related in any meaningful way to the noumena; that the objects and events of the world are essentially unknowable. This simply cannot be. For one thing, Kant's idealism is totally at odds with a twenty-first century world that is awash with science, and hence with a realist stance towards epistemological issues. More importantly, there is the no small matter that, in evolutionary terms, if our organs of cognition did not accord to some minimal extent with the world as it is, we would not survive. Our biological fitness would be hopelessly imperilled. The knowledge that we gain through our cognitive organs may be only partial, incomplete and to some extent inaccurate. However, it is good working knowledge—good enough for us to survive on it. That we survive at all is proof that knowledge is possible and at least partially accurate, an evolutionary epistemological argument that has been presented at much greater length elsewhere (Plotkin 1994).

Lorenz and Shepard are not alone in seeing linkage between Kant's epistemology and evolutionary epistemology: 'The Darwinian view and the Kantian view are thus to an extent complementary; one is the inverse of the other. One starts from the world of things and derives humanity from, so to speak, the outside; the other starts from human subjectivity and attempts to derive the world of things by a "transcendental deduction" from the inside, from the "unity of apperception"' (Smith 1991, pp. 45–46). In the end, whilst the rationalist position does not sit well with the contemporary view that some, perhaps most, knowledge comes to us through our sensory surfaces, the *tabula rasa* view of the empiricists is quite wrong. The rationalists come closer to a science of knowledge of the twentieth and twenty-first centuries than do the empiricists, with Kant's rationalism the closest to a modern, naturalized epistemology.

Thus it is no surprise that a philosopher of mind of the present time should have coined the phrase 'the new rationalism' to describe the form of innatist thinking described in preceding chapters, even though, as noted before, he dislikes the neoDarwinism. It is entirely fitting to end the philosophical part of this book with a quotation from him.

> So, cognition exists to theorize about experience. One uses the concepts at one's disposal to construct the theories; that's what concepts are for. But where does one get the concepts? Some, no doubt, are bootstrapped from the results of previous theorizing, but that process has to stop somewhere (more precisely, it has to *start* some-where). Hence the traditional connection between rationalism and content nativism.

Experience can't explain itself; eventually, some of the concepts that explaining experience requires have to come from outside it. Eventually, some of them have to be built in (Fodor 1998, p. 149).

Is culture unbounded?

The probability in the none-too-distant future of human cloning, genetic engineering at large, the interfacing of brains with computers, damage to the ozone layer, global warming and weapons of mass destruction are some of the reasons for alarm at the power of that specific form of human culture, science, tipping us into a state where we either destroy or transcend our biological nature (Kurzweil 2005 is a recent example of a growing literature). In terms of the structure of knowledge developed in earlier chapters of this book, especially Chapter 6, the control hierarchy which attaches culture firmly to specific forms of cognition, in turn ties individual cognition to individual developmental experience, with all three levels being nested under, and causally a consequence of, evolution. The great difference between culture and other forms of knowledge is that only culture can short-circuit genetic transmission, even within the enriched theoretical conceptions of niche construction and ecological inheritance, and transmit knowledge directly between individuals. Science is a form of culture and, since the individual scientists belonging to that culture, or subculture, do so by virtue of the cognitive processes and mechanisms that allow them to invent and share scientific knowledge, and those cognitive processes and mechanisms are firmly tied to the other levels of the knowledge hierarchy, science and its products is no different from cooking traditions, tool use or art forms.

In that restricted causal sense, culture in any form cannot be considered as a form of knowledge that can be unbounded from our biology—scientists think with their brains. Culture is a part of human biology. Such an argument is not to be confused with the utterly incorrect old sociobiological argument of the 1970s of 'culture on a biological leash' which implied that human culture is constrained in what it may conceive. Cognition is constrained, and culture is causally connected to cognition; but culture itself may conceive of anything that human imagination can contrive. Insofar as we live in a cultural world, some parts of which believe in a Creator, some parts of which believe in an afterlife, and other parts of which believe that the universe is multidimensional and built upon superstrings, the contents of culture, what is shared between cognizing individuals, is entirely unbounded. The causal connections do not determine necessary links of content.

The principal concerns, however, of those who fret at where culture may be leading us have less to do with the contents of culture, and more with its potential for destruction and dehumanization. Human reproductive cloning, especially if it includes engineering for the enhancement of specific physical attributes and cognitive skills, would certainly change the strength of the causal connections between the levels of the knowledge hierarchy. The causal connections, however, would still be in place. Only in a science fiction world of wholly artificial intelligence replacing the humans who invented the devices, would culture be truly unbounded.

The destructive potential and actual consequences of science and engineering, typified by the effects of carbon emissions on climate, is a separate case, with the bleakest scenario of the consequences of culture being death on a large scale. That, of course, is a possibility, if remote. However, any death caused by culture might be construed as showing culture to be an abiological, if not antibiological, force. The potential for destruction of life is not, however, the unique preserve of science and its application. As noted in Chapter 6, social constructions such as ethnic identity, religions and ideologies have been the direct causes of death in warfare that go back at least 3000 years. It is certainly the case that at this point in human history, social constructions have been vastly more destructive of human life than science has ever been. If, then, a finger must be pointed to the destructive, abiological nature of culture, abiological in the sense that it has severed connections with the continuity of knowledge that comes to us through human evolution and individual experience and cognition, it is to social constructions that we must look, not science.

References

Aiello, L.C. and Dunbar, R.I.M. (1993) Neocortex size, group size, and the evolution of language. *Current Anthropology*, **34**, 184–193.

Aiello, L.C. and Wheeler, P. (1995) The expensive tissue hypothesis: the brain and the digestive system in human and primate evolution. *Current Anthropology*, **36**, 199–221.

Aiken, H.D. (1956) *The Age of Ideology*. Mentor Books, New York.

Ancell, L.W. (1999) A quantitative model of the Simpson–Baldwin effect. *Journal of Theoretical Biology*, **196**, 197–209.

Armstrong, E. and Falk, D., eds (1982) *Primate Brain Evolution: Methods and Concepts*. Plenum, New York.

Arnold, H.J. and Fristrup, K. (1982) The theory of evolution by natural selection: a hierarchical expansion. *Palaeobiology*, **8**, 113–129.

Atran, S. (1998) Folk biology and the anthropology of science: cognitive universals and cultural particulars. *Behavioural and Brain Sciences*, **21**, 547–609.

Aunger, R. (2003) *The Electric Meme*. The Free Press, London.

Ayer, A.J. (1980) *Hume*. Oxford University Press, Oxford.

Baldwin, J.M. (1890) *Handbook of Psychology*. Macmillan and Co., London.

Baldwin, J.M. (1895) *Mental Development in the Child and the Race*. Macmillan and Co., London.

Baldwin, J.M. (1896) A new factor in evolution. *American Naturalist*, **30**, 441–451, 536–554.

Baldwin, J.M. (1902) *Development and Evolution*. Macmillan and Co., London.

Baldwin, J.M. (1909) *Darwin and the Humanities*. Review Publishing Co., Baltimore, MD.

Baldwin, J.M. (1930) Autobiography of James Mark Baldwin. In: Murchison, C., ed. *History of Psychology in Autobiography*. Vol. 1, pp. 1–30. Macmillan, New York.

Balinsky, B.I. (1960) *An Introduction to Embryology*. W.B. Saunders, London.

Barkow, J.W., Cosmides, L. and Tooby, J., eds (1992) *The Adapted Mind: Evolutionary Psychology and the Generation of Culture*. Oxford University Press, Oxford.

Baron-Cohen, S. (1995) *Mindblindness: an Essay on Autism and Theory of Mind*. MIT Press, Cambridge, MA.

Baron-Cohen, S. and Cross, P. (1992) Reading the eyes: evidence for the role of perception in the development of a theory of mind. *Mind and Language*, **6**, 173–186.

Bartlett, F.C. (1932) *Remembering*. Cambridge University Press, Cambridge.

Bateson, G. (1979) *Mind and Nature*. Fontana, London.

Bateson, P. (1988) The active role of behaviour in evolution. In: Ho, M-W. and Fox, S.W., eds. *Evolutionary Processes and Metaphors*. Wiley, Colchester, pp. 191–207.

Bateson, P.P.G. (1978) Early experience and sexual preferences. In: Hutchison, J.B., ed. *Biological Determinants of Sexual Behaviour*. Wiley, London, pp. 29–54.

Beach, F.A. (1950) The snark was a boojum. *American Psychologist*, **5**, 115–124.

Beckner, M. (1957) *The Biological Way of Thought*. University of California Press, Berkeley.

Beckner, M. (1969) Function and teleology. *Journal of the History of Biology*, 2, 151–164.

Bingenheimer, J.B., Brennan, R.T. and Earles, F.J. (2005) Firearm violence exposure and serious violent behaviour. *Science*, **308**, 1323–1326.

Bitterman, M.E. (1988) Vertebrate–invertebrate comparisons. In: Jerison, H.J. and Jerison, I. eds. *Intelligence and Evolutionary Biology*. NATO ASI Series Vol. 17, Springer-Verlag, Berlin, pp. 251–276.

Bitterman, M.E. (2000) Cognitive psychology: a comparative perspective. In: Heyes, C. and Huber, L., eds. *The Evolution of Cognition*. MIT Press, Cambridge MA, pp. 61–79.

Blackmore, S. (1999) *The Meme Machine*. Oxford University Press, Oxford.

Blakemore, C. and Van Sluyters, R.C. (1975) Innate and environmental factors in the development of the kitten's visual cortex. *Journal of Physiology*, **248**, 663–716.

Bloch, M. (2000) A well-disposed social anthropologist's problems with memes. In: Aunger, R., ed. *Darwinizing Culture: The Status of Memetics as a Science*. Oxford University Press, Oxford, pp. 189–203.

Boakes, R. (1984) *From Darwin to Behaviourism*. Cambridge University Press, Cambridge.

Boas, F. (1911) *The Mind of Primitive Man*. Macmillan, New York.

Boesch, C. (1996) The emergence of cultures among wild chimpanzees. *Proceedings of the British Academy*, **88**, 251–268.

Bok, W.J. (1980) The definition and recognition of biological adaptation. *American Zoologist*, **20**, 217–227.

Bok, W.J. and van Wahlert, G. (1965) Adaptation and the form–function complex. *Evolution*, **19**, 269–299.

Bolles, R.C. (1970) Species-specific defence reactions and avoidance learning. *Psychological Review*, **77**, 32–48.

Bolles, R.C. and Beecher, M.D., eds (1988) *Evolution and Learning*. Erlbaum, Hillsdale NJ.

Boring, E.G. (1957) *A History of Experimental Psychology*, 2nd edn. Appleton-Century-Croft, New York.

Boyd, R. and Richerson, P.J. (1985) *Culture and the Evolutionary Process*. Chicago University Press, Chicago.

Boyd, R. and Richerson, P. (2000) Meme theory oversimplifies how culture changes. *Scientific American*, **283**, 58–59.

Brainard, M.S. and Doupe, A.J. (2002) What songbirds teach us about learning. *Nature*, **417**, 351–358.

Brandon, R.N. (1988) The levels of selection: a hierarchy of interactors. In: Plotkin, H., ed. *The Role of Behaviour in Evolution*. MIT Press, Cambridge, MA, pp. 51–71.

Brannon, E.M. and Terrace, H.S. (1998) Ordering of the numerosities 1–9 by monkeys. *Science*, **282**, 746–749.

Bratman, M.E. (1992) Shared cooperative activity. *Philosophical Review*, **101**, 327–341.

Breland, K. and Breland, M. (1961) The misbehaviour of organisms. *American Psychologist*, **16**, 681–684.

Brennan, J.F. (1994) *History and Systems of Psychology*, 4th edn. Prentice Hall, Englewood Cliffs, NJ.

Broughton, J.M. and Freeman-Moir, D.J., eds (1982) *The Cognitive Developmental Psychology of James Mark Baldwin*. Ablex Publishing Corp., Norwood, NJ.

Burkhardt, R.W. (1983) The development of an evolutionary ethology. In: Bendall, D.S., ed. *Evolution: From Molecules to Men*. Cambridge University Press, Cambridge, pp. 430–444.

Burkhardt, R.W. (2005) *Patterns of Behavior: Konrad Lorenz, Niko Tinbergen, and the Founding of Ethology.* Chicago University Press, Chicago.

Butterworth, B. (1999) *The Mathematical Brain.* McMillan, London.

Buzsaki, G. and Draghun, A. (2004) Neuronal oscillations in cortical networks. *Science,* **304,** 1926–1929.

Byrne, R.W. and Russon, A.E. (1998) Learning by limitation: a hierarchical approach. *Behavioural and Brain Sciences,* **21,** 667–684.

Byrne, R.W., Barnard, P.J., Davidson, I., Janik, V.M., McGrew, W.C., Miklosi, A. and Wiessner, P. (2004) Understanding culture across species. *Trends in Cognitive Sciences,* **8,** 341–346.

Call, J., Hare, B., Carpenter, M. and Tomasello, M. (2004) 'Unwilling' versus 'unable': chimpanzees' understanding of human intentional action. *Developmental Science,* **7,** 488–498.

Calvin, W.H. and Bickerton, D. (2000) *Lingua ex Machina.* MIT Press, Cambridge, MA.

Campbell, D.T. (1956) Perception as substitute trial and error. *Psychological Review,* **63,** 331–342.

Campbell, D.T. (1959) Methodological suggestions from a comparative psychology of knowledge processes. *Inquiry,* **2,** 152–182.

Campbell, D.T. (1974*a*) Evolutionary epistemology. In: Schillp, P.A., ed. *The Philosophy of Karl Popper,* Book 1. Open Court Publishing Company, La Salle, IL, pp. 413–463.

Campbell, D.T. (1974*b*) 'Downward causation' in hierarchically organized biological systems. In: Ayala, F.J. and Dobzhansky, T., eds. *Studies in the Philosophy of Biology.* pp. 179–186. Macmillan, London.

Carroll, S.B., Grenier, J.K. and Weatherbee, S.D. (2005) *From DNA to Diversity: Molecular Genetics and the Evolution of Animal Design*, 2nd edn. Blackwell, Oxford.

Cavalli-Sforza, L.L. and Feldman, M.W. (1981) *Cultural Transmission and Evolution: A Quantitative Approach.* Princeton University Press, Princeton, NJ.

Chisholm, R.M. (1989) *Theory of Knowledge.* Prentice Hall, Englewood Cliffs, NJ.

Chomsky, N. (1980) *Rules and Representations.* Columbia University Press, New York.

Chomsky, N. (2000) *New Horizons in the Study of Language and Mind.* Cambridge University Press, Cambridge.

Christiansen, M.H. and Kirby, S. (2003) Language evolution: consensus and controversies. *Trends in Cognitive Sciences*, 7, 300–307.

Clark, A. (1993) *Associative Engines: Connectionism, Concepts, and Representational Change.* MIT Press, Cambridge, MA.

Coghill, G.E. (1929) *Anatomy and the Problem of Behaviour.* Cambridge University Press, Cambridge.

Cohen, L.B. and Chaput, H.H. (2002) Connectionist models of infant perceptual and cognitive development. *Developmental Science*, 5, 173–175.

Cohen, L.B., Chaput, H.H. and Cashon, C.H. (2002) A constructivist model of infant cognition. *Cognitive Development*, 17, 1323–1343.

Cohen, L.B. and Marks, S.K. (2002) How infants process addition and subtraction events. *Developmental Science*, 5, 186–212.

Cohen, R.S., ed. (1974) *Biennial Proceedings of the Philosophy of Science Association*, pp. 613–710. Reidel, Boston.

Cohen-Armon, M., Visochek, L., Katzoff, A., Levitan, D., Susswein, A., Klein, R., Valbrun, N. and Schwartz, J.H. (2004) Long-term memory requires polyADP-ribosylation. *Science*, **304**, 1820–1822.

Cole, M. (2006) Culture and cognitive development in phylogenetic, historical and ontogenetic perspective. In: Damon, W. and Kuhn, D., eds. *Handbook of Child Psychology Vol. 2: Cognition, Perception and Language*, 6th edn. Wiley, Chichester.

Cole, S., Hainsworth, F.R., Kamil, A.C., Mercier, T. and Wolf, L.L. (1982) Spatial learning as an adaptation in hummingbirds. *Science*, **217**, 655–657.

Coqueugniot, H., Hublin, J.J., Veillon, F., Houet, F. and Jacob, T. (2004) Early brain growth in *Homo erectus* and implications for cognitive ability. *Nature*, **431**, 299–302.

Corning, W.C., Dyal, J.A. and Willows, A.O.D. (1973) *Learning in Invertebrates: Volume 1*. Plenum, London.

Crain, S. and Pietroski, P. (2001) Nature, nurture and universal grammar. *Linguistics and Philosophy*, **24**, 139–186.

Cranston, M. (1961) *Locke*. Longmans, Green and Co., London.

Dancy, J. (1985) *Introduction to Contemporary Epistemology*. Blackwell, Oxford.

Darwin, C. (1859) *On the Origin of Species by Means of Natural Selection or the Preservation of Favoured Races in the Struggle for Life*. Murray, London.

Darwin, C. (1871) *The Descent of Man and Selection in Relation to Sex*. John Murray, London. (The Modern Library edition, New York.)

Darwin, C. (1872a) *The Origin of Species by Means of Natural Selection*, 6th edn. John Murray, London. (The Modern Library edition, New York.)

Darwin, C. (1872b) *The Expression of the Emotions in Man and Animals*. John Murray, London. (University of Chicago edition of 1965).

Darwin, C. (1887) Autobiography. In: Darwin, F., ed. *Life and Letters of Charles Darwin*. Murray, London. Reprinted in de Beer G., ed. *Charles Darwin and Thomas Henry Huxley: Autobiographies*. Oxford University Press, Oxford, pp. 3–88.

Darwin, C. (1890) *A Naturalist's Voyage: Journal of Researches into the Natural History and Geology of the Countries Visited During the Voyage of H.M.S. Beagle Round the World*. John Murray, London.

Davey, G. (1989) *Ecological Learning Theory*. Routledge, London.

Dawkins, R. (1976a) *The Selfish Gene*. Oxford University Press, Oxford.

Dawkins, R. (1976b) Hierarchical organization: a candidate principle for ethology. In: Bateson, P.P.G. and Hinde, R.A., eds. *Growing Points in Ethology*. Cambridge University Press, Cambridge, pp. 7–54.

Dawkins, R. (1982a) *The Extended Phenotype: The Gene as the Unit of Selection*. Freeman, Oxford.

Dawkins, R. (1983) Universal Darwinism. In: Bendall, D.S., ed. *Evolution from Molecules to Men*. Cambridge University Press, Cambridge, pp. 403–425.

Dawkins, R. (1986) *The Blind Watchmaker*. Longman, Harlow.

Dawkins, R. (2004) Extended phenotype—but not *too* extended. *Biology and Philosophy*, **19**, 377–396.

Deacon, T. (1997) *The Symbolic Species: The Co-evolution of Language and the Human Brain*. Allen Lane, London.

Deacon, T. (2003) Multilevel selection in a complex adaptive system: the problem of language origins. In: Weber, B.H. and Depew, D.J., eds. *Evolution and Learning: The Baldwin Effect Reconsidered*. MIT Press, Cambridge, MA, pp. 81–105.

Degler, C.N. (1991) *In Search of Human Nature: The Decline and Revival of Darwinism in American Social Thought.* Oxford University Press, Oxford.

Dehaene, S., Izard, V., Pica, P. and Spelke, E. (2006) Core knowledge of geometry in an Amazonian indigene group. *Science*, **311**, 381–384.

Dennett, D.C. (1991) *Consciousness Explained.* Allen Lane, London.

Dennett, D.C. (1995) *Darwin's Dangerous Idea.* Penguin Books, London.

Dennett, D.C. (2003) The Baldwin effect: a crane, not a skyhook. In: Weber, B.H. and Depew, D.J., eds. *Evolution and Learning: The Baldwin Effect Reconsidered.* MIT Press, Cambridge, MA, pp. 69–79.

Descartes, R. (1637) *Discourse on Method.* Translated by A. Wollaston. Penguin Books, Harmandsworth.

Descartes, R. (1641) *Meditations.* Translated by A. Wollaston. Penguin Books, Harmondsworth.

Desmond, A. and Moore, J. (1991) *Darwin.* Michael Joseph, London.

de Wolsky, M. I. and Wolsky, A. (1976) *The Mechanism of Evolution: A New Look at Old Ideas.* Karger, New York.

Dickinson, A. and Shanks, D. (1995) Instrumental action and causal representation. In: Sperber, D. Premack, D. and Premack, A.J., eds. *Causal Cognition.* Clarendon Press, Oxford, pp. 5–25.

Donald, M. (1991) *Origins of the Modern Mind: Three Stages in the Evolution of Cognition and Culture.* Harvard University Press, Cambridge, MA.

Doupe, A.J. and Kuhl, P.K. (1999) Birdsong and human speech: common themes and mechanisms. *Annual Review of Neuroscience*, **22**, 567–631.

Dray, W. (1957) *Laws and Explanation in History*. Oxford University Press, Oxford.

Dunbar, R.I.M. (2003) The social brain: mind, language and society in evolutionary perspective. *Annual Review of Anthropology*, **32**, 163–181.

Dunn, J. (1984). *Locke*. Oxford University Press, Oxford.

Durant, J.R. (1981) Innate character in animals and man: a perspective on the origins of ethology. In: Webster, C., ed. *Biology, Medicine and Society 1840–1940*. Cambridge University Press, Cambridge, pp. 157–192.

Durham, W.H. (1991) *Coevolution: Genes, Culture, and Human Diversity*. Stanford University Press, Stanford, CA.

Edelman, G.M. (1987) *Neural Darwinism: The Theory of Neuronal Group Selection*. Basic Books, New York.

Egan, M.F., Kojima, M., Callicott, J.H., Goldberg. T.E., Kolochana, B.S. and Bertolino, A. (2003) The BDNF va166met polymorphism affects activity-dependent secretion of BDNF and human memory and hippocampal function. *Cell*, **112**, 257–269.

Eldredge, N. and Gould, S.J. (1972) Punctuated equilibria: an alternative to phyletic gradualism. In: Schopf, T.J.M. ed. *Models in Palaeobiology*. Freeman, San Francisco, pp. 82–115.

Eldredge, N. and Salthe, S.N. (1984) Hierarchy and evolution. In: Dawkins, R. and Ridley, M., eds. *Oxford Surveys in Evolutionary Biology Vol. 1*, pp. 184–208. Oxford University Press, Oxford.

Elman, J.L. (2005) Connectionist models of cognitive development: where next? *Trends in Cognitive Science*, **9**, 111–117.

Elman, J.L., Bates, E.A., Johnson, M.H., Karmiloff-Smith, A., Parisi, D. and Plunkett, K. (1996) *Rethinking Innateness: A Connectionist Perspective on Development*. MIT Press, Cambridge, MA.

Endler, J.A. (1986) *Natural Selection in the Wild*. Princeton University Press, Princeton, NJ.

Fabricius, E. (1964) Crucial periods in the development of the following response in young nidifugous birds. *Zeitschrift fur Tierpsychologie*, **21**, 326–337.

Farroni, T., Csibra, G., Simion, F. and Johnson, M.H. (2002) Eye contact detection in humans from birth. *Proceedings of the National Academy of Sciences of the USA*, **99**, 9602–9605.

Feigenson, L., Dehaene, S. and Spelke, E. (2004) Core systems of number. *Trends in Cognitive Sciences*, **8**, 307–314.

Feyerabend, P.K. (1968) How to be a good empiricist—a plea for tolerance in matters epistemological. In: Nidditch, P.H., ed. *The Philosophy of Science*. Oxford University Press, Oxford. pp 12–39.

Fitch, W.T., Hauser, M.D. and Chomsky, N. (2005) The evolution of the language faculty: clarifications and implications. *Cognition*, 97, 179–210.

Fodor, J. (1983) *The Modularity of Mind*. MIT Press, Cambridge, MA.

Fodor, J. (1998) *In Critical Condition*. MIT Press, Cambridge, MA.

Fragaszy, D.M. and Perry, S., eds (2003) *The Biology of Animal Traditions*. Cambridge University Press, Cambridge.

Freeman, D. (1974) The evolutionary theories of Charles Darwin and Herbert Spencer. *Current Anthropology*, **15**, 211- 221.

Freeman, D. (1983) *Margaret Mead and Samoa.* Penguin Books, London.

Frith, C. and Wolpert, D, eds (2004) *The Neuroscience of Social Interaction.* Oxford University Press, Oxford.

Frith, U. and Frith, C. (2001) The biological basis of social interaction. *Current Directions in Psychological Science,* **10**, 151–155.

Frith, U. and Frith, C. (2004) Development and neurophysiology of mentalizing. In: Frith, C. and Wolpert, D.M., eds. *The Neuroscience of Social Interaction.* Oxford University Press, Oxford, pp 45–75.

Gallese, V., Keysers, C. and Rizzolatti, G. (2004) A unifying view of the basis of social cognition. *Trends in Cognitive Science,* **8**, 396–403.

Galton, F. (1869) *Hereditary Genius.* Macmillan, London.

Garber, D. (1995) Rationalism. In: Audi, R., ed. *The Cambridge Dictionary of Philosophy.* Cambridge University Press, Cambridge, pp. 673–674.

Garcia, J. (1991) Lorenz's impact on the science of learning. *Evolution and Cognition,* **1**, 31–41.

Garcia, J. and Koelling, R.A. (1966) The relation of cue to consequence in avoidance learning. *Psychonomic Science,* **4**, 123–124.

Garcia, J., Ervin, F.R. and Koelling, R.A. (1966) Learning with prolonged delay of reinforcement. *Psychonomic Science,* **5**, 121–122.

Garstang, W. (1922) The theory of recapitulation: a critical restatement of the biogenetic law. *Journal of the Linnaean Society of London, Zoology.* **35**, 81–101.

Gaulin, S.J. and Fitzgerald, R.W. (1989) Sexual selection for spatial-learning ability. *Animal Behaviour,* **37**, 322–331.

Geary, D.C. (1994) *Children's Mathematical Development*. American Psychological Association, Washington, DC.

Gelman, R. and Butterworth, B. (2005) Number and language: how are they related? *Trends in Cognitive Sciences*, **9**, 6–10.

Ghiselin, M.T. (1966) On semantic pitfalls of biological adaptation. *Philosophy of Science*, **33**, 147–153.

Ghiselin, M.T. (1974) A radical solution to the species problem. *Systematic Zoology*, **23**, 536–544.

Godfrey-Smith, P. (1999) Adaptationism and the power of selection. *Biology and Philosophy*, **14**, 181–194.

Goldberg, T.E. and Weinberger, D.R. (2004) Genes and the parsing of cognitive processes. *Trends in Cognitive Science*, **8**, 325–335.

Goldstein, D.G. and Gigerenzer, G. (2002) Models of ecological rationality: the recognition heuristic. *Psychological Review*, **109**, 75–90.

Gomez, J.-C. (2005) Species comparative studies and cognitive development. *Trends in Cognitive Sciences*, **9**, 118–125.

Goodenough, W.H. (1957) Cultural anthropology and linguistics. In: Garvin, P., ed. *Report of the 7th Annual Roundtable Meeting on Linguistics and Language Study*. Vol. 9 of Georgetown University Monograph Series on Language and Linguistics, Georgetown, Washington, DC, pp. 162–184.

Goren, C.C., Sarty, M. and Wu, P.Y.K. (1975) Visual following and pattern discrimination of face-like stimuli by newborn infants. *Paediatrics*, **56**, 544–549.

Gottlieb, G. (1976) Conceptions of prenatal development: behavioural embryology. *Psychological Review*, **83**, 215–234.

Gottlieb, G. (1987) The developmental basis of evolutionary change. *Journal of Comparative Psychology*, **101**, 262–371.

Gottlieb, G. (1992) *Individual Development and Evolution.* Oxford University Press, Oxford.

Gottlieb, G. (1998) Normally occurring environmental and behavioural influences on gene activity: from central dogma to probabilistic epigenesis. *Psychological Review,* **105**, 792–802.

Gottlieb, G. (2002) Developmental–behavioral initiation of evolutionary change. *Psychological Review,* **109**, 211–218.

Goudge, T.A. (1961) *The Ascent of Life.* University of Toronto Press, Toronto.

Gould, J.L. and Marler, P. (1987) Learning by instinct. *Scientific American,* **256**, 62–73.

Gould, S.J. (1977) *Ontogeny and Phylogeny.* Harvard University Press, Cambridge, MA.

Gould, S.J. (1981) *The Mismeasure of Man.* Penguin Books, London.

Gould, S.J. (1982*a*) Darwinism and the expansion of evolutionary theory. *Science,* **216**, 380–387.

Gould, S.J. (1982*b*) The meaning of punctuated equilibrium and its role in validating a hierarchical approach to macroevolution. In: Milkman, R., ed. *Perspectives on Evolution.* Sinauer, Sunderland, MA, pp. 83–104.

Gould, S.J. (1986) Evolution and the triumph of homology, or why history matters. *American Scientist,* **74**, 60–69.

Gould, S.J. (1991) Exaptation: a crucial tool for an evolutionary psychology. *Journal of Social Issues,* **47**, 43–65.

Gould, S.J. (2002) *The Structure of Evolutionary Theory.* Harvard University Press, Cambridge, MA.

Gould, S.J. and Lewontin, R.C. (1978) The spandrels of San Marco and the Panglossian paradigm: a critique of the adaptationist programme. *Proceedings of the Royal Society B: Biological Sciences,* **205**, 581–598.

Gould, S.J. and Vrba, E.S. (1982) Exaptation—a missing term in the science of form. *Palaeobiology*, **8**, 4–15.

Grant, P.R. (1986) *Ecology and Evolution of Darwin's Finches*. Princeton University Press, Princeton, NJ.

Grant, P.R. (1991) Natural selection and Darwin's finches. *Scientific American*, **260**, 60–65.

Greco, J. and Sosa, E., eds (1999) *Epistemology*. Blackwell, Malden, MA.

Green, P.R. (1982) Problems in animal perception and learning and their implications for models of imprinting. In: Bateson, P.P.G. and Klopfer, P.H., eds. *Perspectives in Ethology: Ontogeny*. Vol. 5, Plenum, London, pp. 243–273.

Greenfield, P.M. (1991) Language, tools and the brain: the ontogeny and phylogeny of hierarchically organized sequential behaviour. *Behavioural and Brain Sciences*, **14**, 531–551.

Greenfield, P.M., Keller, H., Fuligni, A. and Maynard, A. (2003) Cultural pathways through universal development. *Annual Review of Psychology*, **54**, 461–490.

Greenough, W.T., Black, J.E. and Wallace C.S. (1987) Experience and brain development. *Child Development*, **58**, 539–559.

Grene, M. (1972) Aristotle and modern biology. *Journal of the History of Ideas*, **30**, 395–424.

Grene, M. (1987) Hierarchies in biology. *American Scientist*, **75**, 504–510.

Griffiths, P.E. (2004) Instinct in the 50s: the British reception of Konrad Lorenz's theory of instinctive behaviour. *Biology and Philosophy*, **19**, 609–631.

Griffiths, P.E. (2005) Review of 'niche construction'. *Biology and Philosophy*, **20**, 11–20.

Griffiths, P.E. and Gray, R.D. (2005) Three ways to misunderstand developmental systems theory. *Biology and Philosophy*, **20**, 417–425.

Gruber, H.E. (1974) *Darwin on Man (Darwin's Early and Unpublished Notebooks)*. Wildwood House, London.

Gruber, H.E. (1982) Foreword. In: Broughton, J.M. and Freeman-Moir, D.J., eds. *The Cognitive Developmental Psychology of James Mark Baldwin*. Ablex Publishing Corp., Norwood, NJ, pp. xii–xx.

Hailman, J.P. (1967) The ontogeny of an instinct. *Behaviour Supplements*, **15**, 1–196.

Hailman, J.P. (1969) How an instinct is learned. *Scientific American*, **221**, 98–107.

Hailman, J.P. (1982) Evolution and behaviour: an iconoclastic view. In: Plotkin, H.C., ed. *Learning, Development and Culture: Essays in Evolutionary Epistemology*. Wiley, Chichester, pp. 205–254.

Hamilton, W.D. (1964) The genetical evolution of social behaviour, pts. 1 and 2. *Journal of Theoretical Biology*, **7**, 1–16, 17–52.

Hardy, A.C. (1965) *The Living Stream*. Collins, London.

Hare, B. and Tomasello, M. (2005) Human-like social skills in dogs. *Trends in Cognitive Sciences*, **9**, 439–444.

Hare, B., Call, J., Agnetta, B. and Tomasello, M. (2000) Chimpanzees know what conspecifics do and do not see. *Animal Behaviour*, **59**, 771–785.

Hare, B., Call, J. and Tomasello, M. (2001) Do chimpanzees know what conspecifics know? *Animal Behaviour*, **61**, 139–151.

Hare, R.M. (1991) *Plato: Founders of Thought*. Oxford University Press. Oxford.

Harré, R. (1972) *The Philosophies of Science.* Oxford University Press, Oxford.

Harvey, P.H. and Purvis, A. (1991) Comparative methods for explaining adaptations. *Nature,* **351,** 619–624.

Hauser, M. (2005) Our chimpanzee mind. *Nature,* **437,** 60–63.

Hauser, M.D. and Carey, S. (2003) Spontaneous representations of small numbers of objects by rhesus macaques: examinations of content and format. *Cognitive Psychology,* **47,** 367–401.

Hauser, M.D., Chomsky, N. and Fitch, W.T. (2002) The faculty of language: what is it, who has it, and how did it evolve? *Science,* **298,** 1569–1579.

Hebb, D.O. (1949) *The Organization of Behaviour.* Wiley, New York.

Hebb, D.O. (1953) Heredity and environment in animal behaviour. *British Journal of Animal Behaviour,* **1,** 43–47.

Hempel, C.G. (1965) *Aspects of Scientific Explanation and Other Essays in the Philosophy of Science.* The Free Press, New York.

Heyes, C.M. and Galef, B.G., eds (1996) *Social Learning in Animals: The Roots of Culture.* Academic Press, London.

Himmelfarb, G. (1968) *Darwin and the Darwinian Revolution.* Norton, New York.

Hinde, R.A. and Stevenson-Hinde, J. (1973) eds. *Constraints on Learning: Limitations and Predispositions.* Academic Press, London.

Hinton, G.E. and Nowlan, S.J. (1987) How learning can guide evolution. *Complex Systems,* **1,** 495–502.

Hirsch, H.V.B. and Spinelli, D.N. (1970) Visual experience modifies distribution of horizontally and vertically oriented receptive fields in cats. *Science,* **168,** 869–871.

Hirschfeld, L.E. and Gelman, S.A. (1994) *Mapping the Mind: Domain Specificity in Cognition and Culture*. Cambridge, Cambridge University Press.

Ho, M.W. and Saunders, P.T. (1979) Beyond neoDarwinism: an epigenetic approach to evolution. *Journal of Theoretical Biology*, **78**, 673–691.

Ho, M.W. and Saunders, P.T. (1982) The epigenetic approach to the evolution of organisms—with notes on its relevance to social and cultural evolution. In: Plotkin, H.C., ed. *Learning, Development and Culture: Essays in Evolutionary Epistemology*. Wiley, Chichester, pp. 343–361.

Hobert, O. (2003) Behavioural plasticity in *C. elegans*: paradigms, circuits, genes. *Journal of Neurobiology*, **54**, 203–223.

Hodgson, G.M. (2004) Social Darwinism in anglophone academic journals: a contribution to the history of the term. *Journal of Historical Sociology* **17**, 428–463.

Hodos, W. and Campbell, C.B.G. (1969) *Scala naturae*: why there is no theory in comparative psychology. *Psychological Review*, **76**, 337–350.

Horner, V. and Whiten, A. (2005) Causal knowledge and imitation/emulation switching in chimpanzees (*Pan troglodytes*) and children (*Homo sapiens*). *Animal Cognition*, **8**, 164–181.

Hull, D.L. (1974) *Philosophy of Biological Science*. Prentice-Hall, Englewood Cliffs, NJ.

Hull, D.L. (1976) Are species really individuals? *Systematic Zoology*, **25**, 174–191.

Hull, D.L. (1988a) Interactors versus vehicles. In: Plotkin, H., ed. *The Role of Behaviour in Evolution*. MIT Press, Cambridge, MA, pp. 19–50.

Hull, D.L. (1988b) *Science as Process*. Chicago University Press, Chicago.

Humphrey, N.K. (1976) The social function of intellect. In: Bateson, P.P.G. and Hinde, R.A., eds. *Growing Points in Ethology*. Cambridge University Press, Cambridge, pp. 303–317.

Huxley, J. (1942) *Evolution, the Modern Synthesis*. Allen and Unwin, London.

Izquierdo, I. and Cammarota, M. (2004) Zif and the survival of memory. *Science*, **304**, 829–830.

Jablonka, E and Lamb, M.J. (1998) Bridges between development and evolution. *Biology and Philosophy*, **13**, 119–124.

Jackendoff, R. (2004) Précis of foundations of language: brain, meaning, grammar, evolution. *Behavioural and Brain Sciences*, **26**, 651–665.

Jackendoff, R. and Pinker, S. (2005) The nature of the language faculty and its implications for evolution of language. *Cognition*, **97**, 211–225.

James, W. (1880) Great men, great thoughts and the environment. *The Atlantic Monthly*, **46**, 441–459.

Jerison, H.J. (1973) *Evolution of the Brain and Intelligence*. Academic Press, New York.

Jerison, H.J. (1985) Animal intelligence as encephalization. *Philosophical Transactions of the Royal Society B: Biological Sciences*, **308**, 21–35.

Johnson, M.H. (1997) *Developmental Cognitive Neuroscience*. Blackwell, Oxford.

Johnson, M.H. and Morton, J. (1991) *Biology and Cognitive Development: The Case of Face Recognition*. Blackwell, Oxford.

Kalat, J.W. and Rozin, P. (1970) 'Salience': a factor which can override temporal contiguity in taste-aversion learning. *Journal of Comparative and Physiological Psychology*, **71**, 192–197.

Kalikow, T.J. (1975) History of Konrad Lorenz's ethological theory 1927–1939. *Studies in the History of Philosophy and Science*, **6**, 331–341.

Kalikow, T.J. (1976) Konrad Lorenz's ethological theory 1939–1943. *Philosophy of the Social Sciences*, **6**, 15–34.

Kamil, A.C. (1978) Systematic foraging by a nectar-feeding bird, the Amakihi (*Loxop virens*). *Journal of Comparative and Physiological Psychology*, **92**, 388–396.

Karmiloff-Smith, A. (1992) *Beyond Modularity: A Developmental Perspective on Cognitive Science*. MIT Press, Cambridge, MA.

Karmiloff-Smith, A. (1998) Development itself is the key to understanding developmental disorders. *Trends in Cognitive Sciences*, **2**, 389–398.

Karmiloff-Smith, A., Klima, E., Bellugi, U., Grant, J. and Baron-Cohen, S. (1995) Is there a social module? Language, face processing, and theory of mind in individuals with Williams syndrome. *Journal of Cognitive Neuroscience*, **7**, 196–208.

Kauffman, S. (1995) *At Home in the Universe*. London, Penguin Books.

Kenny, A. (2004) *A New History of Western Philosophy: Volume 1 Ancient Philosophy*. Oxford University Press, Oxford.

Kenny, A. (2005) *A New History of Western Philosophy. Volume 2: Medieval Philosophy*. Oxford, Oxford University Press.

Kenny, A. (2006) *A New History of Western Philosophy. Volume 3: The Rise of Modern Philosophy.* Oxford University Press, Oxford.

Kettlewell, H.B.D. (1955) Selection experiments on industrial melanism in the Lepidoptera. *Heredity,* **10**, 287–301.

Kingsland, S. (2005) Following their instincts. *Science,* **309**, 247–248.

Kraut, R. (1995) Plato. In: Audi, R., ed. *The Cambridge Dictionary of Philosophy.* Cambridge University Press Cambridge, pp. 619–624.

Krebs, J.R. and McCleery, R.H. (1984) Optimization in behavioural ecology. In: Krebs, J.R. and Davies, N.B., eds. *Behavioural Ecology: An Evolutionary Approach.* Blackwell, Oxford, pp. 91–121.

Kroeber, A.L. and Kluckhohn, C. (1952) *Culture: A Critical Review of Concepts and Definitions.* Harvard University Press, Cambridge, MA.

Kuo, Z.-Y. (1922) How are our instincts acquired? *Psychological Review,* **29**, 344–365.

Kuo, Z.-Y. (1924) A psychology without heredity. *Psychological Review,* **31**, 427–448.

Kuo, Z.-Y. (1932a) Ontogeny of embryonic behaviour in Aves I: the chronology and general nature of the behaviour of the chick embryo. *Journal of Experimental Zoology,* **61**, 395–430.

Kuo, Z.-Y. (1932b) Ontogeny of embryonic behaviour in Aves II: the mechanical factors in the various stages leading to hatching. *Journal of Experimental Zoology,* **62**, 453–489.

Kuo, Z.-Y. (1932c) Ontogeny of embryonic behaviour in Aves III: the structure and environmental factors in embryonic behaviour. *Journal of Comparative Psychology*, **13**, 245–272.

Kuo, Z.-Y. (1932*d*) Ontogeny of embryonic behaviour in Aves IV: the influence of embryonic movements upon the behaviour of hatching. *Journal of Comparative Psychology*, **14**, 109–122.

Kuo, Z.-Y. (1970) The need for coordinated efforts in developmental studies. In: Aronson, L.R., Tobach, E., Lehrman, D.S. and Rosenblatt, J.S., eds. *Development and Evolution of Behaviour*, Freeman, San Francisco, pp. 181–193.

Kurzweil, R. (2005) *The Singularity is Near: When Humans Transcend Biology*. Viking, London.

Lai, C.S., Fisher, S.E., Hurst, J.A., Vargha-Khadem, E. and Monaco, A.P. (2001) A forkhead-domain gene is mutated in a severe speech and language disorder. *Nature*, **413**, 519–523.

Laland, K.N. (1993) The mathematical modelling of human culture and its implications for psychology and the human sciences. *British Journal of Psychology*, **84**, 145–169.

Laland, K. (2003) Learning to evolve. *Nature*, **425**, 345.

Laland, K.N. (2004). Extending the extended phenotype. *Biology and Philosophy*, **19**, 313–325.

Laland, K.N. and Brown, G.R. (2002) *Sense and Nonsense: Evolutionary Perspectives on Human Behaviour*. Oxford University Press, Oxford.

Laland, K.N., Kumm, J. and Feldman, M.W. (1995) Gene–culture coevolutionary theory: a test case. *Current Anthropology*, **36**, 131–158.

Laland, K.N., Odling-Smee, F.J. and Feldman, M.W. (1996) Evolutionary consequences of niche construction: a theoretical investigation using two-locus theory. *Journal of Evolutionary Biology*, **9**, 293–316.

Laland, K.N., Odling-Smee, F.J. and Feldman, M.W. (1999) Evolutionary consequences of niche construction and their implications for ecology. *Proceedings of the National Academy of Sciences of the USA*, **96**, 10242–10247.

Laland, K.N., Odling-Smee, F.J. and Feldman, M.W. (2000) Niche constructing, biological evolution, and cultural change. *Behavioural and Brain Sciences*, **23**, 131–146.

Laland, K.N., Odling-Smee, F.J. and Feldman, M.W. (2005) On the breadth and significance of niche construction. *Biology and Philosophy*, **20**, 37–55.

Lamarck, J.-B. (1809) *Philosophie Zoologique*. English translation by Hugh Elliott (1914) Macmillan, London.

Larson, A., Prager, E.M. and Wilson, A.C. (1984) Chromosomal evolution, speciation and morphological change in vertebrates: the role of social behaviour. *Chromosomes Today*, **8**, 215–227.

Lashley, K.S. (1938) Experimental analysis of instinctive behaviour. *Psychological Review*, **45**, 445–471.

Laurence, S. and Margolis, E. (2001) The poverty of the stimulus argument. *British Journal of the Philosophy of Science*, **52**, 217–276.

Leahey, T.T. (1987) *A History of Psychology*, 2nd edn. Prentice-Hall, Englewood Cliffs, NJ.

Lees, D.R. (1981) Industrial melanism: genetic adaptation of animals to air pollution. In: Bishop, J.A. and Cook, L.M., eds. *Genetic Consequences of Man Made Change*, Academic Press, London, pp. 129–176.

Lehrman, D.S. (1953) A critique of Konrad Lorenz's theory of instinctive behaviour. *Quarterly Journal of Biology*, **28**, 337–363.

Lehrman, D.S. (1970) Semantic and conceptual issues in the nature–nurture problem. In: Aronson, L.R., Tobach, E.,

Lehrman, D.S. and Rosenblatt, J.S., eds. *Development and Evolution of Behaviour: Essays in Memory of T.C. Schneirla*. Freeman, San Francisco, pp. 17–52.

Leslie, A.M. (2005) Developmental parallels in understanding minds and bodies. *Trends in Cognitive Sciences*, 9, 459–463.

Leslie, A.M., Friedman, O. and German, T.P. (2004) Core mechanisms in theory of mind. *Trends in Cognitive Sciences*, 8, 528–533.

Lewontin, R.C. (1970) The units of selection. *Annual Review of Ecology and Systematics*, 1, 1–18.

Lewontin, R.C. (1978) Adaptation. *Scientific American*, 239, 156–169.

Lewontin, R.C. (1980) Adaptation. In: *The Encyclopaedia Einaudi*. Einaudi, Milan, pp. 235–251.

Lewontin, R.C. (1982) Organism and environment. In: Plotkin, H.C., ed. *Learning, Development and Culture: Essays in Evolutionary Epistemology*, Wiley, Chichester, pp. 151–170.

Lewontin, R.C. (1983) Gene, organism, and environment. In: Bendall, D.S., ed. *Evolution from Molecules to Men*. Cambridge University Press, Cambridge, pp. 273–285.

Lillard, A. (1998) Ethnopsychologies: cultural variations in theories of mind. *Psychological Bulletin*, 123, 3–32.

Lloyd, E.A. (1999) Evolutionary psychology: the burdens of proof. *Biology and Philosophy*, 14, 211–233.

Lloyd, E.A. (2004) Kanzi, evolution, and language. *Biology and Philosophy*, 19, 577–588.

Logan, C.A. (1983) Biological diversity in Avian vocal learning. In: Zeiler, M.D. and Harzem, P., eds. *Biological Factors in Learning: Advances in Analysis of Behaviour*, Vol. 3. Wiley, Chichester, pp. 143–176.

Lorenz, K. (1935) Companionship in bird life. (Der Kumpan in der Umvelt des Vogels) *Journal of Ornithology*, **83**, 137–213. [Translated into English in Schiller (1957) pp. 83–128.]

Lorenz, K. (1937) The nature of instinct. (Uber die Bildung des Instinktbegriffes) *Die Naturwissenschaften*, **25**, 289–300, 307–318, 324–331. [Translated into English in Schiller (1957) pp. 129–175.]

Lorenz, K. (1941) Kant's Lehre vom apriorischen im Lichte geganwartiger Biologie. *Blatter fur Deutsche Philosophie*, **15**, 94–125. [English translation as Kant's doctrine of the *a priori* in the light of contemporary biology in Plotkin (1982) pp. 121–143.]

Lorenz, K. (1950) The comparative method in studying innate behaviour patterns. *Symposium of the Society for Experimental Biology*, **4**, 221–268.

Lorenz, K. (1958) The evolution of behaviour. *Scientific American*, **198**, 49–58.

Lorenz, K. (1965) *Evolution and Modification of Behaviour*. Methuen, London.

Lorenz, K. (1966) The psychobiological approach: methods and results. *Philosophical Transactions of the Royal Society B: Biological Sciences*, **251**, 273–284.

Lorenz, K. (1969) Innate bases of learning. In: Pribram, K., ed. *On the Biology of Learning*. Harcourt, Brace and Janonovich, New York, pp. 13–92.

Lorenz, K. (1977) *Behind the Mirror: A Search for the Natural History of Human Knowledge*. Methuen, London.

Lorenz, K. (1996) *The Natural Science of the Human Species: An Introduction to Comparative Behavioural Research*. (The Russian manuscript 1944–1948.) Translated by R.D. Martin, MIT Press, Cambridge, MA.

Losos, J.B., Warheit, K.I. and Schoener, T.W. (1997) Adaptive differentiation following experimental island colonization in Anolis lizards. *Nature,* **387,** 70–73.

Mamelli, M. and Bateson, P. (2006) Innateness and the sciences. *Biology and Philosophy,* **21,** 155–188.

Marcus, G. (1998) Can connectionism save constructivism. *Cognition,* **66,** 153–182.

Marcus, G. (2004) *The Birth of the Mind.* Basic Books, New York.

Marler, P. (1997) Three models of song learning: evidence from behaviour. *Journal of Neurobiology,* **33,** 501–516.

Marler, P. (2004) Innateness and the instinct to learn. *Anais da Academia Brasileira de Ciencias,* **76,** 189–200.

Marler, P. and Slabberkoorn, H. (2004) *Nature's Music: The Science of Birdsong.* Elsevier, London.

Marler, P. and Terrace, H.S., eds (1984) *The Biology of Learning.* Springer-Verlag, Berlin.

Martin, R.D. (1983) Human brain evolution in an ecological context. *Fifty Second James Arthur Lecture on the Evolution of the Human Brain.* American Museum of Natural History, New York.

Matsuda, R. (1987) *Animal Evolution in Changing Environments with Special Reference to Abnormal Metamorphosis.* Wiley, New York.

Maynard Smith, J. (1978) Optimization theory in evolution. *Annual Review of Ecology and Systematics,* **9,** 31–56.

Maynard-Smith, J. (1987) When learning guides evolution. *Nature,* **329,** 761–762.

Mayr, E. (1961) Cause and effect in biology. *Science,* **134,** 1501–1506.

Mayr, E. (1963) *Animal Species and Evolution.* Harvard University Press, Cambridge, MA.

Mayr, E. (1982) *The Growth of Biological Thought.* Harvard University Press, Cambridge, MA.

McGrew, W. (2004) *The Cultured Chimpanzee: Reflections on Cultural Primatology.* Cambridge University Press, Cambridge.

Medin, D.L. and Atran, S. (2004) The native mind: biological categorization and reasoning in development and across cultures. *Psychological Review,* **111**, 960–983.

Melis, A.P., Hare, B. and Tomasello, M. (2006) Chimpanzees recruit the best collaborators. *Science,* **311**, 1297–1300.

Meltzoff, A.N. (1996) The human infant as imitative generalist: a 20-year progress report on infant imitation with implications for comparative psychology. In: Heyes, C.M. and Galef, B.G., eds. *Social Learning in Animals: The Roots of Culture.* Academic Press, London, p. 347–370.

Meltzoff, A.N. and Moore, M.K. (1977) Imitation of facial and manual gestures by human neonates. *Science,* **198**, 75–78.

Meltzoff, A.N. and Moore, M.K. (1983) Newborn infants imitate adult facial gestures. *Child Development,* **54**, 702–709.

Mikkelsen, T.S. *et al.*; the chimpanzee sequencing and analysis consortium (2005) Initial sequence of the chimpanzee genome and comparison with the human genome. *Nature,* **437**, 69–87.

Minsky, M.L. (1975) A framework for representing knowledge. In: Winston, P.H., ed. *The Psychology of Computer Vision.* McGraw Hill, New York, pp. 211–277.

Morgan, C.L. (1891) *Animal Life and Intelligence.* Edward Arnold, London.

Morgan, C.L. (1894) *An Introduction to Comparative Psychology.* Walter Scott, London.

Morgan, C.L. (1900) *Animal Behaviour.* Edward Arnold, London.

Morrison, G.E. and van der Kooy, D. (2001) A mutation in the AMPA-type glutamate receptor, glr-1, blocks olfactory associative and non-associative learning in *C. elegans. Behavioural Neuroscience,* **115,** 640–649.

Nagel, E. (1979) *Teleology Revisited and Other Essays in the Philosophy and History of Science.* Columbia University Press, New York.

Nidditch, P.H., ed. (1975) *Locke: Essay Concerning Human Understanding.* Clarendon Press, Oxford.

Nisbett, A. (1976) *Konrad Lorenz.* Dent & Son, London.

Nisbett, R.E. and Masuda, T. (2003) Culture and point of view. *Proceedings of the National Academy of Sciences of the USA,* **100,** 11163–11175.

Nisbett, R.E. and Miyamoto, Y. (2005) The influence of culture: holistic versus analytic perception. *Trends in Cognitive Sciences,* **9,** 467–473.

Nisbett, R.E., Peng, K., Choi, I. and Norenzayan, A. (2001) Culture systems of thought: holistic versus analytic cognition. *Psychological Review,* **108,** 291–310.

Norris, C. (2005) *Epistemology.* Continuum, London.

Novak, M.A., Komarova, N.L. and Niyogi, P. (2002) Computational and evolutionary aspects of language. *Nature,* **417,** 611–617.

O'Neill, R.V., DeAngekis, D.L., Wade, J.B. and Allen, T.F.H. (1986) *A Hierarchical Concept of Ecosystems.* Princeton University Press, Princeton, NJ.

Odling-Smee, F.J. (1988) Niche-constructing phenotypes. In: Plotkin, H., ed. *The Role of Behaviour in Evolution.* MIT Press, Cambridge, MA, pp. 73–132.

Odling-Smee, F.J., Laland, K.N. and Feldman, M.W. (2003) *Niche Construction: The Neglected Process in Evolution.* Princeton University Press, Princeton, NJ.

Okasha, S. (2005) On niche construction and extended evolutionary theory. *Biology and Philosophy,* **20**, 1–10.

Oppenheim, R.W. (1982) Preformation and epigenesis in the origins of the nervous system and behaviour: issues, concepts, and their history. In: Bateson, P.P.G. and Klopfer, P.H., eds. *Perspectives in Ethology: Ontogeny.* Vol. 5. Plenum, London, pp. 1–100.

Oppenheimer, J.M. (1967) *Essays in the History of Embryology and Biology.* MIT Press, Cambridge, MA.

Oyama, S. (1982) A reformulation of the idea of maturation. In: Bateson, P.P.G. and Klopfer, P.H.. eds. *Perspectives in Ethology: Ontogeny.* Vol. 5. Plenum, London, pp. 101–131.

Oyama, S. (1985) *The Ontogeny of Information: Developmental Systems and Evolution.* Cambridge University Press, Cambridge.

Oyama, S. (2000*a*) *Evolution's Eye: A Systems View of the Biology–Culture Divide.* Duke University Press, Durham, NC.

Oyama, S. (2000*b*) *The Ontogeny of Information: Developmental Systems and Evolution,* 2nd edn. Duke University Press, Durham, NC.

Oyama, S., Griffiths, P.E. and Grey, R.D., eds (2001) *Cycles of Contingency: Developmental Systems and Evolution.* MIT Press, Cambridge, MA.

Parker, G.A. and Maynard Smith, J. (1990) Optimality theory in evolutionary biology. *Nature*, **348**, 27–33.

Pattee, H.H. (1970) The problem of biological hierarchy. In: Waddington, C.H., ed. *Towards a Theoretical Biology: Drafts*. Edinburgh University Press, Edinburgh, pp. 117–136.

Pattee, H.H. (1973*a*) *Hierarchy Theory: The Challenge of Complex Systems*. George Braziller, New York.

Pattee, H.H. (1973*b*) The physical basis and origin of hierarchical control. In: Pattee, H.H., ed. *Hierarchy Theory: The Challenge of Complex Systems*. George Braziller, New York, pp. 72–108.

Patten, B.C. and Odum, E.P. (1981) The cybernetic nature of ecosystems. *American Naturalist*, **118**, 886–895.

Paul, D.B. and Spencer, H.G. (1995) The hidden science of eugenics. *Nature*, **374**, 302–304.

Pearce, J.M. (1987) *An Introduction to Animal Cognition*. Erlbaum, London.

Peel, J.D.Y., ed. (1972) *Herbert Spencer on Social Evolution: Selected Writings*. Chicago University Press, Chicago.

Perner, J. (1991) *Understanding the Representational Mind*. MIT Press, Cambridge, MA.

Perner, J., Leekam, S.R. and Wimmer, H. (1987) Three year olds' difficulty with false belief. *British Journal of Developmental Psychology*, **5**, 125–137.

Piaget, J. (1953) *The Origin of Intelligence in the Child*. Routledge, London.

Piaget, J. (1971) *Biology and Knowledge: An Essay on the Relations between Organic Regulations and Cognitive Processes*. Edinburgh University Press, Edinburgh.

Piaget, J. (1973) *Structuralism*. Routledge, London.

Piaget, J. (1979) *Behaviour and Evolution*. Routledge, London.

Piaget, J. (1979/1982) Reflections on Baldwin. In: Broughton, J.M. and Freeman-Moir, D.J., eds. *The Cognitive Developmental Psychology of James Mark Baldwin*. Ablex Publishing Corp., Norwood, NJ, pp. 80–86.

Piaget, J. (1980) *Adaptation and Intelligence*. University of Chicago Press, Chicago.

Pinker, S. (1994) *The Language Instinct*. Allen Lane, London.

Pinker, S. (1997) *How the Mind Works*. Penguin, London.

Pinker, S. (2002) *The Blank Slate*. Penguin Books, London.

Pinker, S. and Jackendoff, R. (2005) The faculty of language: what's special about it. *Cognition*, **95**, 201–236.

Pittendrigh, C. S. (1958) Adaptation, natural selection, and behaviour. In: Roe, A. and Simpson, G.G. eds. *Behaviour and Evolution*. Yale University Press, New Haven, pp 390–416.

Plotkin, H., ed. (1982) *Learning, Development and Culture: Essays in Evolutionary Epistemology*. Wiley, Chichester.

Plotkin, H. (1988*a*) Behaviour and evolution. In: Plotkin, H., ed. *The Role of Behaviour in Evolution*. MIT Press, Cambridge, MA, pp. 1–17.

Plotkin, H. (1988*b*) Learning and evolution. In: Plotkin, H., ed. *The Role of Behaviour in Evolution*. MIT Press, Cambridge, MA, pp. 133–164.

Plotkin, H. (1994) *The Nature of Knowledge*. Penguin Books, London.

Plotkin, H. (2000) People do more than imitate. *Scientific American*, **283**, 60.

Plotkin, H. (2002*a*) *The Imagined World Made Real*. Penguin Books, London.

Plotkin, H. (2002*b*) Intelligence as predisposed sceptical induction engines. In: Sternberg, R.J. and Kaufman, J.C., eds. *The Evolution of Intelligence* Lawrence Erlbaum, Mahwah, NJ, pp. 339–358.

Plotkin, H. (2003) We-intentionality: an essential element in understanding human culture. *Perspectives in Biology and Medicine*, **46**, 283–296.

Plotkin, H. (2004) *Evolutionary Thought in Psychology: A Brief History*. Blackwell, Oxford.

Plotkin, H. (2007) The power of culture. In: Dunbar, R.I.M. and Barrett, L., eds. *The Oxford Handbook of Evolutionary Psychology*. Oxford University Press, Oxford, pp. 11–20.

Plotkin, H.C. and Odling-Smee, F.J. (1979) Learning, change and evolution: an enquiry into the teleonomy of learning. *Advances in the Study of Behaviour*, **10**, 1–41.

Plotkin, H.C. and Odling-Smee, F.J. (1981) A multiple-level model of evolution and its implications for socio-biology. *Behavioural and Brain Sciences*, **4**, 225–268.

Polanyi, M. (1968) Life's irreducible structure. *Science*, **160**, 1308–1312.

Popper, K.R. (1972) *Objective Knowledge*. Oxford University Press, Oxford.

Potegal, M., ed. (1982) *Spatial Abilities: Developmental and Physiological Foundations*. Academic Press, New York.

Premack, D. and Premack, A. (2003) *Original Intelligence: Unlocking the Mystery of Who We Are*. McGraw-Hill, New York.

Quartz, S.R. (1999) The constructivist brain. *Trends in Cognitive Sciences*, **3**, 48–57.

Quartz, S.R. and Sejnowski, T.J. (1997) The neural basis of cognitive development: a constructivist manifesto. *Behavioural and Brain Sciences*, **20**, 537–556.

Quinlan, P. (1991) *Connectionism and Psychology.* Harvester Wheatsheaf, Hemel Hempstead.

Ramus, F., Hauser, M.D., Miller, C., Morris, D. and Mehler, J. (2000) Language discrimination by human newborns and by cotton-top tamarind monkeys. *Science,* **288,** 349–351.

Reader, S.M. and Laland, K.N. (2002) Social intelligence, innovation, and enhanced brain size in primates. *Proceedings of the National Academy of Sciences of the USA,* **99,** 4436–4441.

Rendell, L. and Whitehead, H. (2001) Culture in whales and dolphins. *Behavioural and Brain Sciences,* **24,** 309–324.

Richards, R.J. (1987) *Darwin and the Emergence of Evolutionary Theories of Mind and Behavior.* Chicago University Press, Chicago.

Richerson, P. and Boyd, R. (2005) *Not by Genes Alone: How Culture Transformed Human Evolution.* Chicago University Press, Chicago.

Ridley, M. (1996) *Evolution,* 2nd edn. Blackwell, Oxford.

Rizzolatti, G, and Graighero, I. (2004) The mirror-neuron system. *Annual Review of Neuroscience,* **27,** 169–192.

Rizzolatti, G., Fadiga, L., Gallese, V. and Fogassi, L. (1996) Premotor cortex and the recognition of motor actions. *Cognition and Brain Research,* **3,** 131–141.

Rose, G.J., Goller, F., Gritton, H.J., Plamondon, S.L., Baugh, A.T. and Cooper, B.G. (2004) Species typical songs in white-crowned sparrows tutored with only phrase pairs. *Nature,* **432,** 753–758.

Rose, H. and Rose, S., eds (2000) *Alas, Poor Darwin! Arguments Against Evolutionary Psychology.* Harmony Books, New York.

Rose, S. (1997) *Lifelines: Biology Beyond Determinism.* Oxford University Press, Oxford.

Rosenberg, A. (1978) The supervenience of biological concepts. *Philosophy of Science*, **45**, 368–386.

Rosenberg, A. (2001) How is biological explanation possible? *British Journal of the Philosophy of Science*, **52**, 735–760.

Rosenblatt, J.S. (1967) Nonhormonal basis of maternal behaviour in the rat. *Science*, **156**, 1512–1514.

Rosenblatt, J.S. (1970) Views on the onset and maintenance of maternal behaviour in the rat. In: Aronson, L.R., Tobach, E., Lehrman, D.S. and Rosenblatt, J.S., eds. *Development and Evolution of Behaviour: Essays in Memory of T.C. Schneirla*. Freeman, San Francisco, pp. 489–515.

Rosenbleuth, A., Wiener, N. and Bigelow, J. (1943) Behaviour, purpose, and teleology. *Philosophy of Science*, **10**, 18–24.

Rozin, P. and Kalat, J. (1971) Specific hungers and poison avoidance as adaptive specializations of learning. *Psychological Review*, **78**, 459–486.

Rummelhart, D.E. and Norman, D.A. (1985) Representations of knowledge. In: Aitkinhead, A.M. and Slack, J.M., eds. *Issues in Cognitive Modelling*. pp. 15–62. Erlbaum, Hove.

Ruse, M. (1973) *The Philosophy of Biology*. Hutchinson University Library, London.

Ruse, M. (1988) *Philosophy of Biology Today*. State University of New York Press, Albany.

Russell, B. (1946) *History of Western Philosophy*. Routledge, London.

Sage, R.D., Loiselle, P.V., Basasibwaki, P. and Wilson, A.C. (1984) Molecular versus morphological change among Cichild species of Lake Victoria. In: Echelle, A.A. and Kornfield I. eds. *Evolution of Fish Species*. Orono, University of Maine Press, pp. 174–194.

Salthe, S.N. (1985) *Evolving Hierarchical Structures: Their Structure and Representation.* Columbia University Press, New York.

Salzen, E.A. (1970) Imprinting and environmental learning. In: Aronson, L.R., Tobach, E., Lehrman, D.S. and Rosenblatt, J.S., eds. *Development and Evolution of Behaviour.* Freeman, San Francisco, pp. 158–178.

Samuels, R. (2004) Innateness in cognitive science. *Trends in Cognitive Sciences,* **8**, 136–141.

Sarkar, S. (1998) *Genetics and Reductionism.* Cambridge University Press, Cambridge.

Savage-Rumbaugh, S., Fields, W.M. and Spircu, T. (2004) The emergence of knapping and vocal expression embedded in a Pan/Homo culture. *Biology and Philosophy,* **19**, 541–575.

Scerif, G. and Karmiloff-Smith, A. (2005) The dawn of cognitive genetics? Crucial developmental caveats. *Trends in Cognitive Sciences,* **9**, 126–135.

Schaffner, K.F. (1967) Approaches to reduction. *Philosophy of Science,* **34**, 137–147.

Schaffner, K.F. (1974) Reduction in biology: prospects and problems. In: Cohen, R.S., ed. *Biennial Proceedings of the Philosophy of Science Association,* 613–632. Riedel, Boston.

Schank, R.C. and Abelson, R. (1977) *Scripts, Plans, Goals, and Understanding.* Erlbaum, Hillsdale, NJ.

Schiller, C.H., ed. and Trans. (1957) *Instinctive Behaviour.* Methuen, London.

Schmalhausen, I.I. (1949) *Factors of Evolution.* Blakiston, Philadelphia.

Schneirla, T.C. (1956) The interrelationship of the 'innate' and the 'acquired' in instinctive behaviour. In:

Grassé, P.-P., ed. *Instinct dans le Comportement des Animaux et de l'Homme*. Masson, Paris, pp. 387–452. (Reprinted in Aronson, L.R., Tobach, E., Rosenblatt, J.S. and Lehrman, D.S., eds. *The Selected Writings of T.C. Schneirla*. Freeman, San Francisco, pp. 131–188.)

Schneirla, T.C. (1966) Instinct and aggression: a review of two books by Konrad Lorenz. *Natural History*, **75**, 16–20.

Searle, J.R. (1995) *The Construction of Social Reality*. Penguin Press, London.

Segerstrale, U. (2000) *Defenders of the Truth*. Oxford University Press, Oxford.

Seligman, M.E.P. (1970) On the generality of the laws of learning. *Psychological Review*, **77**, 406–418.

Senghas, A., Kita, S. and Ozyurek, A. (2004) Children creating core properties of language: evidence from an emerging sign language in Nicaragua. *Science*, **305**, 1779–1782.

Shepard, R.N. (2001a) Perceptual cognitive universals as reflections of the world. *Behavioural and Brain Sciences*, **24**, 581–601.

Shepard, R.N. (2001b) On the possibility of universal mental laws: a reply to my critics. *Behavioural and Brain Sciences*, **24**, 712–748.

Shettleworth, S.J. (1972) Constraints on learning. *Advances in the Study of Behaviour*, **4**, 1–68.

Shettleworth, S.J. (1998) *Cognition, Evolution and Behaviour*. Oxford University Press, Oxford.

Shettleworth, S.J. (2000) Modularity and the evolution of cognition. In: Heyes, C. and Huber, L., eds. *The Evolution of Cognition*. MIT Press, Cambridge, MA, pp. 43–60.

Simon, H.A. (1962) The architecture of complexity. *Proceedings of the American Philosophical Society*, **106**, 467–482.

Simon, H.A. (1973) The organization of complex systems. In: Pattee, H.H., ed. *Hierarchy Theory: The Challenge of Complex Systems.* George Braziller, New York, pp. 2–27.

Simon, H.A. (1982) *The Sciences of the Artificial.* MIT Press, Cambridge, MA.

Simpson, G.G. (1953) The Baldwin effect. *Evolution*, 7, 110–117.

Siok, W.T., Perfetti, C.A., Jin, Z. and Tan, L.H. (2004) Biological abnormality of impaired reading is constrained by culture. *Nature*, **431**, 71–76.

Skinner, B.F. (1957) *Verbal Behaviour.* Appleton-Century-Crofts, New York.

Smart, J.J.C. (1968) *Between Science and Philosophy.* Random House, New York.

Smith, C.U.M. (1991) Kant and Darwin. *Journal of Social and Biological Structures*, **14**, 35–50.

Smith, R.L., ed. (1984) *Sperm Competition and the Evolution of Animal Mating Systems.* Academic Press, New York.

Sober, E. (1993) *Philosophy of Biology.* Oxford University Press, Oxford.

Soha, J.A. and Marler, P. (2000) A species-specific acoustic cue for selective song learning in the white-crowned sparrow. *Animal Behaviour*, **60**, 297–306.

Sommerhoff, G. (1950) *Analytical Biology.* Oxford University Press, Oxford.

Sommerhoff, G. (1969) The abstract characteristics of living systems. In: Emery, F.E., ed. *Systems Thinking.* Penguin, Harmandsworth, pp. 147–202.

Spencer, H. (1855) *The Principles of Psychology.* Longman, Brown, Green and Longmans, London.

Spencer, H. (1870) *The Principles of Psychology*, 2nd edn, Vol. 1. Williams and Norgate, London.

Spencer, H. (1904) *An Autobiography.* Vols 1 and 2. Williams and Norgate, London.

Sperber, D. (2000) An objection to the memetic approach to culture. In: Aunger, R., ed. *Darwinizing Culture: The Status of Memetics as a Science.* Oxford University Press, Oxford, pp. 163–173.

Sperber, D., Premack, D. and Premack, A.J., eds (1995) *Causal Cognition.* Oxford University Press, Oxford.

Sterelny, K. (2005) Made by each other: organisms and their environment. *Biology and Philosophy,* **20,** 21–36.

Suddendorf, T. and Whiten, A. (2001) Mental evolution and development: evidence for secondary representation in children, great apes, and other animals. *Psychological Bulletin,* **127,** 629–650.

Szathmary, E. and Maynard Smith, J. (1995) The major evolutionary transitions. *Nature,* **374,** 227–232.

Tebbich, S., Taborsky, M., Febl, B. and Blomqvist, D. (2001) Do woodpecker finches acquire tool-use by social learning? *Proceedings of the Royal Society B: Biological Sciences,* **268,** 2189–2193.

Tinbergen, N. (1951) *The Study of Instinct.* Oxford University Press, Oxford.

Tinbergen, N., Broekhuysen, G.J., Feekes, F., Houghton, J.C.W., Kruuk, H. and Szule, E. (1962) Egg shell removal by the black-headed gull: a behaviour component of camouflage. *Behaviour,* **19,** 74–118.

Todd, P.M. and Gigerenzer, G. (2000) Simple heuristics that make us smart. *Behavioural and Brain Sciences,* **23,** 727–741.

Tomasello, M. (1999) *The Cultural Origins of Human Cognition.* Harvard University Press, Cambridge, MA.

Tomasello, M. and Call, J. (1997) *Primate Cognition*. Oxford University Press, Oxford.

Tomasello, M., Carpenter, M., Call, J., Behne, T. and Moll, H. (2005) Understanding and sharing intentions: the origins of cultural cognition. *Behavioural and Brain Sciences*, **28**, 675–735.

Tuomela, R. and Miller, K. (1988) We-intentions. *Philosophical Studies*, **53**, 367–389.

van Schaik, C.P., Ancrenaz, M., Borgen, G., Galdikas, B., Knott, C.D., Singleton, I., *et al.* (2003) Orangutan cultures and the evolution of material culture. *Science*, **299**, 102–105.

von Bertalanffy, L. (1969) Chance or law. In: Koestler, A. and Smythies, J.R., eds. *Beyond Reductionism: New Perspectives in the Life Sciences*. Beacon Press, Boston, pp. 56–76.

Vouloumanos, A. and Werker, J.F. (2004) Tuned to the signal: the privileged status of speech for young infants. *Developmental Science*, **7**, 270–275.

Vrba, E.S. and Eldredge, N. (1984) Individuals, hierarchies, and processes: towards a more complete evolutionary theory. *Palaeobiology*, **10**, 146–171.

Vrba, E.S. and Gould, S.J. (1986) The hierarchical expansion of sorting and selection: sorting and selecting cannot be equated. *Palaeobiology*, **12**, 217–228.

Waddington, C.H. (1952) Selection of the genetic basis for an acquired character. *Nature*, **169**, 278–279.

Waddington, C.H. (1957) *The Strategy of the Genes*. Allen and Unwin, London.

Waddington, C.H. (1959*a*) Evolutionary adaptation. In: Tax, S., ed. *Evolution after Darwin*. University of Chicago Press, Chicago, pp. 381–402.

Waddington, C.H. (1959*b*) Evolutionary systems: animal and human. *Nature*, **183**, 1634–1638.

Waddington, C.H. (1961) The human evolutionary system. In: Banton, M., ed. *Darwinism and the Study of Society.* Tavistock Publications, London, pp. 63–81. (Reprinted in Waddington, 1975.)

Waddington, C.H., ed. (1968) *Towards a Theoretical Biology: Prolegomena.* Edinburgh University Press, Edinburgh.

Waddington, C.H.. ed. (1969*a*) *Towards a Theoretical Biology: Sketches.* Edinburgh University Press, Edinburgh.

Waddington, C.H. (1969*b*) Paradigm for an evolutionary process. In: Waddington, C.H., ed. *Towards a Theoretical Biology.* Vol. 2. Edinburgh University Press, Edinburgh, pp. 106–124.

Waddington, C.H., ed. (1970) *Towards a Theoretical Biology: Drafts.* Edinburgh University Press, Edinburgh.

Waddington, C.H. (1972) *Towards a Theoretical Biology: Essays.* Edinburgh University Press, Edinburgh.

Waddington, C.H. (1975) *The Evolution of an Evolutionist.* Edinburgh University Press, Edinburgh.

Watson, J.B. (1913) Psychology as a behaviorist views it. *Psychological Review*, **20**, 158–177.

Watson, J.B. (1924) *Behaviorism.* Norton, New York.

Weber, B.H. and Depew, D.J., eds (2003) *Evolution and Learning: The Baldwin Effect Reconsidered.* MIT Press, Cambridge, MA.

Wedin, M.V. (1995) Aristotle. In: Audi, R., ed. *The Cambridge Dictionary of Philosophy.* Cambridge University Press, Cambridge, pp. 38–45.

Weiner, J. (1995) Evolution made visible. *Science*, **267**, 30–34.

West-Eberhard, M.J. (2003) *Developmental Plasticity and Evolution*. Oxford University Press, Oxford.

Whitehead, H. (1998) Cultural selection and genetic diversity in matrilineal whales. *Science*, **282**, 1708–1711.

Whiten, A. and Byrne, R.W. (1988) Tactical deception in primates. *Behavioural and Brain Sciences*, **11**, 233–244.

Whiten, A., Goodall, J., McGrew, W.C., Nishida, T., Reynolds, V., Sugiyama, Y., *et al*. (1999) Cultures in chimpanzees. *Nature*, **399**, 682–685.

Whiten, A., Horner, V. and Marshall-Pescini, S. (2003) Cultural panthropology. *Evolutionary Anthropology*, **12**, 92–105.

Whiten, A., Horner, V. and de Waal, B.M. (2005) Conformity to cultural norms of tool use in chimpanzees. *Nature*, **437**, 737–740.

Wicken, J.S. and Ulanowicz, R.E. (1988) On quantifying hierarchical connections in ecology. *Journal of Social and Biological Structures*, **11**, 369–377.

Wilcoxon, H.C., Dragoin, W.B. and Kral, P.A. (1971) Illness-induced aversions in rat and quail: relative salience of visual and gustatory cues. *Science*, **171**, 826–828.

Williams, G.C. (1966) *Adaptation and Natural Selection*. Princeton University Press, Princeton, NJ.

Williams, G.C. (1985) A defence of reductionism in evolutionary biology. *Oxford Surveys in Evolutionary Biology*, **2**, 1–27.

Williams, G.C. (1992) *Natural Selection: Domains, Levels, and Challenges*. Oxford University Press, Oxford.

Williams, M. (2001) *Problems of Knowledge*. Oxford University Press, Oxford.

Wilson, A.C. (1985) The molecular basis of evolution. *Scientific American*, **253**, 148–157.

Wimsatt, W. (1974) Reductive explanation: a functional account. In: Cohen, R.S., ed. *Biennial Proceedings of the Philosophy of Science Association*, pp. 671–710. Reidel, Boston.

Wollaston, A. (1960) *Translations of Descartes' Discourse and Meditations*. Penguin Books, Harmondsworth.

Wozniak, R.H. (1982) Metaphysics and science, reason and reality: the intellectual origins of genetic epistemology. In: Broughton, J.M. and Freeman-Moir, D.J., eds. *The Cognitive Developmental Psychology of James Mark Baldwin*. Ablex Publishing Corp., Norwood, NJ, pp. 13–45.

Wrangham, R.W., Jones, J.H., Laden, G., Pilbeam, D. and Conklin-Brittain, N. (1999) The raw and the stolen: cooking and the ecology of human origins. *Current Anthropology*, **40**, 1–51.

Wright, L. (1973) Functions. *Philosophical Review*, **82**, 139–168.

Wyles, J.S., Kunkel, J.G. and Wilson, A.C. (1983) Birds, behaviour, and anatomical evolution. *Proceedings of the National Academy of Sciences of the USA*, **80**, 4394–4397.

Wynne, K. (1998) Psychological foundations of number: numerical competence in human infants. *Trends in Cognitive Sciences*, **2**, 296–303.

Wynne, K., Bloom, P. and Chiang, W.-C. (2002) Enumeration of collective entities by 5-month-old infants. *Cognition*, **83**, B55–B62.

Yang, C.D. (2004) Universal grammar, statistics or both? *Trends in Cognitive Sciences*, **8**, 451–456.

Zach, R. (1979) Shell dropping: decision making and optimal foraging in Northwestern crows. *Behaviour*, **68**, 106–117.

Ze Cheng, Ventura, M., Xinwei She, Khatovich, P., Graves, T., Osoegawa, K *et al.* (2005) A genome-wide comparison of recent chimpanzee and human segmental duplications. *Nature*, **437**, 88–93.

Zirkle, C. (1946) The early history of the idea of the inheritance of acquired characters and of pangenesis. *Transactions of the American Philosophical Society*, **35**, 91–151.

Index